Contents

Acknowledgements

The author and publishers would like to thank the following for permission to reproduce material in this publication:

Hulton Deutsch for the photographs of Karl Marx and Niccolo dei Machiavelli; Burger King and *The Sun* for the use of their logos; Grand Metropolitan PLC for the photograph of the Lord Sheppard of Didgemere; Topham for the photograph of the Berlin Wall coming down; Mr D. Hodgson and the Beverley School for the Deaf for the British two-handed finger spelling alphabet; Marvin Dunnette for permission to redraw Figure 46 from the *Handbook of Industrial and Organizational Psychology*, edited by Marvin Dunnette, Rand McNally, 1976; Gyles Brandreth and Michèle Brown at Victorama Ltd for the optical illusions from *The Big Book of Optical Illusions* by Gyles Brandreth; Jane Sweet at SCOPE (formerly The Spastic Society) for the photograph of a team-link session at SCOPE; Greenpeace/Culley for the photograph of a Greenpeace expedition to Southern Ocean to protest against Japanese whaling 20.12.91; the House of Commons for the photograph of the House in session; Stephen Hawking and Transworld Publishers for the photograph of Stephen Hawking; Roddy Paine for the photograph of a football goal; Life File for the photographs of a rugby goal and mountaineers at a summit; and The Munch Museum/The Munch-Ellingsen Group/DACS 1995 for *The Scream*.

BEHAVIOUR
at work

British Library Cataloguing in Publication Data

Lynch, Alex
 Behaviour at Work
 I. Title
 302.35

ISBN 0–340–61112–X

First published 1995
Impression number   10   9   8   7   6   5   4   3   2   1
Year   1999   1998   1997   1996   1995

Typeset by Wearset, Boldon, Tyne and Wear.
Printed in Great Britain for Hodder & Stoughton Educational,
a division of Hodder Headline Plc, 338 Euston Road, London
NW1 3BH by Bath Press, Bath, Avon

Introduction

What is an organisation? Can we see it, touch it, smell it, taste it, hear it? We can. An organisation is any group, society, club or business. From cradle to grave we are part of, or subject to, the attention of an organisation. It is the health sector that organises our entry into this world. We may then escape for a few short years, but are soon compelled by one organisation, the government, to attend another, the education sector. At 16 we have choices: to continue within an educational organisation; to work for an industrial, commercial or public organisation; or to become part of a government initiative training scheme. It is possible to escape the clutches of an organisation, but becoming a hermit may not be some people's idea of a good career move. A religious organisation may provide its services following birth, at marriage and may also prove to be the final organisation to provide us with a service. We are an organised society and we live within a society of organisations.

Our interest, in this book, lies in business; that is, those organisations which produce or sell goods, or provide a service. It is the corner shop, British Rail, McDonalds, Marks & Spencer, Adidas. The organs of an organisation are the people, the workers, the employees. These organs may also be seen as the tools which give the organisation its shape and size.

WHERE HAVE YOU BEEN?

How many organisations have there been in your life?
Complete the following list. Compare your list with other people's lists.

Age	*Organisation*
0	e.g. Strathclyde Maternity Hospital
1	
2	
3	
4	
5	e.g. Petworth Primary School, West Sussex
6	
7	
8	
9	
10	
11	
12	
13	e.g. Martins Newsagents
14	
15	
16	
17	
18	
19	
20	

SHAPE AND SIZE OF ORGANISATIONS

Organisations vary in shape and size. However, to begin to understand organisations it is helpful to group them together into different types. The arrangement into types will depend on the viewer's perspective, as no one organisation fits conveniently into one grouping. For example: you have attended a sporting event. The next day you read a report of the game in your newspaper; you may wonder if you had seen the same game – you have a different perspective.

A QUESTION OF CLASS

How would you classify your local NHS hospital? Does it fit into the same grouping as a nearby private hospital? They both have a similar objective in, say, providing efficient and effective patient care. Would you classify one as a 'public service organisation' and the other an 'economic organisation'?

As far as size is concerned, there are small, medium and large organisations. The easiest way to measure an organisation is by the number of people it employs. An organisation employing 50 people or less is small, whereas one with 51 to 250 employees is medium, and one with over 250 is large. Besides being depicted by numbers employed, the size of an organisation can be judged by looking at the amount of money it generates each year through its level of sales.

FURTHER READING

Start using your research skills by looking up commentators on organisations to see how size is defined. Ask for details at your local TEC.

The classification of organisations is important in providing a general picture of organisations, albeit from a variety of angles.

THE WAY YOU SEE IT

Draw a tree on a separate piece of paper.
   Now compare your drawing with those of others. We all know what a tree is, but how we express it will differ widely. It will be the same with organisations.

EMPLOYEE RELATIONS PERSPECTIVE

One way to view organisations is through their behaviour towards their employees, or the way employees or outsiders may view that behaviour.

A **unitary organisation** (a single complete thing) is one that believes that all employees work towards the company goals, with loyalty and complete acceptance of the structure and systems. Such organisations need excellent leadership to maintain steady working relationships and employees dedicated to getting the job done. Their working systems and their methods of communicating with employees are usually very good. They see conflict, or disharmony, as being caused only by people, as it is very unlikely that the way of doing things to their detailed plan and rules is the problem. Unions are not welcome in the company, as they are seen as the creator of divided loyalties; employees can only be loyal to one organisation – the one that pays their wages.

TO BE OR NOT TO BE

List three reasons why employees **should not** belong to a union. Then list three reasons why they **should** belong to a union.

A **pluralist organisation** (concerning many) begins with the understanding that different groups have differing ambitions, and if disharmony results then a solution will be found through compromise. Conflict is seen as healthy to a developing organisation. Unions have an important part to play and are accepted as a reasonable and valued participant in the work of the organisation.

ONE MORE

You have a brief description of unitarist and pluralist. How would you describe the third part of the triangle (not mentioned above), known as Marxist?

I'll be back

STARS, CASH COWS, WILD CATS AND DOGS

The Boston Consulting Group, who must have been avid readers of nursery rhymes, began a classification of private organisations by looking at market growth and market share. They came up with the terms stars, cash cows, dogs and wild cats.

Stars are those organisations with a high market share and a high market growth which have enough profits to pay for further growth. Those who like to work with companies which have progressive methods and systems will do well in this medium to large growing organisation. Such organisations are likely to have very good recruitment and selection methods in order to attract and pay the right person to work within a team framework. The training they provide is there to keep the favoured employee.

Cash cows are organisations with a high market share but a low growth rate which need little money in order for them to hold on to their present position in the market. These are usually large stable organisations perhaps with a mothering approach. They may, however, need to look at how they carry out what they do. They have to be more efficient, but would do it in a way that would not upset the generally smooth-working employee relationships. They have little innovation, may be ripe for a take-over, and must be careful not to turn into a **dog**.

A **dog** has a low share of the market with a low growth and little or no profit. Such companies tend to be declining and medium sized. Dogs are sold to someone who does not know it is a dog, or liquidated. Working for a dog is a walk to redundancy, unless a guardian angel can wave a magic wand.

Wild cats have a low share of the market but a high growth rate and require investment in the business to be greater than the profit they are currently making. According to the consulting organisation Arthur D. Little, organisations of this type require an entrepreneurial style of management. They are also likely to be small and experimental. They need employees with a broad range of skills so that they can be flexible enough to undertake whatever the business needs, as it will operate with the lowest possible level of staffing.

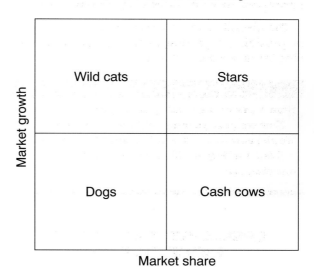

Fig. 1   The Boston Matrix

You will meet this classification again when looking at marketing, as it can also relate to the product life cycle.

STRATEGIC PLANNING, FINANCIAL CONTROL AND STRATEGIC CONTROL

Further groupings continue when you look at companies that own other companies. Look at Dolland & Aitchison, the optician. It began in 1750 with a store in Spitalfields, London. Owners have included Harlech TV, Slater Walker, and Gallaher

3

who are part of the American Brands empire and also own tobacco and whisky producers. When you look at those companies that own other companies, it is worth looking at the work of Goold and Campbell. They give three interesting classifications of organisations: strategic planning, financial control, and strategic control.

Strategic planning organisations attempt to gain the greatest lead in their own particular field of operation. So, if they make cardboard boxes, they want to be the leader in making cardboard boxes. They tend to hold on to poor performing, subsidiary companies. They are supportive of their employees, but do not believe in giving financial rewards, such as bonuses, as they believe that working for the organisation is benefit enough and, they suggest, above individual effort.

Financial control companies are concerned mainly with the organisation's financial performance, not their competitive position. They reward those who succeed very well, and fire those who fail. They view their workers through their contribution to the company profit.

The **strategic control** company, as you may expect, tries to balance both the competitive and financial objectives.

FURTHER READING

For a good summary from a human angle, read Derrek Torrington in *New Perspectives on Human Resource Management*, Ed. J. Storey, Routledge, 1992.

Each has a different parent – who are they?

ORGANISATIONAL STRUCTURE

The reason for having a structure is to have a formal system so that employees are able to perform their jobs within an ordered framework of co-operation. This will help to meet the aims and objectives of the organisation. It brings together people and jobs and gives an indication of what the organisation expects from everyone. The basic structure is normally depicted by an organisation chart. It can look like a family tree (see Fig. 2).

There is no best way to organise, no ideal plan. Most organisations are not planned, they just grow. Good staff can make a poor organisational pattern work, as it forces people and groups to co-operate. However, most people will work better when they know the part they have to play and how they relate to others in the company; team sports would be an obvious example of how this works.

The way in which an organisation is designed helps the performance of the organisation, but it does not get rid of, or provide answers to, ingrained disagreements or arguments from within the organisation. Do not expect a 'good' structure to correct the poor performance of managers or employees.

The size of the organisation will have some effect on the structure to be introduced: the larger it is the more complex the structure.

Mechanistic/bureaucratic and organic structures

A **mechanistic**, and some forms of **bureaucratic**, structure may be described as an organisation where there is a place for everything and everything is in its place. It is excessively concerned with rules and procedures. Everything is done by the book. Those people further up the family tree know more about the organisation's problems and activities than those lower down, and become the source of information, or power. Those lower down the structure need to go upwards to seek the answer to a problem. Such an organisation would produce detailed policy and procedure

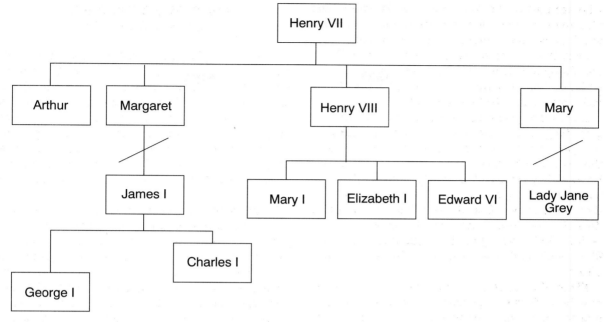

Fig. 2   A family tree

manuals that lower management must refer to before taking a particular action. Conformity is required, through the obeying of instructions from those above, and innovation is frowned upon as this may encourage disobeying organisational policies and procedures.

An **organic** structure is flexible in its design and has the ability to grow and alter to meet changed circumstances. Higher management is not assumed to hold more information than middle or lower management. Decisions are made at the 'lowest' possible level. Job holders are flexible, then they can 'act up' or 'act down'. Policies and procedures are guidelines, not inflexible instructions. Innovation is positively encouraged and rewarded.

The **Scalar Chain** is the term used to describe the chain of command or authority running from the top to the lower levels of the organisation. Communication runs up and down the chain. The authority can be line, staff or functional. **Line authority** allows the manager to allot work, guide and command subordinates and delegate authority. **Staff authority** is where specialist advice is available, say in the human resources management (HRM) department, but no authority exists over those receiving the advice. In **func-**

tional authority there is a mix in which specialist advisers have some authority, for example, the HRM department has the final authority on a dismissal. Line managers have the direct responsibility for achieving company objectives whereas staff managers have an advisory or service role to the line managers.

Tall or flat structures

A **tall** or **flat structure** refers to the number of levels within an organisation. The term can also relate to the size of an organisation.

An organisation with up to 200 staff will normally have around four levels. In one with 1,000 staff you might expect to see around six levels. Companies with around 10,000 staff should not have many more, around seven or eight levels.

Tall structures, as in Figure 3, have advantages. For example, the large number of levels suggests that those given the opportunity can climb the ladder of success, a small, and perhaps, frequent, step at a time. This should then generate commitment to the organisation and improve employee satisfaction.

5

The advantages recorded above for a tall structure have been called into doubt. Can you provide some valid reasons against the advantages given?

There are disadvantages, and these tend to be related to difficulties in communication. The top is seen to be too remote from the 'shop floor', administration costs can increase, and managers may feel that responsibility is restricted. Work passes through far too many, up and down the chain.

A flat organisational structure, as in Figure 4, appears to lower the level of decision making and thus increase the power of the middle ranks in the organisation. A flat structure needs good middle management; management that will delegate, and control a greater number of subordinates, known as increasing the **span of control**. Changing from a tall to a flat structure may initially create promotions, or demotions, but thereafter the promotion prospects may be limited when compared to the tall structure. When Grand Metropolitan bought Burger King they discovered a poor performer with 13 levels of management between chief executive and store manager. Major changes made included moving from the tall to a flat structure.

Choosing a structure

In choosing a structure, management is aware that whichever design is selected, it must help in achieving organisational aims and objectives. The design must reflect the important tasks or mission of the organisation.

The structure can be centralised, that is brought under the control of one central group; or decentralised; where it is organised so that the power is transferred from the one main centre to smaller local units. It must address the question of how much authority is delegated to divisions and at which levels in the hierarchy the decisions are taken.

As well as being tall or flat, the structure can be formal, that is conforming to accepted conventions, and decentralised by product, as in Figure 5, or by geographical area, shown in Figure 6.

The advantages of a product style of organisation are that the activities required to produce and sell a specific product can be brought together by the head of the division who will be accountable for the profit. It will, however, increase administrative costs and has many parts.

In a geographically organised company, similar

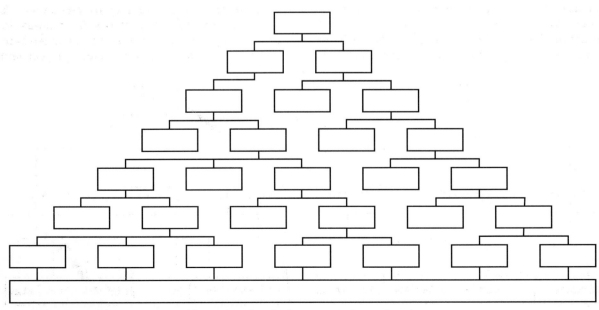

Many tiers/levels from top to lower levels

6   *Fig. 3   An outline of a tall organisation structure*

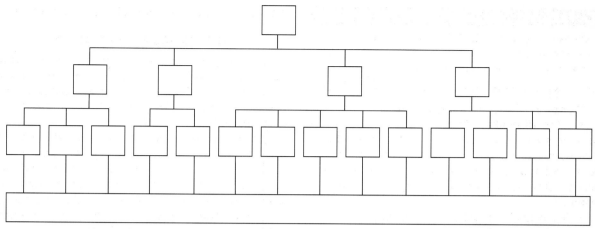

Fig. 4   An outline of a flat organisation structure

activities are undertaken in different locations. Its advantages are that it has direct contact with the customer, and local knowledge can be put to good use. The disadvantages are that there is a duplication of effort in each area – for example six HRM departments and six finance departments instead of one of each, means that administration costs are increased.

A company can be formal and centralised by a functional structure, as in Figure 7. This is the most widely used approach. It is logical and traditional to divide the activities of the company into specialised groups. Problems can arise, however,

where the 'staff' advisers are seen to conflict with the role of 'line' managers.

A company can have an informal centralised entrepreneurial structure, as in Figure 8. This is where everything is organised around the owner or manager with no neat divisions of responsibility. This may be a very apt structure for a small growing company, a wild cat.

A company's structure can be a matrix, as in Figure 9. This is a blending of structures. It requires people to work across boundaries to achieve organisational goals. Its main use tends to be when a company has a particular project and

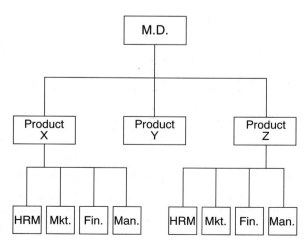

Fig. 5   Organisation structure by product
(from T. D. Weinshall)

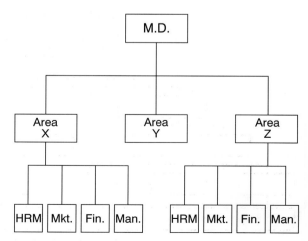

Fig. 6   Organisation structure by
geographical area (from T. D. Weinshall)

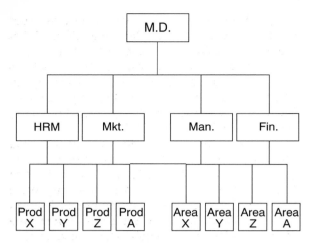

Fig. 7   Functional organisation structure
(from T. D. Weinshall)

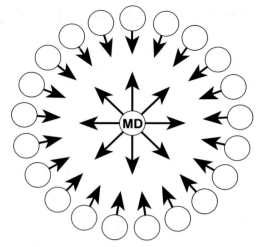

*Fig. 8   Entrepreneurial organisation
structure* (from T. D. Weinshall)

brings together staff from various disciplines and
departments to complete the project, disbanding
when it is completed. It recognises that a manager
cannot have total authority over all the activities
to achieve a goal. However, authorities have to be
clearly known so that major conflicts are avoided.

REORGANISE IT

Obtain a copy of your educational establishment's
organisational structure. If none is available, create
one by interviewing staff. Then redraw it to reflect a
different structure. Give the advantages and
disadvantages of your chosen structure.

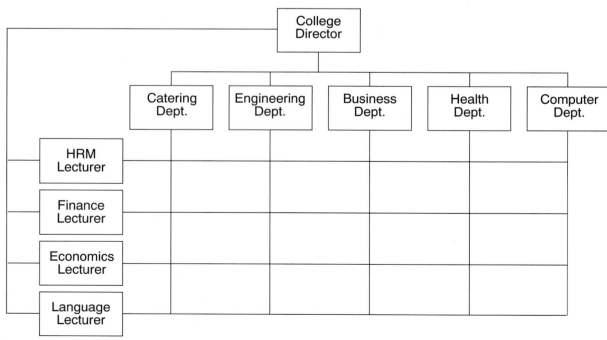

Fig. 9   Matrix organisation structure

INFORMAL ORGANISATIONS

The difference between formal and informal organisations is highlighted in the work of Chester Barnard, plus that of Elton Mayo and F. J. Roethlisberger at the Hawthorne Works of the Western Electric Company in 1927.

As you know, a formal organisational structure need not be inflexible but it is important that an individual's contribution be focused within organisational or group activities. An organisation must be efficient and effective.

IS THERE A DIFFERENCE?

What is the difference between being efficient and being effective?

Organisations need continual change in order to be one step ahead of the competition. What shape will organisations take in the future? The answer may be seen in organisations such as Mercury Communications. The future for organisations is full of new and exciting opportunities. One visionary is Charles Handy: read his *Age of Unreason* and *The Empty Raincoat*.

Following this brief overview of organisational types, we can now look closely at how the management of these organisations behave in leading their employees. We can look at how employees behave as individuals and within groups. We can see how change in any organisation affects the staff. We will look at people's behaviour at work.

The Management

This section sets out to meet the requirements of Element 11.1, 'Investigate management styles'.

On completion of this section you will be able to:

1. Differentiate between management styles used in varying situations
2. Identify the responsibilities of managers
3. Explain why and how managers need to communicate
4. Analyse the barriers to effective communication

INTRODUCTION

How would you like to be a manager? Nice job. You sit behind a big desk and bark out orders to your troops, but you call them employees or staff, and it is well paid. John Lawler, a training consultant, runs management courses on interviewing skills. He noticed that those taking part seemed to bring with them ideas they had already formed as to how managers behaved.

HOW DO MANAGERS BEHAVE?
(JOHN LAWLER)

Which are true and which are false?

- The manager knows everything. *True/False*
- The manager must be in control at all times. *True/False*
- The manager must never apologise. *True/False*
- The manager must concentrate on solving problems, not people. *True/False*
- The manager's agenda must be adhered to. *True/False*

- Managers know best what is best for people. *True/False*
- The manager's plans are best. *True/False*
- Managers are men. *True/False*

By the time you finish this section, you will know the answers.

WHAT IS A MANAGER?

So what do managers do? What does a manager look like? We have all seen one, whether it is in Tesco's or McDonald's. However, just because someone is called a manager it does not mean that he/she takes on the duties that should be expected of a manager. The word *manager* has been in use for over 400 years, but today the title is dished out more as a bonus, to give status and boost morale. It does sound impressive to be called a manager.

Some people do not have the title of manager, but carry out all the activities you would expect of a manager. They include head teachers, company secretaries and chief accountants. So what does this title, manager, mean, what responsibilities does it include?

Collins dictionary gives the definition as:

1   ... a person responsible for running a business or organisation, e.g., the bank manager.
2   The manager of a star is the person who looks after the star's business interests.
3   The manager of a sports team is the person responsible for organising and training it.'

From this we can see that a manager is someone who is responsible for running, looking after, organising and training.

The definition we seek, however, does not lie in the dictionary, but comes from the work of academics and management experts. One such expert was the French industrialist Henri Fayol, who listed five elements of what then became the classic definition of a manager's job:

THE FIVE ELEMENTS NEEDED TO BE A MANAGER (HENRI FAYOL)

1   Forecasting and planning
2   Organising
3   Commanding
4   Co-ordinating
5   Controlling

Fayol's elements are still as appropriate today as when first published in 1916. His text was translated into English in 1929 and by popular demand relaunched in 1949 by Pitman under the title, *General and Industrial Management*.

A MANAGER'S DAY

First: Take one manager, but remember, a manager may not have the title manager. If you cannot find a business manager, take a year tutor.

Now ask that manager to keep a diary of his/her activities for one day. The information may already be available.

Ask the manager to categorise each activity into one or more of Fayol's elements. If an activity does not fit one of the five elements, then create a sixth called 'Other'.

Forecasting and planning: ....
Organising: ....
Commanding: ....

Co-ordinating: ....
Controlling: ....
Other: ....

One further writer to note is Henry Mintzberg, who grouped a manager's role into three parts: interpersonal, informational and decision making. These look more at what a manager does, rather than give a general statement about management. He lists ten roles or characteristics within those three divisions:

THE INTERPERSONAL THREE

1   **Figurehead**   Seen as in charge. A bit like the large wooden model decorating the front of old sailing ships.
2   **Leader**   Motivates, co-ordinates, shows the way. As expected of the manager of the England or Wales football team.
3   **Liaison**   Co-operates with and keeps informed those in and outside the department. A sales manager would need the co-operation of the sales team and the people making the goods.

THE INFORMATIONAL THREE

4   **Monitor**   Controls. This is like a science teacher, who needs to keep an eye on the way in which experiments are done, so that the conclusions are appropriate.
5   **Disseminator**   Communicator. This is rather like a post office, receiving information and making sure that it is delivered to the right person.
6   **Spokesperson**   The voice of the department. The person who has to face others outside the department, to explain how well or badly they have done.

THE DECISION-MAKING FOUR

7   **Entrepreneur**   Takes risks, sees opportunity and assists change. A diluted version of a Richard Branson.
8   **Disturbance handler**   Sorts out unexpected occurrences. The policeman who redirects the traffic at the scene of an accident.

9 **Resource allocator**   Gives out time, money, staff and materials. The one who holds all the cards, shuffles the deck, and deals a hand to the players or employees.

10 **Negotiator**   Reaches agreements. Similar to the person who agrees the price and other contract conditions with a builder.

Perhaps not all managers undertake all roles all of the time, but the range of what they do would still be within the Mintzberg top ten.

Although there are similarities in different managerial jobs, as can be seen through the work of Fayol, Mintzberg and others, it is clear that each management job is different. Similarities most certainly exist and a great deal of the common skills can be transferred from one managerial job to another. However, just because a manager is good in one job it does not follow that he or she will be seen as good in another, even at the same level of authority and responsibility.

RECAP FROM ANOTHER MODULE?

What is the difference between authority and responsibility?

An electrician must be technically skilled, and it takes years to be competent to an acceptable level. When that electrician becomes a supervisor, the previous essential technical skills are less important. When that person reaches a managerial post, the need for those original skills diminishes even further and then it is the people skills that are of most importance.

The popular, and reasonable, view is that a manager, quite simply, gets results through people. The manager will choose people with the technical skills to perform the job to an acceptable standard. The manager no longer needs to fix the electrical socket; the manager needs to fix the situation, to allow the hiring of the right employee to fix the socket, at the right time, place, cost and with the right resources, to meet the required standards.

Managers appear to spend a great deal of their time attending and holding meetings and on the telephone; so they need a high level of communications skills. They also spend considerable time

with their staff; so they need a high level of people skills. Studies of what a manager does each day show that when it comes to forecasting, planning and organising, managers find it difficult to forecast, plan and organise their own working day. More than half their time seems to be spent on unforeseen activities.

JOIN THE DEBATE

There is an age-old argument about managers and management:

- Is management an art or is it a science?
- Are managers born or are they made?

What do you think?

Art, science, politics and magic

In 1986, T. J. Watson, in his book *Management, Organisation and Employment Strategy*, said that management can be viewed as being art, science, politics and magic.

- An **art**: good managers are born with the intelligence, personality and intuition that they can then develop when they become a manager.
- A **science**: good managers are those who have obtained the knowledge, then acquired the ability to put into practice management techniques and skills.
- A manager as a **politician** is one who can play the organisational games and, when they have discovered the unpublished rules, such a manager can play to win the inevitable power struggles that take place within organisations.
- The manager who practices **magic** is the one who can call upon the management saints and gurus to aid in controlling the elements, known as employees.

It was G. Cleverley, in 1971, who suggested in *Managers and Magic* that of all the factors surrounding a manager the '... most unpredictable, least understood and least controllable factor is the behaviour of the people he manages. Not surprisingly therefore, the subject is shrouded in mystique'.

The manager needs to be a leader. A manager needs the commitment of people. In this text only, the terms manager and leader are interchangeable, although I hasten to point out that a manager may not be a leader and a leader need not be a manager. Definitions of a leader exceed the number of Big Macs served in a McDonalds on a Saturday lunchtime.

The work of A. Zaleznik, *Managers and Leaders: are they different?* is one source from which the difference may be gleaned. This may be summarised as:

THREE DIFFERENCES BETWEEN A MANAGER AND A LEADER

Manager	Leader
Impersonal and passive to goals	Personal and active to goals
Low level of emotional involvement	Empathy with people
Regulator of the current order	Searcher for change

In *Leadership, Management and the Seven Keys*, C. M. Watson said that although leaders have to manage, a manager will find it difficult to dominate all the seven elements. These elements and their relationship with a manager and leader are shown as:

WATSON AND THE 7 S'S

A **manager** relies on:
1. Strategy
2. Structure
3. Systems

A **leader** uses:
4. Style
5. Staff
6. Skills
7. Shared goals

Trait or qualities approach

In an attempt to find out what makes a good leader, various researchers have looked at the qualities of some who were regarded as showing excellent examples of leadership. The idea was to look at the person, not the job he or she per-

formed. A list could then be made of the qualities present in these effective leaders and what made them different, enabling an organisation to choose the right person for the job.

It would be wonderful to think that if we could spot all the qualities of a good manager, we could then work towards achieving those qualities. Becoming a good leader is not so simple, however. Consider the following cup of qualities:

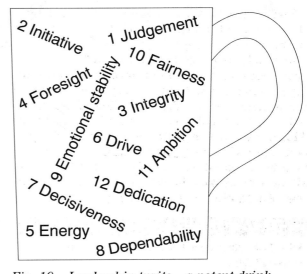

Fig. 10   *Leadership traits – a potent drink*

But how do we define 'drive' or 'dependability'. If we cannot agree what is meant, we have problems. The problems may get worse if we cannot agree on how we see the quality in the way the manager behaves in the working situation.

I WANT TO BE A LEADER

Think about great leaders outside the business environment. Identify someone you consider to have been a great leader, e.g., J. F. Kennedy, Malcolm X, 'Stormin' Norman' of the Gulf War.

1. List their qualities or traits.
2. Now compare your list with other students' lists
3. As a group can you product a list on which you all agree?

Charles Handy, in his book *Understanding Organisations* (Penguin, 3rd ed., 1985), said that in most of those studies a few came up time and time again:

1 **Intelligence**   Good at solving complex and abstract problems. Should be above average intelligence but not at genius level.

2 **Initiative**   The ability to see the need for action and the willingness to do something about it. (He did add that this quality goes down after the age of 40.)

3 **Self-assurance**   Self-confident person who has high expectations of him/herself.

4 **Helicopter factor**   Able to rise above and look at the situation in relation to its surroundings.

5 **Height**   Above or below average height.

6 **Socio-economic group**   Upper socio-economic level in society.

7 **Health**   Good.

So, it's bad luck if you are of average intelligence or a genius. Forget it, if you are over 40 years. No way, if you are a bit miserable on a Monday morning or if you do not think you are the best thing since sliced bread. Alas again, no, if you are of average height from the working classes with a bad chest and get a nose bleed when you go up in a lift.

There are many more; so many more of these lists that it is impossible for a person to have all of these qualities. It is difficult enough to have the first three in Charles Handy's list, and those are regarded as a helpful start.

In your recruitment module you will have discovered that the Personnel Department do look at the qualities in a person which are needed to fill a job. But those qualities will be related to the situation of a particular job in which the successful applicant will find themselves.

MAKE A LIST OF QUALITIES

- List the qualities of a good manager or teacher/lecturer you have known.
- What does your list have in common with those of others?
- How does it differ from your list of the qualities of a great leader?

If toughness is seen to be a requirement by those institutions who invest millions, then the *Sunday Times* discovered in late 1993 the 'Toughs at the top'.

THE TOUGH TEN

1   The Lord Sheppard of Didgemere – Grand Metropolitan
2   Archie Norman – Asda
3   Sir Alastair Morton – Eurotunnel
4   Michael Gifford – Rank Organisation
5   Sir William Purves – HSBC Holdings
6   Nick Newmarch – Prudential
7   Lord Hanson – Hanson
8   Sir Geoff Mulcahy – Kingfisher
9   Lord Stevens – United Newspapers
10   Martin Sorrell –WPP

The tough men, for there are no women on this list, regarded people as the toughest thing they had to deal with.

Tough at the top – The Lord Sheppard of Didgemere

YOU KNOW WHAT I MEAN

What do you think 'tough' means, as a quality in a manager?

Does it mean he/she is: strong, firm, rugged, hard,

vigorous, hardy, rigid, inflexible, unyielding, uncompromising, hard-line, incorrigible, troublesome, severe, ferocious, fierce, a bruiser, a gangster, a hoodlum?

Situational approach

This way of looking at leaders suggests that the best person to lead a group or team is that person who has the knowledge, skills and perhaps qualities to deal with the particular situation or problem. Consider the phrase, 'Authority flows from the one that knows'. It really means that the leader switches, each time, in order to meet changing situations or problems. People with widely differing qualities, backgrounds and age have shown themselves as excellent leaders, but in different situations.

WHO IS IN CHARGE?

Consider the following: a traffic accident occurs, in which two people are injured. Passing by the scene is a car carrying three people: a doctor; a nurse and a para-medic all of whom are off duty. Which of the three would take charge within this situational approach to leadership?

A situational approach to leadership may be applicable in schools and colleges. Here, a group of teachers are brought together for a common purpose, such as the delivery of a bunch of modules, or the teaching of a particular year group. They are all on the same level in the organisation, no one has positional power over the others. The leader is selected for particular knowledge, skills and qualities to deal with the situation. The leader then exercises this wisdom, known as sapiential authority, over the others. There may be a number of such groups or teams and it may be that the leader of one group is a member of another, with the leader of that further group being a member of the former group. But some argue that it is not 'real' authority, and only lasts as long as the members of the team believe the leader still holds the knowledge and skills.

Although there should only be one captain of the ship, that is the manager; it may, however, prove beneficial to the organisation to practise some form of situational approach to leadership, although it may not be too easy to control.

Three-dimensional leaders

Just as we thought that the qualities or trait approach to leadership had seen its day we find it examined further, this time with a built-in situation factor. Carl A. Rodrigues of the School of Business Administration, Montclair State College, New Jersey, says that different situations require leaders with particular characteristics. He proposed that it is the environment that creates the situation, or circumstances, which then influence the behaviour that the leader must pursue in order to be effective.

CHARACTERISTICS OF LEADERS DEMANDED BY DIFFERENT SITUATIONS

- **The innovator**   Does well in crisis situations.
- **The implementor**   Will do well when the vision of the innovator needs to be introduced.
- **The pacifier**   Preferred when the department is in a steady state after all has been introduced and all is running fairly well.

The **innovator** is needed by an organisation or department when it is in trouble; when it needs changes and modernisation. The innovator brings new ideas and is a forceful person who can solve the problem in hand. The innovator is very competitive and will go out on a limb to win. An innovator is not easily rebuffed but gets up and keeps on trying to succeed. An innovator readily takes responsibility for success and failure; takes risks, but not uncalculated ones. An innovator continually searches for new ideas and commits him or herself, and their department, to major courses of action. Innovators want and seek out growth, motivated by the desire to achieve and to be creative. They are most certainly in control of their department and they would stand out from the herd of other managers within the organisation. They fully believe that the business environment can be controlled and manipulated, their thinking is long range and they are able to see the future of the organisation.

15

However, the 'shelf-life' of an innovator, in one organisation or department, is limited. When the vision takes form, the employees may not be able to contend with the style of the innovator, this entrepreneur, or more accurately, 'intrepreneur'. An innovator is not an implementor.

The **implementor** is someone who can put into effect the changes and dreams of the innovator. An implementor is assertive, able to get things done through people, and wishes to exercise power in order to control and influence situations. The implementor is systematic in analysing and solving a problem, with the ability to assume responsibility for decision making. However, there will always come a time when everything has been introduced and the department settles down, and the qualities of the implementor are no longer required.

It is now the turn of the **pacifier**. The pacifier works well within a steady state environment. They look up to authority figures; they are willing and able to do all the administrative paperwork. They like to talk with and work with their employees; keep things friendly; improve the social atmosphere of the department. Although they allow employees to make many of the decisions, any decisions they do make are based on the feedback from earlier similar situations; their decisions are ones which would make the employees reasonably happy. Although they accept that not all decisions are harmonious, those decisions they do make are short range and they observe their results to make sure they satisfy influential individuals. The pacifier likes to be known as a member of the team and does not make waves.

Unfortunately for some, organisations or departments never stand still, they do not settle down for any reasonable length of time. Change in an organisation is continuous; it needs to be, in order to keep up with competitiors, technology and customers' requirements. It is not very practicable, therefore, to begin with an innovator, then, when the innovative part is done, take on an implementer instead who is in turn, replaced by a pacifier. The only time I consider this to be a viable option is in the case of an ailing organisation, perhaps a cash cow in trouble or a dog you do not want to take to the vet.

According to Carl Rodrigues, and others, good managers must have the traits, abilities and behaviour of all three types of leader. They need the skills of an innovator to create new business or projects; they need to implement their own ideas; they need the skills of a pacifier to manage the steady state activities of the department. A good manager must be three-dimensional, a transformational leader. A good manager must be able to identify the problem, know which type of behaviour is appropriate, and act.

The head of Compass, a contract catering company, approached the head of Grand Metropolitan with the innovative idea that Compass introduce Burger King products within its contracts with schools and company restaurants. This would, of course, increase the visibility of Burger King and most certainly improve the competitive edge of Compass. The innovator has completed his job; it is now the role of the implementor to turn the idea into reality and then the pacifier to maintain that idea.

GENDER: INNOVATORS, IMPLEMENTORS AND PACIFIERS

In his article, 'Developing Three-dimensional Leaders' (in the *Journal of Management Development*, Vol. 11, No. 3, 1993, pp. 4–11), Carl Rodrigues tells the tale of a group of managers who focused on gender expectations. That group concluded that it was more likely that males would be innovators, whereas females would be expected to take on the role as pacifiers. They further suggested that females are looked upon negatively if they behave as an innovator.
What do you think?

FURTHER READING

For an examination of innovators read B. Ritchie and W. Goldsmith, *The New Elite*, Weidenfeld & Nicholson, 1987, which looks at British hero managers such as John Harvey-Jones and Michael Edwardes.
Read John Harvey-Jones' own book, *Making it Happen*, Collins, 1988. Look up Donald Trump and his book, *Trump: The Art of the Deal*, Arrow, 1987, or the man who liked the product so much he bought the company, Victor Kiam, *Going for it: How to succeed as an Entrepreneur*, Fontana, 1987.

POWER

Power is the ownership of control or command over others. Power is something most of us would like to have; to hold it, to keep it and to use it as we see fit. Lots of people have power, some more than others. Power is like the old fairy tale, *The Emperor's New Clothes*; it is there because people believe it to be there. It may vanish, if a subordinate refuses to recognise that their superior has the power, or if the use of power is challenged.

We will look at a manager's individual power and the source of that power. We will look at power in countries which claim that they support equality at work for all, such as the UK, where the open use of power is not respected.

According to John French and Bartram Raven, in their *Studies in Social Power* published through the University of Michigan, in 1959, there are five sources of power:

SOURCES OF POWER

- Physical
- Resource
- Position
- Expert
- Personal

Physical power is the might of superior energy. This is the bully; those who rule their country through fear; teachers who set detentions unnecessarily; or, in some countries, those who make sure the work is done otherwise the student gets a beating. Employees may not get detention, or a physical beating, but they can still be subjected to abusive behaviour at work. The mere presence of a boss is enough to cause some employees extreme nervousness.

Abusive behaviour can go some way to demolishing an organisation and ruining the self-esteem of its employees. The way in which abusive behaviour shows itself takes many forms. What is important is how the employees view the manager's behaviour towards them, not how the manager may see his/her own conduct. The employees may describe the conduct of their manager as offensive, rude, aggressive, nasty, hateful, threatening, impertinent or insulting.

More research is being conducted in this previously neglected area, such as the work undertaken by Emily Bassman and Manuel London. They remind us that a bully manager can, with consummate ease, inflict physical and/or psychological harm to employees. Bassman and London ('Abusive Managerial Behaviour', *Leadership & Organisational Development Journal*, Vol. 14, No. 2, MCB University Press.) have raised two distinct answers to why managers may behave in this abusive way.

There is the **psychopathological** answer, which suggests that such behaviour is a result of a personality disorder. This is where the manager is unable to control his/her aggressive impulses. The manager is, to some degree, mentally ill and behaves in an extreme and uncontrollable fashion. So, when an employee does not match up to what the manager expects of him/her, or the manager dislikes the employee the manager, instead of controlling any of those negative emotions, cracks and hits out verbally, if not physically. Such managers make a nonsense of the old saying. 'Sticks and stones will break my bones but words will never hurt me'. Words can hurt.

There is also the **social-cultural** answer, where the manager acts in a manner contrary to the beliefs and norms of business society. The abuse is directly linked to a work-stress overload. An article in *Business Week* by E. J. Smith said that because of continually increasing organisational pressure, at least 45 per cent of American managers bear far too much stress. This overload results in managers developing abusive, intolerant and dictatorial habits. There seems to be a vicious

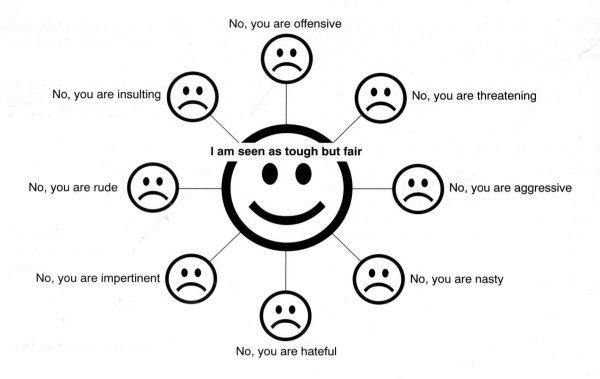

Fig. 11   To see ourselves as others see us

circle, as R. W. Walters and Associates comment in *Behavioural Sciences Newsletter*, with research showing that two of the top factors contributing to job stress are deadlines and (as a result) long working hours. These add to an unacceptable level of stress and abusive behaviour by the boss or manager.

It seems then, that stress overload may be caused by organisational Frankenstein pressures from the top, resulting in the creation of a managerial monster, who then frightens the employees. The employees may respond to this abusive behaviour by reacting in kind, or by some devious means, such as sabotage. If not, they may in turn abuse others who are defenceless. They might go home, shout at their partner, who then shouts at the children, and the children kick the cat. The employees' pent-up frustration needs an outlet.

Perhaps some companies should follow the example of a Japanese organisation which has set aside a room containing dummies, to which are attached the photographed faces of various managers, so the employee can express his/her frustration appropriately.

Regardless of the method of expression, abuse can clearly lead to a reduction in work performance, lessening of employee commitment and a decrease in employee motivation.

THE WHISTLE BLOWER

Abusive behaviour by management towards employees is a very serious and sad occurrence. It is hidden, because employees do not want to speak about it; perhaps because they feel shamed; perhaps because if they become a 'Whistle Blower' it is they that will be shunned and made to feel guilty. How do you suggest an organisation deals with this problem?

Resource power is retained by a manager who is able, for example, to give or deny a pay rise, grant a company car, or provide bonuses. The manager who has control over the departmental budget has a distinct advantage over those who do not; it is a material power held over the employee.

Position power is the power a manager holds

18

simply because he/she has a particular position in the organisation. The corporal has that power over the private; the sergeant has that power over the corporal. In the army the soldiers salute the uniform, of, say, the captain, not the person inside that uniform; it is the uniform that represents the position power, not the person. Position power also brings with it certain unseen benefits: information, access and the power to organise.

- **Information** is power, it can be reserved by the manager for distribution at selected times or to selected people. However information can be set free, from the clutches of the selfish manager, so that all who need it can function effectively. It is easy to hold on to information and make others rely on your largess.
- **Access** is the way into a network of managerial contacts, where it is who you know and not just what you know that counts. A manager may sit on a number of committees which will provide information to add to the information power.
- It is the manager who has the right, because of his/her position, to **organise** and reorganise employees and their work. According to A. M. Pettigrew, a manager's level on an organisational chart is an asset of power.

Expert power is that power vested in a manager, or consultant, because he or she is believed to have some recognised expertise. We all go to an expert when we need advice or guidance on a subject in which we lack knowledge or experience. It is a form of power most of us would like to have. Charles Handy adapted the old proverb, 'In the country of the blind, the one-eyed man is king; until he with two eyes comes along.'

Personal power is charisma. This is power of personality. Many think they have charisma when all they have is position power. Did Margaret Thatcher have charisma or was it simple position power? Does the President of the USA have position power, or is it charisma? It is difficult to define, difficult to operate. However, if we think again about the qualities or trait approach to leadership, we see that it gives prominence to the importance of charisma in a leader or manager.

A. Conger and R. N. Kanungo, in 'Toward a behavioural theory of charismatic leadership in organisational settings', *Academy of Management Review*, Vol. 12 (1987), have provided us with their idea of the behavioural ingredients of charismatic and non-charismatic leaders. It may be partly summarised as follows:

CHARISMATIC AND NON-CHARISMATIC LEADERS

Status quo

Non-charismatic

Best to keep things as sweet as they are.

Charismatic

To move on we need to change and after that change again.

Future goal

Non-charismatic

To get where I need to be I do not have to travel far.

Charismatic

My achievement horizon is still a long way off.

Likeableness

Non-charismatic

People like me because we have the same outlook.

Charismatic

I am the Pied Piper.

Expertise

Non-charismatic

I am good at using what is available to achieve my goals, all within the existing order.

Charismatic

There is another way.

Behaviour

Non-charismatic

There is nothing wrong with the present code of behaviour.

Charismatic

If I behave like everyone else I shall start to think like them.

Power Base

Non-charismatic

I need only rely on position power and personal power, based on reward, and expertise.

Charismatic

I rely on personal power, based on expertise, respect, and I have no equal.

Leader-follower relationship

Non-charismatic

I seek consensus; if it does not work then I prod or order people to share my views.

Charismatic

I admit to being élitist, an entrepreneur and a model for people to share the radical movements I advocate.

Negative power is used to stop things happening. It is the secretary blocking calls to the boss; the post room sending data in the wrong direction; and the computer programmer who inserts a time bomb in the systems ready to go off a year after his or her departure. It is an awesome power that needs to be limited and can often be linked directly to the results of a manager's contrary behaviour to employees.

Employees can use negative power to slow down changes. One team I met were able to stop changes to their department through the simple device of talking. They used the consultation mechanism to seek clarification, suggest amendments, further research, ask for the formation of sub-teams to look at particular issues and request the contribution of people outside the department. They also considered the unusual step of taking out a grievance, suggesting that the changes recommended would produce added and unnecessary stress. The department was closed down within 12 months.

We have already discussed how management

can be viewed as being an art, a science, as political and as having some magic (see page 12). The political part can also be seen as an element of power. All managers play a game of politics. The rules, as you will recall, are difficult to determine. For the winner the prizes can be promotion, money and/or status. For the loser it can mean excess stress, losing money, losing status or the sack. Some managers just dip their toes in this shark-infested water, others dive straight in. The manager can give information to unauthorised persons, start a rumour, form cliques, complain, moan, or more usually, try and sway opinion on behalf of, or against, another person or decision. Although one manager's behaviour, in itself, will not lead to the downfall, or indeed the growth, of the organisation, it can propel towards either.

POWER: WHAT WOULD INFLUENCE YOU?

Types of power: physical, resource, position, expert, personal

The teacher/lecturer has a problem with one particular group. The assignment profile of the group has been good: 10 per cent Pass, 40 per cent Merit and 30 per cent Distinction. However, lately attendance has been poor and the majority of the class do not seem to be doing any preparation, as evidenced by the low level of classroom discussion. You are one of those students. Indicate which type of power would influence you most and which least in:

(a) the short term, and
(b) the long term.

How would you view the teacher/lecturer exercising each type of power?

FURTHER READING

Understanding Organisations by Charles B. Handy, especially the chapter on 'Power and Influence'. I recommend you devour any of the works of Charles B. Handy.

MANAGEMENT SCHOOLS OR FAMILIES

The behaviour of management towards their employees has been influenced by a variety of people, especially those who have had their visions brought to the fore through academics and popular writers. The message of these management saints, may lose something in the journey from the originator to the user. The purity of the original may be diluted or altered through the interpretation of a writer or speaker and further corrupted by the manager who wishes to put that idea into action; a case of Chinese whispers.

Ideas have come and gone over the years, whilst some have lingered. Some ideas may well have been valid at a particular time. The economic situation of a country or an organisation, together with managerial readiness, have allowed the embracing of that idea. Ideas may not always change to fit the times; but the time or situation permits the acceptance of ideas.

It is useful to group these ideas into schools of thought, or families:

- Bureaucracy
- Scientific management
- Classical management
- Human relations
- Neo-human relations

Bureaucracy

Bureaucracy is a term that seems to be used today to indicate hindrance, often by means of complex procedures that are not required or desired, such as someone saying that you cannot do that until you fill in form XYB275. A bureaucratic company has a well-prepared organisation structure with well-organised employees. There is a place for everything and everything is in its place. Neat. Managers are obeyed, as the employees understand and accept that the manager is acting in accordance with rules and regulations.

Max Weber, the German sociologist and philosopher, presented bureaucracy as stability and predictability. It was seen by Thomas Carlyle, the Scottish historian and philosopher, as a Continental nuisance. John Stuart Mill, the English economist and philosopher, warned us to be very careful as a bureaucracy always tends to become what he referred to as a **pedantocracy**. This is an organisation which lays excessive stress upon detail or upon the strict adherence to rules. Mark Twain gave a nice example of a pedantocracy in action in his book, *The Prince and the Pauper*, when describing the dressing of Edward VI.

How to dress a Prince
First a shirt was taken up by the Chief Equerry-in-Waiting,
who passed it to the First Lord of the Buckhounds,
who passed it to the Second Gentlemen of the Bedchamber,
who passed it to the Head Ranger of Windsor Forest,
who passed it to the Third Groom of the Stole,
who passed it to the Chancellor Royal of the Duchy of Lancashire,
who passed it to the Master of the Wardrobe,
who passed it to Norroy King-of-Arms,
who passed it to the Constable of the Tower,
who passed it to the Chief Steward of the Household,
who passed it to the Hereditary Grand Diaperer,
who passed it to the Lord High Admiral of England,
who passed it to the Archbishop of Canterbury,
who passed it to the First Lord of the Bedchamber,
who put it on the young king.

FURTHER READING

Look at the index in a number of books on management or organisations and search for references to bureaucracy and the writers: P. Blau, W. Brown, M. Crozier, E. Jaques and M. Weber.

Scientific management

Scientific management, as we know it, really began with Charles Babbage, the Cambridge professor and father of the computer; but it is through the work of the trio, Taylor, Gantt and Gilbreth, and their time, that it has gained such importance in the minds and actions of managers. Scientific management examines the way jobs are done, the mechanics of the job. To some extent it separates the person from the job. By improving the method and training staff in that new method it is possible to work out a standard time for working within a standard method.

Frederick Winslow Taylor, the father of scientific management, urges management to manage; to work with employees in order to determine how things should be done, and not to leave these important decisions to the employees, as has been done in the past. Taylor saw his ideas as providing a 'fair day's work for a fair day's pay'. He said the application of scientific management techniques would increase production without expending more human effort or energy. In one famous study at the Bethlehem Steel Works, Taylor revised the methods of working so that the work of approximately 500 men could easily be undertaken by 140 men. The remaining 140 men received a 60 per cent pay increase. Taylor also advised managers to work towards harmony with employees and not to promote discord.

Henry Lawrence Gantt worked with Taylor for 14 years, and left more to management than the 'Gantt Chart' (a type of bar chart used by managers to organise, plan and control working activities). He assisted the application of scientific management through devising bonus plans, charts and methods of production control. Regarded as a good leader, although liable to sudden bursts of irritation, he did see that in all the problems of management, the human element was the most important one.

Frank Bunker Gilbreth and Lilian Gilbreth, partners in life and work, were strong supporters of Taylorism, and while Frank advocated the Taylor principles, Lilian, an industrial psychologist, stressed the need to look at the employees first; to try and understand their personality and needs. Frank was the pioneer of 'motion study', the investigation and measurement of all movements involved in any work task, with the idea of eliminating avoidable effort. In one study, Frank was able to more than double the production of bricklayers by reducing the movements needed to lay a brick, from 18 to 5, with no increase in effort. Frank said that his quest in life was to discover the one best way to do the work.

It is interesting to return to F. W. Taylor and his speech to a Committee of Congress at a time when his work was not well accepted. He said that scientific management is not just:

- any efficiency device
- a new system of reducing costs
- a new scheme of paying men
- holding a stop watch on a man and writing about him
- time study or motion study
- divided or functional management

Scientific management, he suggests, is a complete mental revolution of management and employee thinking. It requires that both substitute exact scientific investigation and knowledge in lieu of the opinion or judgement of each side. Taylor, although a dogmatic individual, saw management as providing a service to the employees to ensure that they had all the resources and training needed to do their job effectively. Those ideas may be looked upon favourably today, but at that time the business world was not ready for all his ideas. Although the philosophy of Frederick Winslow Taylor did not survive, his systems of scientific management did. Taylor suggests that another type of scientific investigation should receive special attention: 'the accurate study of the motives which influence men'.

The image of scientific management, however, is still someone with a stopwatch hovering over an employee, recording how long he or she takes to do a job, and telling the employee how long it should take, and how to do it better.

Can you meet the requirement of that person with the stopwatch? Can you do the job within the recommended time? Test yourself. Take a pack of cards. Get someone to time you. Deal all the cards into four hands, the deal should be reasonably neat and the hands 30 cm. apart. How long did you take? 30 seconds would be an acceptable time. But if you want to earn a bonus then I would expect your time to be nearer 22 seconds.

Write to David Charleton at the Institute of Management Services, 1 Cecil Court, London Road, Enfield, Middlesex and see if you can arrange for someone from their local branch to come along and give a short talk on the work of the Institute and how they use scientific management principles today.

Look at the index in a number of books on management or work study, management techniques, organisation and methods, and search for references to scientific management and F. W. Taylor, H. Gantt and F. and L. Gilbreth.

Classical management

Based on the experience of Henri Fayol and his followers, such as Mary Parker Follett, Lyndall F. Urwick and others, the **classical management** school of thought tends to regard employees as numbers, cogs in the wheel. It looks at employees in relation to the organisation's structure, the scalar chain, the span of control. Employees are seen as people who come to work to earn as much as they can. It is up to management to design systems to meet that need; through increased productivity, the organisation's profits will grow. Managers and employees must be seen to behave in a way that will promote organisational aims and objectives.

The classical management school places emphasis on managerial authority, the right to get things done. The tools of management include people, as well as systems and techniques. The classical school is somewhat akin to the bureaucratic school in that they both forget to give due attention to the motivation of the individual. People from different backgrounds have been grouped under the classical school. Lyndall Urwick was, for a considerable time, a colonel in the army; others worked in General Motors, Rowntree at York, and public administration in the USA. Their thoughts were all based on their own experiences. So, although they are grouped together it does not mean that they all had the same thoughts.

It was Bruno Lussato, in his book, *A Critical Introduction to Organizational Theory* published by Macmillan in 1976, who brought together components which he believed made up the common theme of classical management.

- **The scalar chain** The further up the family tree you climb, the more authority you have.
- **Exception principle** Day-to-day tasks should be done at the lowest part of the scalar chain. More difficult tasks or decisions should be given to those further up.
- **Unity of command** Wherever you are on the scalar chain you can only have one person telling you what to do; you can only have one boss.
- **Span of control** This relates to how many people one person can effectively manage.
- **Organisational specialisation** Organise the company on the basis of activities such as product, specialisms or geography.
- **Scientific methods** Do not forget to use logical scientific methods in the running of the organisation and management.

Look at the index in a number of books on management, organisations or behaviour at work and search for references to classical management or administrative management, in particular references to C. Barnard, H. Fayol, M. P. Follett, J. D. Mooney and L. F. Urwick.

Human relations

The **human relations** family was a natural growth from the systems of scientific manage-

23

ment, not perhaps as an adverse reaction to F. W. Taylor's original principles. It dealt with the problems left behind by the actual management-selective practice of scientific management, and entails more than being nice to employees. It has, as its centre, people rather than the mechanics of the job. Employees are people within an organised environment, the workplace. It is essential that employees are motivated and that motivation should be directed towards teamwork, but then it must be directed towards the company, in order to meet the needs of the individual employee and the organisation. The organisation and the employee share the wish to achieve maximum output with the minimum of input. This school of thought sees the first line supervisor as the linchpin, who has direct contact with the shop-floor employee.

The work of Elton Mayo, a Harvard Business School professor, F. J. Roethlisberger and W. J. Dickson showed that productivity and human relations were related, especially those of groups or teams. The power of groups or teams could manipulate the individual and productivity. It is the human relations school of thought that brought to the fore, once again, the idea of the organisation as a family. It also brought with it a move towards a Unitarist approach (discussed earlier, p. 2), where trade unions represented an expression of employee dissatisfaction which could not be allowed to disrupt organisational family loyalty. It became regarded, however, as a continued form of authoritarianism. It was also seen as a means of breaking the back of unionism in America, at a time when unions were having an influence on organisations that some thought inappropriate.

According to Mayo bonus schemes were not the way ahead. What was needed was a participative style of management. However, in time, a participative style was interpreted as meaning telling employees what has been decided and what will be done. Mayo did not advocate consultation of employees or any stronger forms of democratic management.

THE HAWTHORNE EXPERIMENTS

From 1924 to 1927 The National Research Council in America conducted some experiments with a team of employees at the Western Electric Company. The experiment was to find out the effect of lighting and other conditions upon the employees and their productivity. They considered the experiment a failure. The reasons for this were that every time they improved the lighting the productivity of the team improved; but every time they reduced the lighting the productivity still improved. Elton Mayo, a Harvard professor, however, continued with the experiments, at the Hawthorne Works. He not only increased and reduced the lighting, he further shortened then lengthened the rest periods and did the same with the working day; introduced and removed incentive pay schemes. No matter what he and his researchers did with this team of employees, productivity still generally improved.

What do you think were the reasons for this apparently strange occurrence?

FURTHER READING

Look at the index in a number of books on management, managing people, behaviour at work or industrial psychology, and search for the work of E. Mayo, W. Brown, F. J. Roethlisberger and W. J. Dickson, in relation to the Hawthorne Experiments. These include the studies of the Relay Assembly Rooms, the Bank Wiring Room and the Mica Splitting Group.

Neo-human relations

Neo-human relations ideas were a new and improved approach to human relations problems. This put forward the idea that employees should be permitted to grow and develop in the work they do. If employees were given responsibility and they could see that their work had some purpose in life, then this would promote a positive attitude, thus making the aims and objectives of the organisation more readily achievable. Organisations were encouraged to trust their employees. This school of thought sought to get rid of traditional forms of structures. The views of this school are given greater prominence in this section of the text, as they have had the greatest impact on the behaviour of management towards their employees today.

Masters of the neo-human relations (NHR) school, McGregor, Blake and Mouton, Likert and others, moved management away from looking at the employee as a cog in the wheel to seeing the employee as a real, living, breathing, feeling being. They also suggested that their principles can be applied to all organisations, despite their differences – a hospital is the same as a factory that makes guns. However, rhetoric and reality do not always lie comfortably together.

MANAGEMENT STYLE

Style is the manner of doing something. Here we are particularly concerned with the manager's style, as manager, that is, the way in which he or she behaves to an employee or team of employees. We view the manager through the eyes of the neo-human relations school or family. One manager with a very individual style was David Dworkin, the erstwhile chief of Storehouse, which owns Mothercare and BHS. He wore jeans to work, was a bit moody and was reputed at board meetings to pull a banana from his briefcase and eat it. His informal style, however, including the use of psychologists, was a serious attempt to get away from the traditional hierarchical order.

The main protagonists in this drama of management and employees are:

FROM THE 1940s

The **Ohio Studies** with **A. E. Fleishman** and their styles of **consideration** and **structure**.

FROM 1960

Douglas McGregor and his assumptions about human nature that lead to a particular management style, **Theory X or Theory Y**.

FROM 1961

Renis Likert, who gave us **Systems 1, 2, 3 and 4** with the goal of **participative management**.

FROM 1964

Robert Blake and **Jane Mouton** who would plot **management** on a **grid** and propose the preferred style to be 9.9.

FROM 1964

Robert Tannenbaum and **Warren Schmidt**, who, in choosing a leadership style, provide us with a range, or leadership continuum, **boss centred – subordinate centred** and suggest that the one that is preferred is the one that fits the situation.

FROM 1968

John Adair tells us that management is **action-centred leadership** and must balance the needs of the individual, the team and the task they are all undertaking.

FROM 1977

Paul Hersey and **Kenneth Blanchard**, who show us a **model of situational leadership** and advise on the most appropriate style to use on a willing and able employee and a not so willing and able employee.

with a special appearance by
the path goal theory

Ohio studies

The Ohio State Leadership Studies looked at the behavioural aspects of leaders. The resultant two-dimensional approach provided those measurements with the labels **consideration** and **structure**.

Consideration is all about how much attention a manager gives to the needs of an individual employee, through a two-way form of communication. The manager may talk, but also listens. Consideration also relates to the level of trust a manager places in his/her employees; the interaction that takes place between manager and employee; and the support and consideration a manager gives to his/her employees.

Structure is the degree of attention the manager gives to getting the job done, by the use of techniques that are very much work orientated. This fits in well with part of the list provided by Henri Fayol, especially organising, planning, and controlling employees' efforts towards the work goal. From this two-dimensional view, four types of leaders arise. These are illustrated in Figure 12.

A **high structure** but **low consideration** manager as in Figure 12A, would see production as being at a very acceptable level, but the human relations cost could be measured by the high employee leaving rate. Departures would proba-

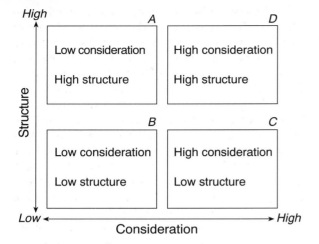

Fig. 12   Four types of manager (Ohio studies)

Jo runs a department that always meets and, at times, exceeds organisational expectations. However, there is a very high turnover of employees. Is there a problem? If so, how would you investigate and deal with it?

As an introduction, try and get hold of the popular and worthwhile *Management and Organisational Behaviour* by Laurie J. Mullins, published by Pitman, 1989.

bly follow numerous complaints about the way they have been treated. Complaints are not always expressed, however, and employees may keep silent and just leave the company.

The manager **low** on both **consideration** and **structure**, as in Figure 12B, seems to be landed with not only a poor level of productivity, but also an unhappy staff with grievances and complaints followed by a high level of resignations. This manager cannot keep productivity at a reasonable level, nor can he or she keep the employees.

The manager who is **low** on **structure** but **high** on **consideration**, (Figure 12C) finds a low rate of production, but the energy devoted to attending to the employees results in a good retention rate and a minor level of moans, groans and grievances. A happy crew, but not a lot of productivity to show for it.

Our ideal manager, **high consideration** and **high structure** (Figure 12D), expects a very good standard of work output from a contented team of employees. The manager knows the requirements of the job and the needs of the employees and acts accordingly.

It is evident that a manager has to perform a complex balancing act between carrying out the job in hand and paying attention to employees, in order to achieve a 'best style' result from both. The results of the Ohio Studies were of considerable value, but were not deemed conclusive, as it was thought that attention to situational factors should, perhaps, have been part of the equation.

Theory X and Theory Y

Douglas McGregor continued the 'best style' approach by putting forward two ideas about human nature and behaviour at work. He called them **Theory X** and **Theory Y**. Although the theories are based on contrasting opinions about people at work, the Theory X manager and the Theory Y manager should not be seen as poles apart in the way their behaviour is expressed. Newer ideas have been put forward and found favour, but McGregor and his X – Y is still a popular topic of discussion with managers.

Read each of the ten statements below, then circle the appropriate letter.

   A – I agree
   B – I tend to agree
   C – I tend to disagree
   D – I disagree

1 It is best for the boss to set the work targets for employees.

   A B C D

2 It is essential to set up meticulous controls in order to ensure that the work is being done.

   A B C D

3 It is best to supervise employees closely so that they perform at their maximum level.

   A B C D

4 It is best to intervene straight away if all is not going to plan.

   A B C D

5 Continual meetings must take place to make sure the boss knows what is going on.

A B C D

6 It is best to check at the start of each working day to see if employees need the help of the boss.

A B C D

7 The boss should never push employees to meet targets.

A B C D

8 Employees should set their own targets.

A B C D

9 It is much better if employees plan their own work.

A B C D

10 There is nothing wrong with allowing employees to make important decisions.

A B C D

Score

On statements 1 to 6 give the following points to your selection

A – 2
B – 4
C – 6
D – 8

On statements 7 to 10 give the following points to your selection

A – 8
B – 6
C – 4
D – 2

Add up your score and plot it on the graph to see if you have a tendency to X or Y

Theory X_____ Theory Y
  20   40   60   80

HOW A THEORY X MANAGER SEES EMPLOYEES

1 They are lazy and it is in their nature to dislike work.

2 Most must be coerced, controlled, directed and scared with discipline, if the organisation is to achieve its objectives.

3 The average person avoids responsibility like the plague, and prefers to be directed; they lack ambition and value holding on to their job most of all.

McGregor advises us that a manager who follows the X line, believing that their workers are naturally lazy, will treat those workers in a certain way. Such managers will rely on giving out rewards, similar to a bribe; they will make promises; they will provide incentives; they will intimidate and use any other enforcing managerial tool. Theory X has a hard style and a soft style. The hard style of Theory X behaviour is the use of coercion, threats, stifling supervision, and very tight control. The soft style of Theory X behaviour is being persuasive and achieving harmony. Theory X is reminiscent of an old police film, where, when two policemen question a suspect, one acts as a bad cop, the second as a good friendly cop; but each holds the same attitude; the hard Theory X and the soft Theory X.

At the other end of the spectrum is the Theory Y manager.

HOW A THEORY Y MANAGER SEES EMPLOYEES

1 People want to work as much as they want to rest and play.

2 People are committed to getting their work done, and will exercise self-direction and self-control in this aim.

3 If treated correctly, the average worker can learn to accept responsibility and will seek it.

4 The potential for creativity in helping to solve problems at work is widely available in the work-force.

5 The intellectual capacity of the work-force is under-utilised.

Theory Y is seen to be a more accurate description of employee attitudes towards work. Managers must harness employees' natural energy and willingness to co-operate; they should realise that employees are capable of self-control; they should encourage personal initiative and release employees' creativity. Tom Peters, a management guru of the 1990s, said that employees were very creative, except between the hours of nine and five; an obvious reference that managers blocked creativity while employees were at work.

McGregor also suggested that workers' needs are quite closely related to the actual undertaking of the work. They are more interested in doing a good job than in such things as fancy surround-

27

ings or a mouthwatering menu in the canteen; although he does not say that the latter should be ignored. Thus a manager cannot wave a magic wand to meet the prime needs of the employee, as these needs are within the very being of the employee. The manager's job, from this viewpoint, is to create the conditions which would allow employees to meet these needs themselves. Managers do this by leading and managing their employees, by guiding the employees' efforts, in a way that will also meet the needs of the organisation – that is, enable it to achieve its targets. According to McGregor, employees are neither servile or meek, nor warlike or militant; but anxious to take on responsibility, to co-operate with management, and want to share their managers' objectives.

He is not saying that Y behaviour is always appropriate. It is clear that in certain circumstances an X approach would be in order. McGregor, and indeed others of the neo-human relations school, did not question the authority of management to organise. Although he provided us with a manager's X and Y Theory of employees, McGregor did not provide an employee's X and Y Theory of managers.

McGregor should be read in conjunction with the motivation theory of Abraham Maslow, raised later in this text (see pages 136–8).

Looking at McGregor's Theory X and Theory Y on managers' assumptions about employees, how would you rewrite the theories, this time basing them on a teacher's or lecturer's Theory X and Theory Y assumptions with regard to students? Try to make a list. Discuss your list with the class and attempt to reach a consensus.

FURTHER READING

You should be able to find many references to McGregor's Theory X and Theory Y. Look through the management books in your library. List all the references and work towards a fuller understanding of X and Y.

System 4 management

Renis Likert, like McGregor, still has a considerable effect on the way managers see their behaviour. Management, we are told, has a direct influence on the quality and quantity of work through the way in which the manager governs the work of his/her employees. Likert, still pursuing an idea, followed close on the heels of McGregor by presenting his four-dimensional model of management influence, **Systems 1, 2, 3 and 4**.

- The **System 1** manager is **exploitive** and **authoritative**. The one who uses and abuses. The one who sees employees as a necessary evil needed to get the job done. This style would result in creating either hostile or cowering employees.
- The **System 2** manager is **benevolent** and **authoritative**. This one acts like the head of a family giving out occasional sweets as a reward for good behaviour. Employees may feel stifled by this approach, and may want greater freedom, but they are not hostile.
- The **System 3** manager is **consultative**. This sort of manager takes the employees' views into account when making decisions. It is the manager who makes all the decisions but he/she does listen to employees.
- The **System 4** manager is **participative**. This is the one who shares his/her role with the employees and has trust and belief in the value of their contribution. This bringing together has a positive effect in developing the individual and teams, and in getting the job done.

Systems 1 and 2 are reminiscent of McGregor's Theory X, while System 4 has similarities with Theory Y. Systems 1 and 2 managers, as Likert suggests, may produce a high productivity rate and keep financial costs low, but the human relations costs may be high, as achievements made are most likely to be short term, and through the use of fear. System 4 should be promoted by managers and be the goal of all managers. The advocates of this form of industrial democracy claim that it will pay long-term dividends, in reduced labour turnover, increased productivity, and more effective use of equipment and materials. A System 4 manager will demonstrate support

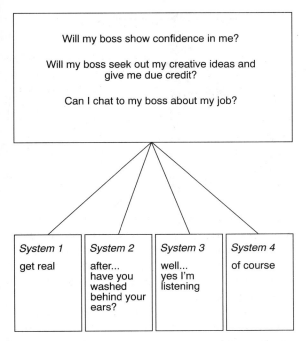

Fig. 13   *Systems 1, 2, 3 and 4 – my boss and me*

through his/her behaviour towards employees. Likert promotes team development, and reminds us that it is the manager who is responsible for the organisation of individuals into effective groups. The achievement of high accomplishments, desired by both management and employees, is via a decision-making process which should be based on group participation.

Although Likert argued for the integration of individual employees through a team structure, he envisaged that they were intended to fit within a hierarchical organised structure. He did not advocate the destruction of that structure but did think that democracy in management would bring its just rewards.

A TOUGH FIT – SYSTEM 1, 2, 3 OR 4

Where would you place The Lord Sheppard of Didgemere of Grand Metropolitan, who has described his own management style as 'management by a loose grip on the throat'? Where would you place Archie Norman of Asda, who has said that he has 65,000 people to motivate, and that they need to feel looked after? However he does not see his job as being in a popularity contest.

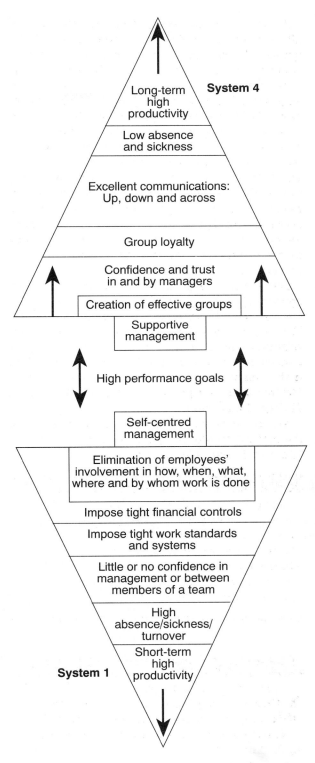

Fig. 14   *Systems 1 and 4: A separate journey to high productivity*

The leadership grid

A further way of describing management style is by means of the grid devised by Robert Blake and Jane Mouton. Similar to the Ohio Studies and strongly reminiscent of Likert's Systems 1–4, the **leadership grid** is a well packaged and well presented review of management styles.

The grid provides the opportunity to plot the style adopted by a manager. On the horizontal axis we can look at the level of importance a manager gives to getting results, his/her **concern for production**. On the vertical axis we can chart the degree to which the manager is people orientated, his/her **concern for people**. As you can see from Figure 15 the scale is from 1 to 9.

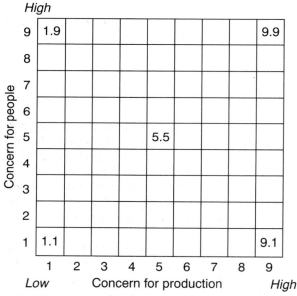

Fig. 15   The leadership grid

Although there are 81 possible results, most managers will tend towards one of the five listed below. Blake and Mouton suggest that, for each manager, one style is dominant but he/she has a back-up style if the dominant one does not work in a particular situation.

LEADERSHIP STYLES

- at **1.1**, the impoverished manager
- at **9.1**, the task-orientated manager
- at **1.9**, the country club manager
- at **5.5**, the middle-of-the-road manager
- at **9.9**, the team manager

The **impoverished manager** (**1.1**) will do little to enhance production or staff relations. He/she just cannot be bothered. This manager is present without being seen. This manager encourages neither creativity nor initiative. This manager aims to survive, does not want to contribute and tries to lie low until retirement. He/she evades conflict at all costs. He/she may need redirecting; either out of the front door or to the door of a counsellor.

The **task-orientated manager** (**9.1**) rates getting the job done as more important than any concern for people. He/she is autocratic. He/she uses people as a tool to get the work done and ignores the psychological and social aspects of work. He/she suppresses conflict by increasing managerial control and is a follower of the techniques developed through the scientific school of management. Managers tend towards this style when there is a recession.

The **country club manager** (**1.9**) likes everyone to be happy and avoids trouble; he/she considers production a poor second to keeping the staff content; a real softie. Neither creativity nor conflict is encouraged, as they are both seen as disturbing the happy balance of the group.

The **middle-of-the-road manager** (**5.5**) is able to maintain a moderate concern for production and people. He/she desires creativity within the group as long as it is regarded as 'safe'. When there is conflict, he/she will compromise. This is the one whose school report says 'Not realising their full potential. Could do better.'

The **team manager** (**9.9**) maintains a high concern for production and people. He/she creates the situation which enables staff needs to be focused on organisational objectives. Employees are free to state their opinions. Creativity is through group participation. This manager sees conflict as not only inevitable but also desirable. He/she faces up to problems openly and with honesty. He/she makes his/her employees feel that they have a stake in and are a valued part of the organisation. This is the ideal manager, the one that all managers should be working towards.

Blake and Mouton suggest that any manager's dominant style will have been greatly influenced by four particular background factors.

- **The organisation**   the type of organisation, e.g. bureaucratic or an *adhoc*racy.
- **The manager's own values**   his/her beliefs in the way people should be treated to get results.
- **The manager's personal history**   how things have worked in the past in specific and similar situations.
- **Chance**   managers are not always aware that problems may be approached from different angles, perhaps because of lack of significant past experiences.

What is an *adhoc*racy?

The work of Blake and Mouton is worthy of much further study, as they provide an analysis of motivation, conflict, behaviour and consequences, recognising the style and recommendations for change. They have said that to change a company, it was necessary for those at the top to lead that change. It is also of interest to note that their grid approach has been applied to other fields such as partnership relations, stress management, sales management, managerial leadership in nursing and social work, to name but a few.

Create your own version of the management grid. Base it on the work of teachers or lecturers or that of any other profession known to your group.

If you are able to get hold of them read: R. B. Blake and J. S. Mouton, *The Managerial Grid*, 1964, *The New Managerial Grid*, 1978, and *The Managerial Grid III*, 1985, all published by the Gulf Publishing Company. These same authors have written a number of other useful books.

Boss-centred – subordinate-centred style

Robert Tannenbaum and Warren Schmidt are the authors of one of the most popular works on leadership behaviour, *Control in Organizations* (McGraw Hill, 1968). They present us with a continuum with two extremes: boss centred, which is very like McGregor's Theory X, and subordinate centred, which is akin to McGregor's Theory Y. However, in Tannenbaum and Schmidt's model, we can move from boss centred to subordinate centred and back again, meeting different styles that can be identified by the level of control exercised by the manager. Neither extreme is perfect, as there are always limitations placed upon authority and freedom.

Tannenbaum and Schmidt's four main styles of management are labelled:

- telling
- selling
- consulting
- joining

Telling is where the manager makes the decision and announces it to the employees and then expects them to carry out any instructions. This represents an autocratic, or dictatorial, style.

Selling is where the manager still makes all the decisions, but, anticipating conflict, tries persuasion as a means of gaining the acceptance of the employees.

Consulting is where the manager presents the problem to the team, asks for advice and then listens to suggestions. Those suggestions are then taken into account before the manager makes the final decision.

Joining is where the manager presents the problem to the team and, subject to organisational and/or external limitations, allows the team to make and implement the decision. The manager acts as a member of the team. This represents a democratic approach.

Tannenbaum and Schmidt further suggest that there are three forces of particular importance in deciding which location on the continuum is desirable and practicable.

- **Forces within the manager**   these will include their own background, personality, knowledge and experience.
- **Forces within the subordinate**   the

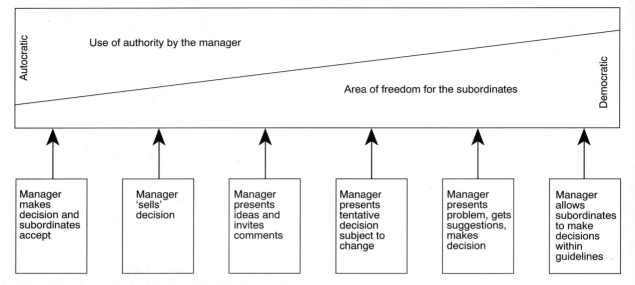

Fig. 16   A continuum of leadership behaviour

manager will have to take into account the employees' personalities and their expectations of themselves and the manager.

- **Forces within the situation**   the manager must give consideration to time pressures, the type of organisation and the character of the team.

Good managers should be recognisable by the fact that they are fully aware of these forces and how they may affect their behaviour at a specific time. They can then behave according to their understanding of themselves, the team, the individuals and the organisation.

MILITARY MINDS WITH TANNENBAUM AND SCHMIDT

If Sir William Purves, of the Hongkong & Shanghai Bank, brought with him the style of management encountered when he served in the armed forces, what would that be?

FURTHER READING

Tannenbaum and Schmidt are popular enough to be referred to in nearly all books with a section on leadership. You may also find in these books references to the continuum autocratic or dictatorial to laissez-faire. You may wish to consider the practicability of these extremes.

Functional approach

The work of John Adair and his action-centred leadership looks at the way in which a manager behaves. This model examines how the manager needs to balance the needs of the organisation to meet the **task** in hand, the need to keep the **group** or team together and the needs of the **individual** within the team. Adair shows these as three interlocking circles (see Figure 17).

Adair was fully aware that a perfect balance of the three needs is not readily achievable, so it is up to the manager to identify what is happening, and to take managerial action.

ADAIR'S EIGHT MUSTS FOR MANAGERS

1 Design the task
2 Plan
3 Brief the team/individual
4 Control
5 Evaluate
6 Organise
7 Motivate
8 Set an example

The listing is reminiscent of Fayol and Mintzberg, but all the items relate to the behaviour of the manager, functioning as an effective leader of the team and the individuals in it.

The manager is required to pay attention to the

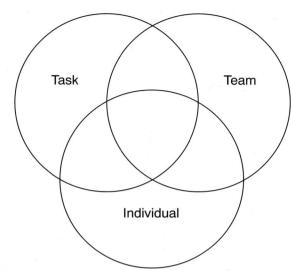

Fig. 17   Action-centred leadership

Seven things a manager must do in relation to the **Task**

Task

1 Plan the work
2 Allocate resources
3 Organise duties and responsibilities
4 Define group tasks
5 Control quality and check performance
6 Review progress
7 Achieve the objectives

Six things a manager must do in relation to the **Team**

Team

1 Appoint sub-leaders
2 Train team
3 Weld the team together as a working team
4 Maintain morale and team spirit
5 Set standards and maintain discipline
6 Set standards of communication within the team

Five things a manager must do in relation to the **Individual**

Individual

1 Train the individual
2 Meet the needs of the individual within the team
3 Attend to personal problems
4 Fix conflicts between the team's needs and the individual's needs
5 Give praise and status

Fig. 18   The manager's function

needs of the task, the team and the individual. The degree of the manager's involvement must relate to what is required, when it is required, how to take action to meet those requirements, and also what impact actions taken in one area, or circle, will have on the other areas or circles. So if the manager expends too much effort on the task, what will be the resultant effect on the individual and the team?

Adair defines the manager's functions in each area as shown in Figure 18.

Action-centred leadership recognises three different parts and it is the manager who must ensure that all receive appropriate attention in order that the whole operates effectively. The requirements of the group or team and the needs of the individual will be examined in greater detail in later sections of this text.

AN ACTION-CENTRED TRIP

Every school and college arranges trips. Why don't you get involved, as an **individual** within a **group**, to arrange such a **task**.

From your **group** select a **leader**, and in addition to the core group appoint two or more observers. The observers will record how the leader deals with the task through his/her concern for the group and the individuals within the group. As a check-list the observers could use the three circles in Figure 18, which indicate the way a leader should behave.

33

The observers may also note how the role of leader moves from the appointed leader to others within the group in order to meet particular situations.

FURTHER READING

Read John Adair, *Effective Leadership*, Pan Books, 1983.

Situational leadership model

Paul Hersey and Kenneth Blanchard present us with a further form of situational leadership, previously known as the life-cycle theory of management, in which the behavioural style of the manager relates and reacts to particular aspects of the employee.

Theirs is, perhaps, a return to, a re-examination and conclusion of the Ohio Studies, Likert traits, the Blake and Mouton Leadership Grid and the Tannenbaum and Schmidt progression model. The difference between their work and that of their predecessors is the importance and weight put upon the employees' so-called maturity.

The model looks at employees or, as Hersey and Blanchard call them, **Followers** and their readiness to follow. This they express on the by now familiar two-dimensional model. The two dimensions are, **task relationships** and **people relationships**.

These dimensions have nothing to do with the personality of the employee or follower; they refer to how **ready** a person is to perform a specific job. This is judged by the person's **ability**, which includes the necessary knowledge, experience and skill. It further looks at the person's **willingness**, that is, does he or she have the confidence, motivation and commitment to do the job?

This readiness (**R**) is shown as having four stages, one following another (a continuum) where, **R1** is **low**, **R2 low** to **moderate**, **R3 moderate** to **high**, and **R4** is **high**.

Low follower readiness (**R1**) is identified through lack of commitment and motivation and such people are seen as unable; in addition they are unwilling, or rather, they are insecure in themselves.

Low to **moderate** followers (**R2**) are unable to do to the job but show they are willing. They do not have the ability but are motivated enough to have a go. They may have confidence, but this does not match their ability.

Moderate to **high** followers (**R3**) are able but unwilling. They can do the job but do not want to do it. They may be perfectly capable but rather insecure, or are unsure of themselves.

High followers (**R4**), as you would expect, are able and willing. They have the ability and commitment. They display their confidence.

R3	R2
Able but unwilling or insecure	Unable but willing or confident
Able and willing or confident	Unable and unwilling or insecure
R4	R1

Fig. 19   Readiness within the situational leadership model

The behavioural style a manager should use involves a mixture of relationships, some focused on the work to be done, and others that are focused on paying attention to the employees as people. The **task** relationship, or behaviour, indicates how much the manager will concern him/herself with providing instructions as to the what, when, where, and how of targeting and performing the work. The **people** relationship shows the level of activity the manager puts into talking with the employees, hearing what they have to say, giving help and reassurance.

Hersey and Blanchard provide four basic management styles, the use of which enables a manager who knows the readiness of his/her employees to cope with those identified as R1, R2, R3 or R4. These styles (**S**) are defined as **S1 – Telling**, **S2 – Selling**, **S3 – Participation** and **S4 – Delegating**.

S1 involves telling the employee what work to

do, and how to do it. Taking the employee by the hand. This style may be appropriate when a department is going through some change. It would be suitable for dealing with new employees, and dealing with a sudden request or problem that requires a quick response. This directing style fits well with **Low follower readiness** or **R1**. It also fits with an **R2** when a new and complex job needs to be done. An **R2**, **R3** or **R4** would not appreciate a directing style as the norm. If a manager adopts this as his/her major style then he/she may be seen as a despot.

S2 is selling the idea, explaining why and how decisions have been reached, clarifying any problem areas. A manager with this style makes the decisions but tells employees the reasons for those decisions. It is a form of coaching and is best for those with **Low to moderate follower readiness** or **R2**. It can work for developing an **R1** who has done well under close supervision. It would also help an **R3** who was backsliding, or the **R3** who needed to meet a tight schedule. It would help those who need some information or knowledge. It is a reasonable style to use in order to check out an employee on a new task.

A manager would not employ this style with a clear **R1**, as it gives more encouragement and conferring than should be required. A clear **R3** would see it as over-direction and an **R4** as over-supportive. The over-playing of a coaching style would be seen as questioning the efforts of the employee.

Participation is the key to the **S3** approach. The manager shares the ideas, and facilitates the decision-making process by talking matters through with the employee. This nourishing, 'working together', style is most suitable with employees who have **High to moderate follower readiness** or **R3**.

A manager would also use this style with, say, an **R4** who has a personal problem or a temporary obstacle in the quality or amount of his/her work. It could be used with the employee who needs a little extra understanding and help, particularly if he/she is engaged on a task with which he/she is not fully familiar. This style is not suitable for rescuing a situation that the employee could perfectly well have worked through him/herself. The manager must not blanket the employee with support or be seen to be mothering him or her.

Delegating (**S4**) occurs when the manager lets

the employees make the decisions and also allows them to be responsible for implementation. This fulfilling style is best suited to the **High readiness follower** or **R4**.

However it is preferable not to use this style if giving an **R4** an unaccustomed task or if the department is in the throes of change. This style is not a excuse for the manager to fail to monitor an employee's performance.

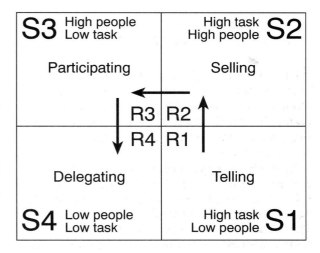

Fig. 20   Styles to meet readiness within the situational leadership model

It may be noticed that in terms of readiness the follower at **R1** is unwilling and insecure; at **R2** is willing and confident; but at **R3**, becomes unwilling and insecure again. This seeming inconsistency is explained by Hersey and Blanchard. They suggest that at R1 the follower is directed by the manager, S1, and is told what to do and how to do it; this style is very task orientated. In order to reach **R4**, which is follower directed, the employee appears to lose confidence as the move from task to people relationships begins to become evident.

Although the model has been called into question, it still has considerable support and is widely used in management training programmes. Managers are able to work with the situational model, as it appears to have validity, it is simple to understand, and can be very quickly put into practice. The situational model is seen as a potent management tool, especially if it can be attached to the path goal model, and the manager can then work out the most appropriate method of behaviour to deal with a variety of situations and employees.

Path goal theory

This theory, devised by R. J. House and G. Dessler, is closely linked with the motivational expectancy theory examined later in section 3, on the individual.

SIX REQUIREMENTS FOR BECOMING AN EFFECTIVE MANAGER

1 The manager must identify what he/she wants from the employee, what the employee wants from the manager, and what the employee wants for him/herself.

2 The manager must give rewards equal to the employee's productivity.

3 The manager must show the employees how they can get what they want, provided, of course, that it can be given by the manager.

4 The manager must help the employees to see the kind of effort that leads to good levels of performance. This is where the manager is concerned with the motivation of the employee.

5 The manager must ensure that the employees have all the necessary materials, equipment, knowledge and skills to perform to a good standard. If they do not have them, then he/she must make provisions and train them.

6 The manager must give the employees work that they will find interesting, challenging and stretching, that is, intrinsically satisfying. The manager must also give them other work that will bring rewards, that is, work that is extrinsically satisfying.

In the **Path Goal model** the manager is able to select one of four styles:

1 The **directive** style – this is the familiar telling what to do and how to do it.

2 The **supportive** style – a sort of paternalistic approach, he/she shows concern for the employee.

3 The **participative** style – where the manager consults with the employee, taking into account what the employee has to contribute, before the manager makes the decision.

4 The **achievement-orientated** style – when the manager expects (and there is evidence that it may happen) a high level of performance from the employees and looks for further improvements.

The manager stretches the employees and shows confidence in their ability to meet the challenge.

Choice of style

The choice of style demands a close look at the situation. It is important that a manager looks at the employees' ability and then selects the style which would have an impact either immediately or in a reasonable time. The manager should be asking: what style would suit that particular employee? It must not be forgotten that the manager must keep an eye on the task and its need in relation to the overall aims and objectives of the department and organisation.

Gurus

In the 1980s and 1990s management's attention was drawn to the ideas of what may be regarded as the high-profile equivalent of new age spiritual teachers, or gurus. The reason for their popularity, for they are the equivalent of the managerial pop or film star, may be that managers are still seeking the definitive solution to the employee problems they encounter. These gurus are seen to bring a practical solution, they put flesh on the bones of theory. They are the leaders of large successful organisations. They are management consultants who have an acquaintance with successful innovative organisations and they distil that success into management action plans. It is not suggested, however, that Ernest Saunders, Robert Maxwell or Asil Nadir be used as role models.

Some of the gurus' wisdom related to management behaviour includes:

THE TO BE ATTITUDES OF MANAGEMENT

- Blessed are the managers that help employees to do a better job.
- Blessed are the managers that ensure their employees receive continuing education and training.
- Blessed are those managers that remove management by fear, and then manage by example.
- Blessed are those managers that have an inspiring vision and also give employees vision and values, as they both have ownership of the organisation.
- Blessed are those managers that make employees aware that their best performance is needed and that they will reap the rewards of the organisation's success.

the management

AN ASSESSMENT OF STYLE

The purpose of this activity is to identify your leadership style and your relative concerns for tasks or people, and locate it in terms of three 'types' of leadership.

1 Fill in the T–P Leadership Questionnaire, following the instructions given.

2 Now look at the Profile Sheet.

3 Scoring is as follows:

   (a) Circle the statement number for statements 8, 12, 17, 18, 19, 30, 34 and 35.

   (b) Write the number 1 in front of a *circled statement number* if you responded S (Seldom) or N (Never) to that item.

   (c) Also write a number 1 in front of *statement numbers not circled* if you responded A (Always) or F (Frequently).

   (d) Circle the number 1s which you have written in front of the following statements: 3, 5, 8, 10, 15, 18, 19, 22, 24, 26, 28, 30, 34 and 35.

   (e) Count the *circled number 1s*. This is your score for concern for people. Record the score in the blank following the letter P at the end of the questionnaire.

   (f) Count the *uncircled number 1s*. This is your score for concern for tasks. Record this number in the blank following the letter T.

4 Now follow the instructions given on the Profile Sheet to plot your T–P Leadership Style Profile.

T–P LEADERSHIP QUESTIONNAIRE

Directions: The following items describe aspects of leadership behaviour. Respond to each item according to the way you would most likely act if you were the leader of a work group. Circle whether you would most likely behave in the described way:

always **A**, frequently **F**, occasionally **O**, seldom **S**, or never **N**

A	F	O	S	N	*1*	I would most likely act as the spokesman of the group.
A	F	O	S	N	*2*	I would encourage overtime work.
A	F	O	S	N	*3*	I would allow members complete freedom in their work.
A	F	O	S	N	*4*	I would encourage the use of uniform procedures.
A	F	O	S	N	*5*	I would permit the members to use their own judgement in solving problems.
A	F	O	S	N	*6*	I would stress being ahead of competing groups.
A	F	O	S	N	*7*	I would speak as a representative of the group.
A	F	O	S	N	*8*	I would needle members for greater effort.
A	F	O	S	N	*9*	I would try out my ideas in the group.
A	F	O	S	N	*10*	I would let the members do their work the way they think best.
A	F	O	S	N	*11*	I would be working hard for a promotion.
A	F	O	S	N	*12*	I would tolerate postponement and uncertainty.
A	F	O	S	N	*13*	I would speak for the group if there were visitors present.
A	F	O	S	N	*14*	I would keep the work moving at a rapid pace.
A	F	O	S	N	*15*	I would turn the members loose on a job and let them go to it.
A	F	O	S	N	*16*	I would settle conflicts when they occur in the group.
A	F	O	S	N	*17*	I would get swamped by details.
A	F	O	S	N	*18*	I would represent the group at outside meetings.
A	F	O	S	N	*19*	I would be reluctant to allow the members any freedom of action.
A	F	O	S	N	*20*	I would decide what should be done and how it should be done.
A	F	O	S	N	*21*	I would push for increased production.
A	F	O	S	N	*22*	I would let some members have authority which I could have kept.
A	F	O	S	N	*23*	Things would usually turn out as I had predicted.
A	F	O	S	N	*24*	I would allow the group a high degree of initiative.
A	F	O	S	N	*25*	I would assign group members to particular tasks.
A	F	O	S	N	*26*	I would be willing to make changes.
A	F	O	S	N	*27*	I would ask the members to work harder.

A	F	O	S	N	28	I would trust the group members to exercise good judgement.
A	F	O	S	N	29	I would schedule the work to be done.
A	F	O	S	N	30	I would refuse to explain my actions.
A	F	O	S	N	31	I would persuade others that my ideas are to their advantage.
A	F	O	S	N	32	I would permit the group to set its own pace.
A	F	O	S	N	33	I would urge the group to beat its previous record.
A	F	O	S	N	34	I would act without consulting the group.
A	F	O	S	N	35	I would ask that group members follow standard rules and regulations.

T _____   P _____

T–P LEADERSHIP STYLE PROFILE SHEET

Directions: To determine your style of leadership, mark your score on the **concern for task** dimension (T) on the left-hand arrow below. Next, move to the right-hand arrow and mark your score on the **concern for people** dimension (P). Draw a straight line that intersects the P and T scores. The point at which the line crosses the **shared leadership** arrow indicates your score on that dimension.

Shared leadership results from balancing concern for task and concern for task and concern for people

Autocratic leadership:	Shared leadership:	Laissez-Faire leadership:
High productivity	High morale and productivity	High morale

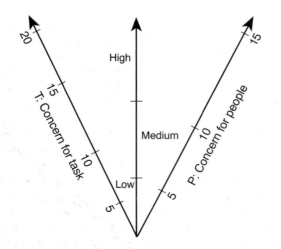

THE STYLE SHOW

This is a team activity.

Your production company has been commissioned by Channel 4 to make a programme on **Managers and their Style**. You are to fill a slot, Sunday afternoon, 6.30 p.m. to 7.00 p.m., with presentations, interviews and a panel discussion, AND IT IS LIVE.

Remember you have exactly 28 minutes (not 30) less 2 minutes for advertising. The adverts occur at the 13th and 14th minutes. Your timing must be spot-on, as the various Channel 4 regions run adverts tailored for their own region. You also have to make the adverts for your own region; they may be pre-recorded. The whole, although live, must be taped for a showing on a later 2.00 a.m. slot.

Throughout your preparation a number of observers will make a record of the management methods and styles your team used to complete the assignment. The observers will get together with the tutor to discuss their assessments of the manager, the team and individual behaviour. You should keep a record of your contribution and the contribution of others.

NB: Keep the recording and your notes as you will need them later when looking at groups.

FURTHER READING

Your research is not yet complete. Find and read: Charles Handy and his 'Best Fit' Approach, F. E. Fielder and his Contingency Model, V. H. Vroom and P. W. Yetton on their Contingency Model.

Look up and read some of the gurus of the 1990s: W. E. Demming, Tom Peters, Edward de Bono and Ken Blanchard.

COMMUNICATIONS

British two-handed finger spelling alphabet

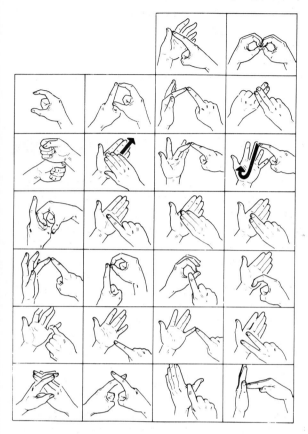

When you see a sign reading 'Wet Paint', do you touch it? When you see a sign reading 'Trespassers will be Prosecuted', why do you not believe it? A miser was in trouble in the local swimming pool and two people came to the rescue. The first reached out and said, 'Give me your hand', the second said, 'Take my hand'. Which was the better communicator?

Since managers achieve results through people, then one aspect of the manager's role is to communicate with the employee. Perhaps more than 60 per cent of a manager's time is taken up in some form of communication – talking, listening, reading and writing. Managers also need to make sure that they are being understood and that, they, in turn, understand their employees.

To communicate effectively is not an easy task. Take your teacher/lecturer for example. Did you know that if you just sit there and listen to him or her talking at you, and then a few weeks later you

were asked to recall the content of that lecture, you would only have retained about 5 per cent of what the teacher had said? If you are given something to read then the recall rate creeps up to 10 per cent. It is obvious that the teacher/lecturer needs to use additional methods in order to communicate effectively some abstract theory or method of performing a practical task. The use of audio-visual aids increases the recall rate to 20 per cent; demonstration moves it up to 30 per cent; discussion groups to 50 per cent; practising the task increases it to 75 per cent and if you then have to teach someone else, or apply that learning immediately, the recall rate is up to 90 per cent. Managers are no different from the teacher/lecturer; they have to use all means at their disposal to ensure their message is received and understood.

YOU HEARD IT – NOW TELL IT

Pick a subject from the core or perhaps from this option, it does not matter which, but ensure all the group choose the same subject. Now, individually, jot down a few notes from your memory, on the content of that subject as you learnt it two weeks ago. What was it all about? What was the message? Take 15 minutes. Re-form as a group and share your understanding. If your understanding of the topic is different from other people's, why is this? Is it a problem related to the person that delivered the sessions, or to you as the recipient?

Managers, as we have seen, need to plan and co-ordinate the working activities of their employees, they need to communicate. Managers also need to co-operate with other departments within the organisation so that they may all work towards the achievement of organisational and departmental aims and objectives, again, they need to communicate. Employees need to know what the organisation and department expects from them, so they need to communicate. Employees need development in order to realise their full personal and work-related potential, again, they need to communicate.

Poor communication can cause misunderstanding between management and the employee, and this could result in confusion, wastage of time, materials or money. It could be the cause of mistakes and accidents and could even be the basic reason for a strike. Poor communications can lower morale, demotivate employees and decrease production. As an organisation gets bigger so will the problems of communicating to the different parts within that organisation.

As communication is the process of passing on information and understanding from one person to another it is quality, not quantity, that is important. Communication, then, is the giving and taking of information between a sender and a receiver and the deduction, by both, of the meaning and purpose.

Direction of communication

The direction of communication in an organisation may be vertical, horizontal or diagonal.

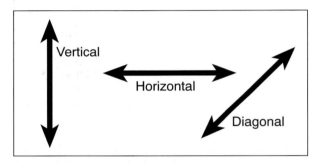

Vertical communication is communication that goes down the organisation scalar chain, from the top to the bottom, or from the manager to the employee. It also moves up the organisation, from the employee to the manager and, perhaps, further towards the top of the organisational tree.

Horizontal communication is between those on the same grade or ranking in the organisation. It is within a team of employees and also with those of similar status in other departments. Horizontal communication is the most common form within an organisation.

Diagonal communication is between those of different levels working in different departments. The human resources department, for example, will communicate with managers in order to advise on discipline and grievance matters, they may also communicate directly with an employee requiring advice on a welfare matter. Diagonal communication usually relates to advisory issues where the persons concerned do not have a direct line relationship.

Formal and informal communication

Formal communication is that which is necessary within a department and with other departments in order to aid and co-operate in the meeting of organisational aims and objectives.

Informal communication is welfare associated in that it is supportive of the well-being of the individual. It may be vertical, as when the manager provides help to an employee who may be finding it difficult to cope. It may be diagonal, for example between the human resources management department which provides a counselling services to employees. It may be horizontal, between employees seeking mutual support, who may form as discussed in Section 2, kinship–friendship groups; cliques and sub-cliques (see p. 62). These are groups, formed by those with no formal authority, and designed to be self-supportive. Such forms of communication, like the grapevine, can help or harm the organisation. It is up to the management of the organisation to harness the power of such communication for the benefit of the organisation.

Process of communication

The process of communication may also be described by the examination of a model (Fig. 21).

It can be seen that any communication needs seven elements.

THE SEVEN COMMUNICATION NEEDS
1 Message
2 Sender
3 Encoding
4 Medium or transmission
5 Receiver
6 Decoding
7 Feedback

The **message** may be necessary because a person wants to inform others of something, provide instructions to a particular individual or team, check facts, or seek clarification. The message has to have a source, that is, the **sender**, who needs a way to put the message into a suitable form. This is the thinking process – or how to impart the meaning of the message – that is, how

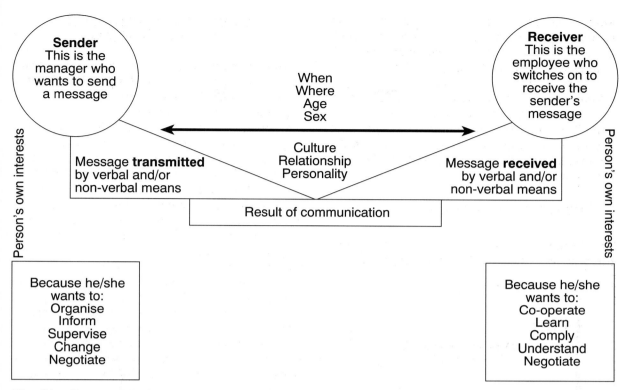

Fig. 21   One model of communication

to **encode** it. The message could be in writing or spoken – that is what is meant by the **medium** or **transmission**. The right individual or team has to hear or read and understand the message; this person is a **receiver**, who will then **decode** the meaning of the message. In addition the sender needs **feedback** to ensure that the message has been received and understood.

Communication has been likened to a radio transmission. As with a radio, problems can occur when there is **interference**, **distortion** or **noise**, because the sender or receiver is not tuned into the proper wavelength. Unless the manager can effectively communicate his/her ideas and instructions to the individual or team, those ideas and instructions will be lost in the atmosphere.

Communication systems

If the system of communication is restricted, then it shows that the manager wants to retain control of communication. Such a manager speaks to a limited number of employees and discourages employees from engaging in cross-communication. This type of system may be seen as the

equivalent of the manager speaking to each employee through individual radio channels (see Figure 23).

The manager must encourage and control an open system of communication, which is more akin to a web (see Figure 24). The web system is somewhat similar to the way in which the manager of my local leisure centre communicates

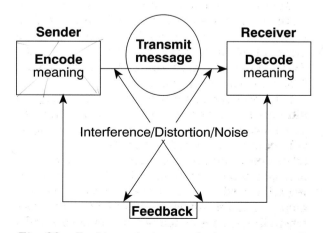

Fig. 22   Problems in transmission

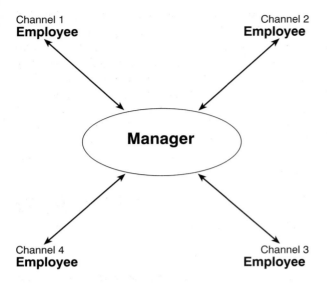

Fig. 23   *The satellite or wheel system where there is no formal connection between employees*

instructions to staff. Each employee has a two-way radio. The manager calls a particular employee to give an instruction or piece of information, and the employee responds. However, the radio channel is open so that all employees hear the communication, both ways.

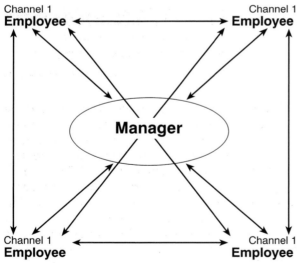

Fig. 24   *The web system*

Grapevine

The restricted system encourages the use of the grapevine. The grapevine does not replace formal communication, but operates within it and is fast. The grapevine is an informal route used to pass

on gossip and rumour. It may be seen as a leakage of bits of information. Bits are half a story not a whole, and the grapevine fills in the rest, in the absence of management providing the whole information. The result is plausible, but can be a bit of a fairytale.

For example this illustration represents the leakage of information:

The grapevine provides additional information to clarify the picture, allowing the employees to interpret the information and see one picture. This might not, however, be the picture the management intended to portray; they might have provided entirely different information to complete the picture.

WHAT DO YOU SEE?

There are two images in the picture above. Do you see what the manager said? Or do you see something different?

To prevent distortion by the grapevine, management must get to and inform employees in advance and plug any leak, or, when a distorted message is brought to their attention, stop it with the facts.

There is always one person, or more, who loves to spread rumours in order to discredit the manager and lower the morale of the team. The manager must identify the rumour-monger as soon as possible, so as to correct any distortion, to find out why he/she is behaving in such a way, and then stop him/her. Should malicious rumours continue the manager may be forced into taking disciplinary action against those responsible in order to prevent the disintegration of a team of employees.

The manager must not attempt to destroy the grapevine, as it is a natural and essential part of organisational life. The manager must live with it, and perhaps use it as a valid form of communication. He/she must harness the grapevine and make it work towards the achievement of organisational aims and objectives.

Channels of communication transmission

There are a number of channels available to the manager which aid communication with employees. Communication is most commonly verbal, (meaning 'expressed in words') and can be either written or oral. Another channel of communication, used when the sender and receiver can see one another, is body language. The manager must first decide which mode of transmission is best for the specific circumstances. The communication must be:

F.O.C.U.S.E.D.

Formality – is this an official communication? If it is, then it should be in writing. Minutes of a meeting or disciplinary letters are obvious examples. But a manager does not always get it right. Employees who have received a memorandum of appreciation for a task well done would perhaps prefer the 'positive stroke' face to face. The formality of the communication would not achieve the desired result, unless it were preceded by a direct personal pat on the back.

KEEP IT FORMAL

List three situations where it is important that a manager keeps communications with employees on a formal basis.

Objective – will it do what I want it to do? Will the method of communication get the employee to act accordingly? Would it be better to telephone someone inviting them to join a working group than to write to them? Some people seldom react to written requests for information on time. They believe that if the matter is important enough the sender will send a reminder or telephone them. More often than not, as if to prove them right, the telephone call or written reminder does not come.

ALL RISE

If the manager wants a 10 per cent increase from his/her 20-strong sales team, how would he/she communicate this information?

Confidentiality – is it for the eyes or ears of the intended receiver only? What effect does it have on the receiver, when a manager tells an employee off about poor standards of work in front of others? Even worse, if the manager asks another to deliver the message? Oral communication may be appropriate, but in private, please.

KEEP IT TO YOURSELF

What method(s) of communication would be appropriate in advising an employee of a pay rise?

Understood – will the receiver understand the message in the form provided? Would it be more effective if it were in the form of a team discussion? Would they have problems with the language in a written communication? What level of language would you use to ensure comprehension? What feedback is needed to check understanding? Consider how the receiver will feel when he/she receives the communication; what is the status of the receiver, are they superior or subordinate? This may, in itself, dictate the method of transmission.

ALL CLEAR?

Give two methods you would use to check a student's understanding of a lecture?

Speed – what is the degree of urgency? Must the message be delivered now? If so, telephone or go and visit in person. If not, consider arranging a meeting or writing a memorandum.

Provide three examples of when speed would be of the essence to a manager in communicating with employees.

Expenditure – is the cost really necessary, can it be done more cheaply? It is cheaper to write to your auntie in Australia than to speak to her on the phone for half an hour. But it is obvious what your auntie would prefer. In business think of the cost of the time it takes to draft a memorandum, get it typed and put it through the internal mail – why not phone? A meeting can be effective, but think of the cost of bringing all the team together. While they are at the meeting they cannot be getting on with other work and just add up the cost of, say, the salaries of ten persons for a one-hour meeting, plus the cost of their travelling to and from the meeting.

You are working for a recruitment agency and need to get ten CVs to New York by close of business tomorrow. How would you do it and how much will it cost?

Dependability – will the message get to the person or persons who need to know? If the management wish to advise all the staff about an important issue, the most obvious place would be on the notice board. Obvious, that is, until you realise that few people read the notice board, they are too busy walking past it. The sender must be sure that the message will arrive at its intended destination, otherwise why bother? Try the most suitable route. Do not, for example, deliver a talk to a group of employees in the canteen, especially if people are digging up the road just outside the window, as the message will not get through to its destination.

What is the most dependable way to inform 100 students (four classes of 25) that, following a visit from the moderator, they are required to undertake an additional finance assignment over the Christmas period?

Written communications

The manager may choose to communicate in writing. This method would be chosen if the information must be recorded or it is to be circulated. If there is not such need then the manager should consider an alternative.

1 **Letters**   used to transmit information outside the organisation.
2 **Memoranda**   used to transmit information within the organisation.
3 **Electronic mail**   (or 'E-Mail') is an increasingly popular way of communicating via computer, where the message is stored in the receiver's 'mailbox' and retrieved when the receiver wishes.
4 **Reports**   used where complex ideas or proposals are recorded and it is necessary for a number of people to review the contents of the report and then use this information as the basis for an important decision or future plans.

Managers should not generate unnecessary paperwork. It has been known, for some newly appointed managers to issue a great many memoranda and new and revised forms, almost as if this proliferation of paperwork provides a justification of their appointment.

Managers need to keep their writing to a minimum, they should keep their written communications short and simple. A notorious exception to this may be found in a document issued by the Welsh Office, National Health Service Directorate. Below are the first 46 words of their 167-word definition of an item common to all homes, hotels and hospitals.

A device or arrangement that may be used to permit a patient to lie down when the need to do so is a consequence of the patient's condition rather than a need for active intervention such as examination, diagnostic investigation, manipulative treatment, obstetric delivery or transport. . .

What is that item? You may need time to sleep on it.

If the manager wants to tell or instruct, then he/she should put across that message in the first sentence. Managers should never assume that the receiver will read all that is written. Keep it short and simple – **KISS**.

List three other forms of written communication within an organisation, eg notice boards, and suggest the advantages and disadvantages of each. Consider which form of written communication you would use to inform staff of redundancies, a change in the way the bonus is calculated, a trip to the theatre, and a rise in the prices in the canteen.

Oral communications

I used to experience some communication problems when I worked with an American company. It was the age-old problem of words or phrases having different meanings. My American manager used to ask, 'Do you hear me?' My first thought was that maybe she thought I was deaf, or that I looked as though I was not paying attention. No, what she meant was, 'Do you understand what I am saying and are you aware of the full implications of what I have said?' I spent some time working in Liverpool, and when I first arrived I used the same words I used in Edinburgh and London, but though the way, the form and the context in which I used those words were fine in 'Old Reekie' and 'The Smoke' they could have got me arrested in 'The Pool'.

Provide a list of English words the British usage of which differs from the American usage. Or a list of words the usage of which differs from one part of the UK to another.

A manager should be aware that speaking to an employee or a team is one of the most important skills of a manager. If a manager needs to express substantial ideas then he/she must try to do so in a simple form. The delivery is just as important as the message that has to be conveyed. The degree of enthusiasm will show through when the manager speaks. He/she must not show aggression or indeed impatience with the employee or team, nor be passive. The manager should try and stick to the matter in hand, and not just say whatever springs to mind – as that may cause him/her to stray from the point. The manager should keep the message short and should even try to copy the teacher (because, after all, teaching is part of the manager's role), perhaps by using visual aids when they are speaking. As feedback is vital, the manager needs to know that his/her message has been received and understood, so a manager must always look for signs of interest or disinterest among his/her audience.

Body language

Each time we speak to someone we also communicate with them through our body language. That is, we either confirm or deny what we have said by the body movements we make. Those movements are made as we speak. The listener also has a message to impart through his or her body language. Imagine a manager listening to an employee talking about a personal problem. The employee is looking sad and hurt, hunched up in a chair explaining a rather difficult personal problem. The manager is tapping a pen on his/her desk and looking round the room with a supercilious grin on his/her face, but speaks the words that say he or she is listening. What message does this give the employee? The message is simply that the manager does not care. A lack of trust will result between that employee and the manager.

Many books have been written on body language, and when you read some, you might think that they provide the key to enable you to unlock the door to a brand new world in understanding the truth behind the spoken word: you always knew that politicians were economical with the truth, now you can have it confirmed by reading their body language; you can spot the salesperson who is lying and the liar at interview. Alas, most of what is written is at the 'pop psychology' stage and while you are busy reading that someone who is scratching his/her nose is about to lie, the liar is reading the same book that tells him/her how to disguise body language in order to give a positive message to the receiver.

It is worth remembering that one signal on its own is not confirmation of a particular interpretation. What is or may be of value, is a series of signals linked to the spoken word which then provide a deeper understanding of the spoken message.

Although care should be taken not to arrive at snap judgements there are some non-verbal signs that have been given common interpretation:

Five non-verbal signals

- Eye contact
- Facial expression
- Body posture
- Gestures
- Voice

Although **eye contact** will vary within cultures there are some general interpretations. Direct eye contact can suggest that the person means what he or she is saying, but staring can be a bit aggressive. Looking away or lowering the eyes can suggest a lack of confidence or submission.

Does the **facial expression** match with what the person is saying? Can you tell the difference between a sarcastic smile and a genuine smile?

A slouching **body posture** with the head down can suggest a lack of confidence; stick out your chin and that can be seen as being aggressive. The norm to indicate assertiveness as opposed to aggression is the upright yet relaxed stance.

A **gesture** such as pointing the finger may indicate aggression, the wringing of hands or fiddling with something may suggest that the person is a bit nervous. There are some people who find it difficult to talk without moving their hands and arms. If such movements appear natural and relaxed then they are used simply to add emphasis to what they are saying.

SPIRAL STAIRCASE

Describe a spiral staircase without using any gestures.

The **voice**, if too loud, can reveal aggression, whereas a soft voice can give the impression of non-resistance. You can hear the whinger, the

seducer and the bully in the tone of voice. If someone ends on a downward note, then he or she appears certain in what they are saying. If a person ends on an upward note, he or she may have some doubts.

TELL ME MORE

What interpretation would you place upon each of the following gestures?

1 Twiddling with the ear
2 Rubbing the chin
3 Keeping hands immobile
4 Foot tapping
5 Not looking the listener in the eye

Feedback

If a manager is convinced that an employee needs to do better, the subject should not be turned into a personal matter. Take, as an example, the teacher as a manager and the student as an employee. A student has handed in an assignment that the teacher considers needs considerable extra work before it will reach a pass standard. The last thing the teacher should do is call the student stupid or thick or any variation of the two. Like a manager, the teacher must apply a 'sandwich' technique, two pieces of medium-cut high fibre brown bread, holding in between the main ingredient. Starting with the top layer of bread, the teacher should tell the student what is good about the assignment. (There must be something, otherwise the teacher's – or manager's – selection process or their ability to manage should be called into question.) Next, the teacher must move into the main ingredient and tell the student what improvements can be made, not that this is wrong and that is wrong. Finally, the other layer of bread: the teacher and student should agree a programme for improving the standards, in behavioural terms, perhaps by close supervision by the teacher/manager, or additional coaching, or the student/employee reviewing the time and or energy put into the task. Whatever the mutually agreed third stage, it must be one that moves the task and the employee forward, where both participants are aware of the problem, the reason for that problem and then the resolution to that problem. Now, if the manager (teacher) stuck to calling the employee (pupil) stupid or thick, there would be no improvement, the employee would not listen to the manager, there would be a complete communication breakdown and, the employee should then have the sense to take out a grievance against that manager.

General problems in communicating

TWELVE GOOD REASONS WHY COMMUNICATIONS FAIL	
1	Not enough information
2	Too much information
3	Body language
4	Differences in background
5	Status
6	Emotions
7	Social class
8	Race
9	Educational level
10	Age
11	Expectations
12	Time

Not enough information or too much information – if there is not enough information to act upon then it may be disregarded; if there is too much information then important bits may be overlooked, there is too much to handle. The sender must ensure that the information given is in manageable, meaningful, useful chunks.

Body language not matching the spoken word – the receiver may hear what the sender has to say but the non-verbal signs, such as facial expression, posture and other body language, may not match the spoken word.

Differences in background – an information technology (IT) expert may have problems communicating with someone who is not familiar with the technical jargon of an IT specialist, especially if that specialist insists on using the same language he or she would normally use when speaking to others in the same field. The technical jargon becomes a foreign language and the receiver may nod his or her head, pretending to understand, so as not to look stupid. It is like a lecturer delivering an economics lecture to a group of MBA students, then the following day delivering

exactly the same lecture to a group of GNVQ Advanced students. If sender and receiver do not speak the same language then communication problems are bound to occur.

Status – the value put on what a person has to say is related to the status of the person saying it. The senior manager will be listened to closely, because he/she is the boss. Those regarded as experts have the ear of others, as they are seen as people with something important to say. However, an employee on the shop floor, who may have something very valuable to say, will not have the same credibility so may experience difficulty in finding an audience willing to listen.

Emotions – if a receiver/employee or indeed a sender/manager is angry, irate, afraid, anxious, apprehensive, nervous, or shy, emotions could retard the transmission of information. Any conflict or discord between the sender and the receiver will hinder the receiver, in that he/she will hear what they want to hear and neglect that which they do not wish to take in. If the receiver/employee distrusts the sender/manager he or she may look for a hidden meaning in the transmitted message.

Social class, **race** or **educational level** – differences in, or any prejudice about, these matters can impede good communication, especially if sender or receiver expresses or feels superior to the other.

Age – differences in age can cause problems if, for example, an older person considers a younger person to be pushy and lacking experience of the real world, or if a younger person thinks that the older person is either a 'has been' or has never made it. My favourite sign in a fast food outlet says: 'Hire a teenager today while they know everything'.

Expectations – people now have higher educational standards and now expect to be consulted, advised, informed of all that will affect them at work. Employees' expectations in these respects are not always met.

Time – managers are subject to growing pressure to meet deadlines and achieve targets. Each departmental manager is required to take on the role of trainer, counsellor, financial controller, marketing, sales and personnel manager. All these burdens consume the scarce commodity of time.

Listening

Do you have a problem listening? I do. Listening to a lecturer or teacher droning on and on makes me want to fall asleep. It is not necessarily the subject, it is partly the fault of the sender, it is partly the fault of the transmission. Alas, the greater fault lies with me, the receiver.

If the lecturer adopts a delivery style that would be better suited to relaxation classes, or explains in a monotone the thrill of getting a trial balance to equalise first time, then it is no wonder that I cannot keep up my concentration. However, I have had the pleasure of listening, enthralled, to a few lecturers – speaking on what some would suggest were dull, boring, dusty subjects – who were able to enthuse the students with their eagerness and excitement. The manager must also enthuse employees by his/her communication. If they do not, the listeners (employees) will think that the manager does not care, and the organisation does not care. Work should be an activity that people look forward to, the manager should make their day, not ruin it.

Another problem I have is daydreaming, or mind travelling. It is because I am not listening, perhaps something distracts me, or the transmission is subjected to interference. At one conference I managed, before the morning coffee break, to mind travel throughout Europe and solve all the national disputes and still have time to receive my Oscar for top film director and the Nobel Peace Prize. All I need is a trigger. The trigger may be boredom, it may be a word or it may be a picture. When watching a management video, as soon as a particular actor appeared, I began to wonder what else I had seen him in, was it in a soap, or a film? Whatever it was, all I know is that I did not see or hear about a minute of the video and I lost another minute or so trying to catch up with what was going on.

The manager must listen as intently to their employees and team as he/she would to their boss. In making important decisions, a manager must listen carefully to the views of the team, especially when conducting a disciplinary interview, or when approached on a personal matter. Distractions, or excessive noise, impair a manager's ability to listen, a determined effort to remove such distractions should be made. It is very difficult to listen if you have a closed mind, and a manager should keep an open mind to receive ideas from the team. As a manager would most certainly not expect to be interrupted when speaking, then he/she in turn should respect others by not interrupting them.

Where have you been for the last few seconds, or is it minutes?

Gap searching

When someone is speaking to you, do you find it difficult to continue to listen because you want to interrupt – either in order to correct a statement the speaker has made or to get him or her to explain something you just do not understand? If so, you are gap searching. Consider a manager speaking to an employee. The manager/sender expresses an opinion or suggests an idea for increased productivity. The employee/receiver hears that opinion or idea and wishes to respond. However, the employee's concentration moves from listening to what is being said to listening for an opening or gap so that he or she may interrupt the manager in order to seek clarification or react to what the manager has said. The employee has effectively stopped listening to what the manager has to say. Once a gap, however small, has been found, the listener/receiver jumps in and becomes a sender. The indiscipline of listening may then continue if the manager starts to search for an opening. Time taken in searching for that gap is simply time wasted, as the receiver is not tuned in to the sender's transmission.

Team briefing

Charles Handy, in his book, *Understanding Organisations*, reported that good communications imply a well designed healthy organisation. However, he did recall the work of Pigeon Savage Lewis Inc., who found out through their research into 100 organisations that, where information was given out by the head of the organisation only 63 per cent of those on the first level down remembered receiving any. At the third level down only 40 per cent recalled receiving the information and at the fifth level from the top only 20 per cent.

It is therefore important that management pay

greater attention to data intended for general consumption within the organisation. One system that is widely used for this purpose is that of **team briefing**. The aim of team briefing is obviously to improve communication between employees and management and, through the use of the system, to prevent misunderstanding. It also sets out to reinforce the leadership position of management and to obtain the commitment of employees, as they will be aware of and understand what is occurring within their organisation.

Team briefing is the process of cascading key information from management down the scalar chain. The information supplied results from managerial decisions, and it is those decisions and their rationale that form the subject of information shared in a systematic way. Team briefing also provides a formal means for employees to voice their concerns on matters that are raised by asking questions, and most importantly, getting a response.

Team briefing is seen as an interactive communication system, whereby in an organisation, from top to toe every person is briefed, in groups of no more than 15 persons, at regular intervals – at least once per month.

THE FOUR ps OF TEAM BRIEFING INFORMATION

- progress
- policy
- people
- points for action

The information on **progress** may include: safety comparisons, records of accidents, productivity throughout the organisation, organisational success and failures, plans for the future.

Data on **policy** may refer to: legal aspects of employment, employee relations, training, job evaluation, welfare, redundancies, short-time working.

Those matters relating to **people** may include: sickness, absenteeism, new appointments, vacancies, resignations, retirements, staff turnover.

Points for action would include: correcting the distortions of the grapevine, quality issues, standards, new procedures.

The listing is not exhaustive. Some people would consider some of the items included to be the province of communication between management and an employee representative or union. The items have, however, been chosen deliberately, to reinforce the view that unions cannot be regarded as the only legitimate way of communicating with the employees on such matters as those listed above. Unions, it is felt, have no responsibility to management to pass on information in the way that management intends or to ensure that the meaning management wishes to convey reaches the work-force. Team briefing should not be used as a device to ignore trade unions as a communication channel. Jenny Davenport, a communications specialist, has said that to bypass unions as a means of communication would be asking for trouble.

Team briefing is not negotiation, nor is it consultation. Both of these processes must take place before a decision is made and it is that decision that is the focus of team briefing. It is also important to recognise that team briefing does not take over from existing forms of communication; it is to complement them, not replace them.

A team-link session at SCOPE

Many organisations have introduced team briefing, and one such organisation worthy of note is **SCOPE** previously known as The Spastic Society. Their mandatory system of briefing was introduced in late 1993 and operates under the title **Team Link**. They have appointed a team link co-ordinator, who has the role of ensuring the successful implementation of the system.

Between the chief executive of SCOPE and the main work-force there are three main levels of

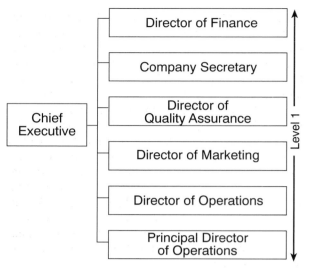

Fig. 25 The structure of SCOPE (Level 1)

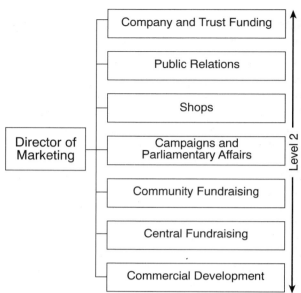

Fig. 26 The structure of SCOPE (Level 2)

management. Those at level 1 (Figure 25), the senior management team, meet on the second Tuesday of each month and prepare a core brief.

On the following day, the second Wednesday of each month, each of the level 1 directors meets with those on their team at level 2 (Figure 26). The level 1 director conducts the briefing and the team have the opportunity to task questions. Any questions raised throughout the whole system must be answered, if not immediately, then within five working days. The person taking the briefing session is required to complete a feedback form and send it to his/her immediate superior and the team link co-ordinator. The feedback form provides a record of the meeting, questions asked and the answers, and identifies items of specific interest and any suggestions or new ideas arising from the meeting. Those at level 2 would then prepare a further brief which would include items particularly relevant to the members of their own team.

Within ten days of the briefing of those at level 2, those at level 3 and all the rest of SCOPE's employees must be briefed.

SCOPE takes care to ensure that any employees who are unable to attend a briefing session are identified on the feedback form and are briefed as soon as they return to their workplace. The team link co-ordinator produces a bulletin of key issues that result from an analysis of the feedback forms. This bulletin is displayed on the staff notice board. An outcome of the system is that it confirms that managers and team leaders are to be regarded as **leaders** and that they are the authoritative source of information.

TAKING THE BRIEF

Now that you have been introduced to team briefing, you have to provide a manager with advice on **how** to conduct a team briefing session, lasting about 30 minutes. The manager in question has never conducted a meeting before and would like about two pages of advice in the form of 'bullet' points.

In 1994 the Industrial Society conducted a survey of around 1,000 organisations and found that a sum equal to £300 for each employee was spent each year on employer/employee communication, with little being done to check whether that money had been well spent. They found that by far the single most effective way to communicate with staff was through team briefing. Staff meetings, newsletters, noticeboards were much less effective.

FURTHER READING

Pick up almost any book on management or supervision and you should find a section, or part, devoted to communication.

ASSIGNMENT FOR SECTION 1, THE MANAGEMENT

Roentegen health care

Dr John Williams persuaded banks to lend him the money to buy a small, badly organised private hospital. In five years he paid back all that he owed and turned this facility around from one which had a low market share and low market growth to one with high market growth and a potentially high market share. To expand he sought further funding from the city in order to purchase two adjoining buildings. He planned and succeeded, over a three-year period, in developing his facility fourfold, introducing state-of-the-art technology and sophisticated management systems of information and control. He also provided a heavily subsidised staff restaurant and very comfortable rest area. Dr Williams owned 70 per cent of the shares, each of his two sons 2.5 per cent, his daughter 2.5 per cent and his wife 2.5 per cent. The remaining 20 per cent of the shares and equity in the business was owned by Balfour Finance.

Dr Williams interviewed and employed the hospital director and each of the senior managers. He also insisted on giving final approval to all other appointments. Middle managers would bring their proposed candidate to Dr Williams' executive suite and he would signify his approval or otherwise after a very brief introduction.

Senior and middle managers would receive their annual objectives and targets from Dr Williams. All senior and middle managers attended monthly financial budget meetings. Managers who wished to spend more than their budget allowed had to obtain approval from Dr Williams, supplying him with a report on the financial benefits of such expenditure.

Although profits were healthy enough to finance growth, Dr Williams was not happy with quality standards. Quality was of prime importance to Dr Williams and he was well known in business circles for following a philosophy of customer care. He also took action to discourage the advance of trade union membership and most certainly would not permit a trade union to negotiate on behalf of the staff. He firmly believed that when there was a recession in the private health care sector, only those with high levels of quality would survive.

Dr Williams was seriously considering calling in a management consultant; but before doing so he felt it important that he look at a few outstanding managerial staff problems. He called in Jane Bolton, his Support Services senior manager. Jane looked after cleaning (16 staff), catering (30 staff), stores (3 staff), transport (4 staff), maintenance (10 staff), porters (6 staff) and security (9 staff). Although, overall, her staffing budget was financially on target, some quality issues needed to be addressed. These problems were in the cleaning and the catering departments. Jane was surprised that all was not well. She believed that the 7 staff reporting directly to her were very happy in their job and this convinced her that they would do what was needed of them and provide a good service.

Jane was aware that Millie, the cleaning department manager, had a very high turnover of staff, however this was to be expected as Millie had difficulty communicating with this largely ethnic minority group. It then followed, Jane suggested, that Millie could have little trust in her staff to show initiative and they worked best with close supervision and daily orders posted in their changing room. It surprised Jane to learn that following a number of staff exit interviews a confidential report had been prepared by the Personnel department and given directly to Dr Williams. The report said that the majority of staff who had left the cleaning department had given reasons which indicated that they had little confidence in Millie, she was not approachable. Dr Williams also told Jane that following a complaint, made directly to him he carried out a random inspection of the cleaning standards, and over a period of three days found considerable room for improvement. Jane responded by advising Dr Williams that she felt sure Millie would respond positively and discipline those responsible.

Dr Williams then drew Jane's attention to the rather unimaginative and repetitive nature of the staff restaurant menu. Although it was disappointing to note that the numbers using the restaurant were declining, queues were still forming due to the slow pace of service. Jane mentioned that Peter, the catering manager, could not be described as dynamic and remained in his office more than perhaps he should. She was aware of the situation, but had held off talking to him until he was fully recovered from his recent illness.

Dr Williams then called in his Administrative Services senior manager, Darious Chaggar, who looked after finance (12 staff), office services (12 staff) and patient records (6 staff). The main area of concern was in the continuing delay in the collection of outstanding accounts. Darious put it all down to staffing problems. He said that 'The caring and sharing attitude of two of my supervisory staff is fine, but this is only relevant when the books are in order.' He went on to complain about Helen, the main culprit, who supervised debt recovery. 'The problem started when Helen returned from a training course. She seems to let her staff do their job in the way they feel fit, she does not seem to care when they leave their desk for a little walk. I asked her yesterday how many decisions she had made in the past week. I was shaken by the reply, it was none, zero. She said she left the decisions to her staff. She commands little respect as she seldom calls staff into her office, she sits at their desk. She appears over-interested in their personal problems and does not see herself as a work-orientated person.' Darious assured Dr Williams that he would 'Get things back on track, in a timely manner by focusing on the bottom line and redirecting the thinking of the human resources.'

The next morning Dr Williams dismissed Jane Bolton, Millie, Peter, Darious Chaggar and Helen. He then called in the services of a management consultant.

*　　　*　　　*

Describe each player's managerial styles and the organisation within which each functions. The description should not be one that you have invented yourself, but must, in your own words, reflect the work of appropriate writers.

MULTIPLE CHOICE AND QUESTIONS

Questions 1, 2 and 3 relate to the following information:

Schools or families of management that have had a great influence upon the behaviour of management towards their employees have included:

a Bureaucracy
b Scientific Management
c Human Relations
d Neo-Human Relations

Which of the above refers to the descriptions below?

1 Managers are obeyed, as the employee understands that the manager is acting in accordance with rules and regulations.

2 Management and employees should not use opinion or judgement to determine how a job **should** be done, but substitute an exacting study of how the job **is** done so as to improve productivity.

3 Management must recognise that employees should be permitted to grow and develop in the work that they do and see that their work has some purpose in life.

4 The management trait that would be appropriate for a department or organisation in crisis would be:
a Innovator
b Implementor
c Pacifier
d Participator

5 Which of the following would describe the power source of a human resources manager giving advice to a departmental manager on the dismissal of an employee?
a Resource
b Position
c Personal
d Expert

6 Douglas McGregor put forward a theory on the manager's view of human nature at work, which he called Theory X and Theory Y.

Decide whether each of the following statements is true or false in relation to Theory X:

(i) A manager needs to rely on giving rewards.

(ii) A manager needs to apply tight controls, threats and coercion.

a (i) is True   (ii) is False
b (i) is False   (ii) is True
c (i) is True   (ii) is True
d (i) is False   (ii) is False

7 There are similarities between Douglas McGregor's Theory X and Theory Y and Renis Likert's Systems 1, 2, 3 and 4. McGregor's Theory X is similar to which of Likert's Systems models?

a System 4
b System 2
c System 1
d System 3

8 The Blake and Mouton grid is based on a two-dimensional model. Those dimensions are:

a Concern for people and concern for production
b Consideration and structure
c Telling and joining
d People relationships and task relationships

9 A **1.1** manager on the Blake and Mouton grid is known as an impoverished manager. Such a manager's style would be best described as:

a Likes everyone to be happy and avoids trouble
b Rates getting the job done above all else
c Does little to enhance the work being done and little towards staff relations
d Creates situations which allow the positive attitude of employees to focus on the organisations objectives

10 The continuum in the Tannenbaum and Schmidt boss-centred to subordinate-centred approach is based on the degree of:

a Use of authority by the manager to area of freedom for the employee
b Concern for production to concern for people
c Level of managerial expertise to readiness of the employee
d Competence of the manager to skills of the employee

11 John Adair, in his functional approach to leadership, highlighted that the manager must pay due accord to the needs of:

a Money, materials and manpower
b Product, price and promotion
c Individual, group and task
d People, policy and progress

12 The Hersey and Blanchard model of situational leadership raises the question of the readiness of the follower. Decide whether each of the following is true or false.

(i) readiness relates to the employee's ability and willingness to do the job

(ii) readiness relates to the employee's level of knowledge, experience and skills with the motivation, confidence and commitment to do the job

a (i) is True   (ii) is False
b (i) is True   (ii) is True
c (i) is False   (ii) is False
d (i) is False   (ii) is True

13 Using the situational model of Hersey and Blanchard, decide whether the participative or S3 style would be suited for one of the following situations:

a An insecure employee who lacks commitment
b An employee who is very motivated but lacks the work skill
c An employee who is rather insecure in tackling the job but has the required knowledge and skills
d An employee who has a high level of commitment and motivation and holds the necessary aptitude

14 Express in a simple diagrammatic format the communication process.

15 The **grapevine** is a method of communication which may be best described as:

a Informal
b Formal
c Satellite or wheel system
d Restricted system

16 Which one of the following must take the form of a written communication?

  a Confirming a final warning within the disciplinary procedure

  b Congratulating a member of staff on a job well done

  c Calling employees to an urgent meeting

  d Checking an employee's progress

17 There is a silent form of language which takes place during oral, face-to-face communication. Is it?

  a Gap searching

  b Listening

  c Body language

  d Verbal communication

Questions 18, 19 and 20 relate to the following information. General problems in communication include:

a Differences in background

b Emotions

c Time

d Expectations

Which of the above is most appropriate to the situations below?

18 A personnel manager is having difficulty in explaining to an employment agency temp. the difference between a Contract of Service and a Contract for Services in relation to sick pay.

19 Conducting an investigation interview with the victim of sexual harassment.

20 An IT specialist giving advice to a newly appointed wages clerk on debugging the system.

REFERENCES

Adair, J., 1983, *Effective Leadership*, Pan.

Bassman, E., and London, M., 1993, 'Abusive Managerial Behaviour', *Leadership & Organisational Development Journal*, Vol. 14 No. 2, MCB University Press.

Blake, R., and Mouton, J., 1964, *The Managerial Grid*, Gulf Publishing.

——, 1978, *The New Managerial Grid*, Gulf Publishing.

——, 1985, *The Managerial Grid III*, Gulf Publishing.

Blanchard, K., and Hersey, P., 1982, *Management of Organizational Behaviour*, Prentice-Hall.

Conger, A., and Kanungo, R. W., 1987, 'Toward a behavioral theory of the charismatic leader in an organisational setting', *Academy of Management Review*.

Fayol, H., 1949, *General and Industrial Management*, Pitman.

French, J., and Raven, B., 1959, *Studies in Social Power*, University of Michigan Press.

Handy, C. B., 1985, *Understanding Organisations*, 3rd Ed., Penguin.

Harvey-Jones, J., 1988, *Making it Happen*, Collins.

Kiam, V., 1987, *Going for it: How to succeed as an Entrepreneur*, Fontana.

Likert, R., 1961, *New Patterns of Management*, McGraw-Hill.

McGregor, D., 1960, *The Human Side of Enterprise*, McGraw-Hill.

Mintzberg, H., 1973, *The Nature of Management Work*, Harper and Row.

Pfeiffer, I. W., and Jones, J. E. (eds.), 1974, *A Handbook of Structured Experiences for Human Resources Training*, Vol. 1 (revised), San Diego, CA University Associates.

Ritchie, B., and Goldsmith, W., 1987, *The New Elite*, Weidenfeld & Nicholson.

Rodriques, C. A., 1993, 'Developing Three Dimensional Leaders', *Journal of Management Development*.

Smith, E. J., 1958, 'Stress: The test the Americans are failing', *Business Week*, 1.

Tannenbaum, R., and Schmidt, W., 1968, *Control in Organizations*, McGraw-Hill.

Trump, D., 1987, *Trump: The Art of the Deal*, Arrow.

Urwick, L., and Brech, E. F. L., 1951, *The Making of Scientific Management*, Pitman.

Walters, R. W. and Assoc., 1991, 'Is Job Stress too High?', *Behavioural Sciences Newsletter*.

Watson, T. J., 1986, *Management, Organisation, and Employment Strategy*, Routledge.

The Group

This section sets out to meet the requirements of Element 11.3,

'Examine the behaviour of groups in the workplace'.

On completion of this section you will be able to:

1 Describe the different roles in groups in the organisation
2 Analyse how work groups behave
3 Develop approaches to achieving targets through a work group

INTRODUCTION

A friend of Socrates visited a place with twin peaks called Delphos, famed for its temple to Apollo and the oracle therein, who made predictions about the future. The oracle said that no one was wiser than Socrates. The meaning of this statement was seen to be that Socrates *knew that he did not know*, whereas others *thought they knew something and they did not.* So perhaps if we bring together a collection of people who think they know something, then maybe, if they talk it through, the group may then think they know a little more, or perhaps a little less, than before. The management, the group and the individual may then benefit from the process.

Try as we might it is very difficult to work in isolation. Whatever we do it has an impact on others. We need the help of others to do our job effectively, and others need our help. At work we may be a member of a section which is part of a department which in turn is part of an organisation. At play we may be a member of a football or hockey team. We have friends we socialise with and strangers we meet who may become part of our friendship group. We share work interests and we share social interests. We are members of a family.

A group is greater than, and not just, a collection of people who have been brought together through fate or design. If that collection of people share a purpose and have a leader, then they are a group. A good example is that of a disaster movie. Imagine a ship taking passengers on an exotic cruise, it strikes a reef and sinks, and the surviving passengers struggle on to a deserted desert island. Whereas before they were merely a collection of people on a journey, now they become a group with a common purpose – survival, and a leader is likely to emerge – the individual who can rise to the situation.

The group we are interested in may be referred to as a 'psychological group'. It consists of two or more persons who interact with each other; they see themselves as a group that is quite different from any other group. They are able to communicate with each other and all give their skills and knowledge to the achievement of the group goal. The individuals in the group know what to expect of each other, via the rules or standards of expected behaviour, known as the group norms.

HOW MANY?

List all the social and work groups of which you
consider yourself to be a participant.

Groups are powerful: consider pressure groups.
These groups can help change the laws of the
country. We would not be talking about green
issues today if it had not been for pressure
groups. However groups can also have negative
power: they can be formed to stop things happening. Take, for example, a group that was formed
for the sole purpose of stopping a local mansion
being turned into a rehabilitation centre for persons who found it difficult to cope with day-to-day
living.

A little can take on a lot

PRESSURE POINTS

Find a pressure group that is of particular interest to
you. It may have local, national or international
interests. A local group may be interested in, say
stopping or minimising a new road network, a
national group may be interested in promoting the
needs of disadvantaged groups, such as the disabled,
an international group may be interested in an issue
like the abolition of slavery. Find out their
membership size, their aims, their successes.

Look back at the list you prepared on the qualities or traits of a manager in Section 1. I have little
doubt that when comparing your list with those of
others, you discovered opposing qualities. One
may have suggested that a manager must be
forceful, another that a manager must be sensitive
to the feelings of the employees. It is likely that, if
you had a long list of qualities, you would not be
able to find many people to meet your requirements. Such people are in very short supply, so
organisations have to make do with what is available. Where one person cannot do all that is
required, a group will be able to do much more
than that individual.

Organisations today do not recruit individuals,
they recruit team players. If a person is rejected
for a job this does not mean that that person is
unemployable with that organisation, it perhaps
means that the person does not fit the needs of a
specific group. The person may fit perfectly well
in another group.

Just because there is today an interest in group
working, however, it does not mean that we can
forget the individual, since it is a collection of
individuals that form the group. An individual's
contribution to the goals of the group can
enhance or diminish the effectiveness of that
group.

There has been interest in groups for many centuries. In the past the main source of this interest
was the part they played in wars. It was the work
of Elton Mayo and his Hawthorne experiments in
the late 1920s that drew our attention to groups in
a working environment. These studies clearly
showed that people want to be a member of a
group, an individual's wanting to belong is very
important. An individual's attitude to work is
strongly influenced by the working group he or
she is in. Equally, the way in which a group
behaves has a great influence on the motivation of
individuals within the group, and should not be
underestimated.

The introduction of GNVQ programmes in
education recognises the need to hold skills in a
number of areas. There are core skills in communication, information technology and application
of number. Working with others, an essential skill
required more and more by employers, should
also be recognised as a core skill.

TIME OUT

Take time out and read BTEC's description of working with others skills (your teacher should be able to provide this). Discuss how these skills will help you in your present situation and in your working life.

A **behavioural approach** to groups means that it is the behaviour of persons **within the group** that is of importance, rather than the **singular** behaviour of individuals. It is always interesting to see how an individual behaves when alone and then to watch how that same individual behaves as part of a group. The person's behaviour is often quite different.

Using companies that had moved to a group-based working system from their previous practices, a survey by the American Society for Training found that:

1 productivity showed an increase in about 80 per cent of the organisations
2 just over 70 per cent reported improvements in the quality of work
3 more than half experienced reductions in waste
4 around 65 per cent claimed an improvement in job satisfaction
5 almost 60 per cent said that there had been an improvement in customer satisfaction.

Claims abound that groups have been responsible for increased morale and that they are an important factor in resolving strife at work. The positive power of the group is recognised by the management guru, Tom Peters, who promotes working in groups as a means of obtaining greater innovation and employee commitment.

At an occupational conference of the British Psychological Society, Professor Richard Hackman of Harvard University, cast a cloud over the alleged wonders of group work. He said that when he looked at 33 groups, only 4 were clear success stories. His message was a cautionary tale: group working should not be played with, the benefits of group working are not easy to achieve. It needs a change of thinking within the whole organisation. It is not something that is an add-on, it is an integral part of the total organisation.

Renis Likert suggested that the design of an

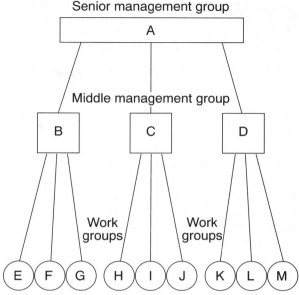

Fig. 27   Group structure based on Likert

organisational structure should be based on groups rather than individuals, as groups have a considerable impact upon the behaviour of the whole organisation.

NATIONAL CULTURES

If you were working with people from other countries, would you expect them to behave differently from you? Organisations are global, communications are global, your future working life may be seen as global, or at the very least within the European Union.

Geert Hofstede did a great deal of research over a number of years on the value systems of national cultures. Four dimensions emerged from these studies as being of importance in indicating differences between people from different cultures:

• power distance
• uncertainty avoidance
• individualism
• masculinity

Power distance is concerned with the measure of the acceptance of inequalities. Some people may consider striving for equality of opportunity and equal association with others to be the norm. Others may recognise the inequalities between people in terms of their status in life, but see such inequalities as normal. In relation to organisations, if there is a small power distance, employees expect to be consulted and there is a harmonisation of conditions and benefits. A large power distance is evident in organisations where employees are kept in their place and the bigger car, the bigger desk, and the perks go with the higher status in the hierarchy.

Small power distance — Large power distance

- All should have equal rights
- Those in power are entitled to privileges
- The system is to blame
- The underdog is to blame
- Inequality in society should be minimised
- There should be an order of equality, everyone in their place

Fig. 28   The power distance dimension
Source: Based on G. Hofstede, 'Motivation, leadership, and organization: do American theories apply abroad?', *Cultures and Organizations: Software of the Mind*, 1991, *McGraw-Hill.*

Power distance

Equality is normal(1) _____ (10) inequality is normal

Uncertainty avoidance is concerned with the degree of flexibility preferred. Values expressed range from those with a preference for flexibility and vagueness to those with a preference for a more bureaucratic, structured approach. People in organisations where uncertainty avoidance is low see uncertainty as a normal part of day-to-day working life. They are motivated by achievement and see work rules as guides not barriers. Organisations with high uncertainty avoidance prefer security, systems and structure as the means to combat imprecision, which they fear may jeopardise the *status quo*.

Weak uncertainty avoidance — Strong uncertainty avoidance

- More acceptance of conflict
- Must achieve consensus
- As few rules as possible
- Must have written rules and regulations
- Hard work, in itself, is not a virtue
- There is an inner urge to work very hard

Fig. 29   The uncertainty avoidance dimension
Source: Based on G. Hofstede, 'Motivation, leadership, and organization: do American theories apply abroad?', *Cultures and Organizations: Software of the Mind*, 1991, McGraw-Hill.

Uncertainty avoidance

Unstructured (1) _____ (10) Structured

Individualism, as you would expect, looks at preference for an individual approach as opposed to being part of a collective. Organisations that recognise individualism look at a person's personal contribution in relation to organisational expectations. Although they recognise the individual's right to have his or her say, the main priority is getting the job done. On the other hand, organisations that take a more collective approach tend to look at relationships within a group setting and see relationships as more important than a task-centred approach.

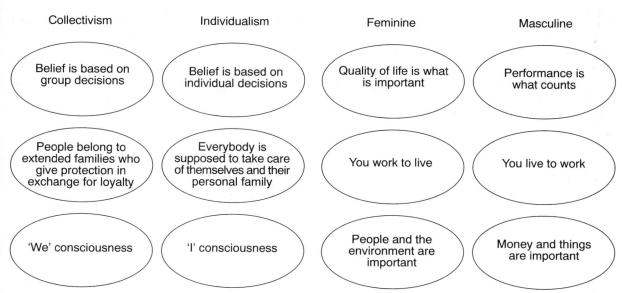

Fig. 30   The individualism dimension
Source: Based on G. Hofstede, 'Motivation, leadership, and organization: do American theories apply abroad?', *Cultures and Organizations: Software of the Mind*, 1991, McGraw-Hill.

Fig. 31   The masculinity dimension
Source: Based on G. Hofstede, 'Motivation, leadership, and organization: do American theories apply abroad?', *Cultures and Organizations: Software of the Mind*, 1991, McGraw-Hill.

SCORE YOURSELF

Individualism

Collectivism (1) _____ (10) Individualism

Masculinity is concerned with the value put on performance as opposed to care for others. Preferences range from the hard man, macho approach to the misnamed opposite, the softer or feminine approach which values others and has a high regard for the quality of life. A masculine organisation needs people to go for success in material terms, such as more money, greater promotion, and such an organisation sees beings that are there to work, and work hard. It is not masculine to fail. However, the feminine side recognises that failure is not negative, as it is a learning experience and something to build upon. People have to work in order to live. Compromise, negotiation and the quality of working life are seen as the appropriate model.

SCORE YOURSELF

Masculinity

Macho (1) _____ (10) Caring values

THROUGH THE TUNNEL

You have given yourself a score, but how do you perceive other nationalities? What attitudes and behaviour do you think they would express towards work? How would you rank different countries on a score of 1 to 10?

Germany? USA? France? Italy? Spain? Greece?

Power distance

Equal is normal (1)_____ (10) inequality is normal

Uncertainty avoidance

Unstructured (1)_____ (10) Structured

Individualism

Collectivism (1) _____ (10) Individualism

Masculinity

Macho (1)_____ (10) Caring values

On power distance the UK would score around 3 to 4 with Germany and the USA much the same. The others would have a higher score, but none higher than France with 6.

On uncertainty avoidance, again the UK would   59

score around 3 to 4, the other countries would be higher, with Greece approaching 10.

On individualism the UK would score 9 and the USA would be slightly higher. All others would have a lower score, with Greece at 4, and the remainder ranging from 5 to Italy, with just over 7.

When it comes to masculinity, the UK, with 6 to 7 scores higher than Spain, France and Greece, slightly higher than the USA and Germany, but behind Italy.

The scores on individualism are of particular importance for organisations attempting to promote working in groups as the norm. Professor Richard Hackman of Harvard University said that in the USA people were very individualistic and that their education system does not prepare them for teamworking. As the UK also has a high preference score towards individualism would you agree that:

- the education system in this country does not prepare people for teamworking, and
- this country does not have the culture to take seriously the concept of group working?

For a really good look at organisational behaviour within an international perspective, try to get hold of Terence Jackson, *Organizational Behaviour in International Management*, Butterworth Heinemann, 1993.

THE NATURE OF GROUPS

Groups are part of a larger whole. Their life and productivity are influenced by factors outside the group's control as well as those within it. They are affected by the organisation's strategic plans. If an organisation is expanding this would have a positive effect on a group. However, if the organisation is shedding jobs, referred to as downsizing, but better known as making jobs and people redundant, then this will naturally have a negative impact upon a group.

If an organisation is bureaucratic in its structure and/or its systems – that is, you do it this way and no other – then this will limit freedom of action within a group. The allocation of resources

will have a modifying effect on how a group behaves and limit what it can do with its allowance of money, materials, people and time.

If an organisation believes in rewarding individual effort and achievement rather than group-based performance, then this will conflict with group co-operation. Some local authorities have abandoned the setting of individual targets and rewards as they found that where people needed to work closely together in a group setting, these targets and rewards had inadvertently introduced inappropriate negative group conflict.

Fig. 32   External influences on groups

Formal and informal groups

Formal groups are created by management to undertake specific activities. Informal groups are created by individuals within organisations for social purposes and mutual support. The life of a group may be either **permanent** or **temporary**.

There are many reasons why an organisation or management assemble groups.

1 To aid the management and control of work activities. The organisation creates a formal structure, the family tree, to make managing easier.

2 To get commitment from an individual and in turn to help motivate the individual. This is done by ensuring that the individual takes part in group activities and thereby comes to accept the standards and values of the group, and in turn those of the organisation.

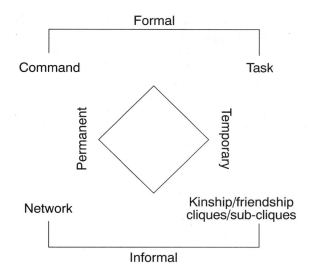

Formal

Command — Task

Permanent — Temporary

Network — Kinship/friendship cliques/sub-cliques

Informal

Fig. 33   Forms and lifespan of groups
Source: Based on M. Higgs and B. Rowland, 'All pigs are equal', *Management Education and Development*, Vol. 23/4, 1992, p. 355.

3 To bring together skills that cannot all be held by one person, so as to perform a short or continuous task.

4 To hold a post-mortem. What happened? What lessons could be learned from the past? How could we do it better? Who could do it better?

5 To bring together an assorted collection of minds to focus on the answering of a problem, or to think up new ideas or make suggestions.

6 To make deals or to sort out dissension within the ranks of the organisation.

OVER TO YOU

Can you add to the list of reasons above the particular reasons why a formal group would be established?

There is also a host of reasons why an individual would want to join and use a group.

SEVEN GOOD REASONS WHY PEOPLE WANT TO JOIN GROUPS

1 Joining helps to satisfy their needs for social interaction or to have a sense of belonging.

People need to chat with others and they want to fit in.

2 Joining helps them to see where they and their own job fit into the organisation as a whole, and how they relate to other employees in the department.

3 People need help and support when things are not going to plan in their personal and/or working lives. They can also give help and support to others.

4 Joining is a means of caring and sharing in the performance of the work they are doing.

5 People may not like to appear different, so they seek the protective cloak of a group. That group could be a trade union, which could wield the power an individual would not have.

6 An individual may gain in status through membership of a group, the more so if it is one that has been given recognition for its achievements. In large Japanese organisations highly successful groups have their achievements publicised throughout the organisation, world-wide. The individual rightly feels proud of his/her contribution to that success.

7 Being part of a group may help to make a person feel important.

Whatever the individual may need and obtain from a group he/she in turn will have to yield to the requirements of the group. An individual may get what he or she wants, but will also have to give what the group wants. It is part of the role of a manager to attempt to ensure that the individual and group all work towards the organisation's objectives. The needs of the individual, the group and the task must all converge.

Formal groups

Organisations use groups for particular reasons that relate to the achievement of the organisation's aims and objectives. Such groups are sometimes referred to as **official groups**. They have a formal structure and are organised for the performance of the work given to them. The organisation sets the terms of reference for the creation and continuance of a formal group and also selects the members of the group.

Formal groups may be permanent or temporary. **Permanent** groups, have no predetermined time limit of existence. They may be referred to as **command groups**, and can be seen on a body's organisational chart. **Temporary** groups are usually formed for a particular purpose – to start and finish a task within a set time – and are referred to as **task groups**. They may have a multi-disciplinary membership drawn from across, as well as up and down, hierarchical boundaries.

As the above description shows, groups may be brought together to perform a number of functions or purposes. Those different functions need different behaviour patterns and perhaps even a different group structure. For example, the agenda of a meeting may include items that require group members to wear very different behavioural 'hats'. At one point a group may be pouring over ideas for an annual social gathering, then the agenda moves straight on to a discussion of the future staffing levels of the department. Group members may find such a switch of behavioural hats rather difficult. That is not to say that a group is incapable of tackling these two quite dissimilar items. It is simply that the switch is difficult and the members would not perform to their full potential unless there is a separation of the items, either by time or by space.

An adult class was asked to comment upon the qualities of a particular activity. That activity had proved to be a rather negative experience. Thus, an item which was expected to take 20 minutes to discuss took one and a half hours. It was an emotionally draining exercise for a number of group members. When they were finished they were then asked to move straight on to discuss the application of the Transfer of Undertakings Act 1981. They found the switch impossible. They needed time out. The meeting had to be reconvened at a later time that day.

FURTHER READING

Charles Handy in his book, *Understanding Organisations* (Penguin, 3rd ed., 1985), provides wonderful examples of groups when he tells the tale of Bull Dogs and Red Devils (pp. 157–9).

Informal groups

An informal personal group does not have the official recognition of an organisation. Such groups are alliances that are not under the direction or creation of management. Informal groups meet the needs of social interaction, although they exist for more than just social purposes. An informal group is an organisation within an organisation and is classified by sociologists as:

- a kinship-friendship group
- a clique
- a sub-clique

A **kinship–friendship** group exists for social purposes both at work and away from it. Members share information and gossip, they support one another, they share the joys of the good news of one of their members and the sadness of the leaving of another.

Cliques are formed among those with a close working relationship in a department or section. they may hold 'meetings' around the coffee machine or huddle together at a canteen table, they are undemocratic and formed for the protection of their membership. They circle their wagons against the arrows of the enemy, who is usually seen as the employer.

A **sub-clique** is the inner circle of a clique, and has control over it. As the clique in turn may hold sway over a large formal group within the organisation, the result is that many people are controlled by a few, who have no formal authority.

An informal group can help or harm an organisation. It is the difficult task of management to harness the power of such groups toward the aims and objectives of the department and the organisation.

CLIQUE NOW

Identify the cliques in your class or place of work. Do they have sub-cliques? Why are you part of those cliques? What influence does this informal grouping have over the rest of the class or department?

There are also informal work groups which are sometimes known as **network groups**. These groups arise where individuals see the need to develop contacts throughout the organisation, up, down and across the scalar chain. Such groupings are not the result of organisational design, but the organisation may encourage them as it realises the individual needs to build working relationships with others. This networking may extend to customers, suppliers, and other outside business contacts. Crafted networking helps people to progress within their organisation and within their chosen occupation.

NETWORK UK

Have you begun to form your own personal network? What contacts have you made that will or may prove useful later? Do you think it is not what you know but who you know that helps you along?

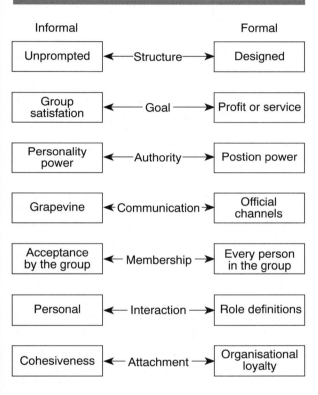

Informal		Formal
Unprompted	←—Structure—→	Designed
Group satisfaction	←—Goal—→	Profit or service
Personality power	←—Authority—→	Postion power
Grapevine	←Communication→	Official channels
Acceptance by the group	←—Membership—→	Every person in the group
Personal	←—Interaction—→	Role definitions
Cohesiveness	←—Attachment—→	Organisational loyalty

Fig. 34 Formal and informal groups

GROUP PROCESSES

The group process is the way in which members of the group behave with others in that group. It is the manner in which they go about solving problems and reaching decisions.

Group functions

It was in 1962 that Bernard Bass said that there are three functions that take up a group's space, time and effort:

- task-oriented behaviour
- interaction-oriented behaviour
- self-oriented behaviour

Task-oriented behaviour is centred on the achievement of group objectives or goals. This is any 'doing' activity that gets the work done. It is the visible evidence that the work is being carried out.

Interaction-oriented behaviour is the group process. This refers to the group's activities in setting standards of behaviour, supporting each other, sorting out any conflicts within the group, reaching agreement for the good of the whole group.

Self-oriented behaviour is that behaviour in which the time and energy of the individual is used to satisfy his or her own needs, even though such actions may well rival the needs of the group. Additionally, these activities may, or may not, help to further the task of the group. Self-oriented behaviour includes such things as emphasising one's own worries, hopes, fears, desires. Such behaviour may also cause time wasting, and the individual may try to dominate the talking by continued interruptions; this sort of approach usually indicates a lower level of listening skills.

Every group will develop its own way of working with these three functions. A **closed group** will confine itself to the accomplishment of the task, so will give little or no attention to the interaction-oriented function (unless, that is, it suits their purpose because they see it as necessary in order to accomplish the task). A closed group positively discourages self-oriented behaviour and is not particularly interested in any individual's personal problems.

Other groups are more permissive towards the interaction- and self-oriented functions. Indeed there are some groups that seem to exist for the promotion of self-oriented behaviour, and interaction-oriented behaviour is used for the purpose of supporting the needs of individual members.

CLOSED FOR BUSINESS

Are you able to recognise and describe a closed group you belong or belonged to, in relation to the three functions identified by Bernard Bass?

Fifteen years after Bass developed his theory, in 1977, W. C. Boshear and K. G. Albrecht added 63

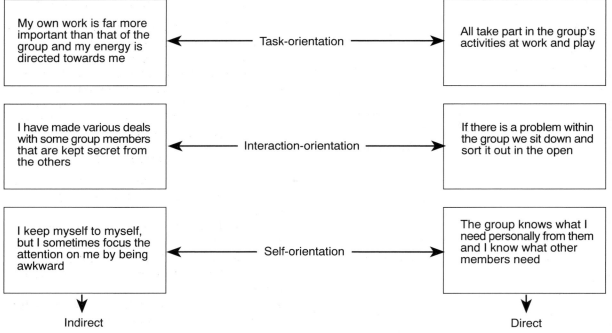

Fig. 35   The three group functions with their direct and indirect influences

the concepts of **direct** and **indirect activities** to the functions of groups. These relate to an individual's behaviour within the group.

When an individual is engaged in behaviour of a direct nature it means that his or her declared reason for doing something is in fact the real reason. But when someone behaves in an indirect way, that means that he/she has an ulterior motive. This concealed reason is, of course, not made available to the group. An example is the employee who agrees with the suggestion of a boss, not because it is a good idea that he/she fully supports, but because doing so helps the employee gain favour with that boss.

Task and maintenance functions

Some years before Bass, Morton Deutsh put forth his theory on co-operation and competition in groups in industry. Receiving considerable academic support he referred to:

- task functions
- maintenance functions

These functions are comparable to Bass's task-oriented and interaction-oriented behaviour.

Task functions are those which assist a group to reach its work goals. The group must clearly define what the task is before they make any decisions, they must work together to find the best way. These functions are all about getting the job done.

Maintenance functions are actions which keep things on a person-to-person level, and keep people working together. They keep the group working as a single unit so that it runs at a fast but safe speed. These functions are all about sorting out disputes, mutual support, the emotional side of the group.

The work of Deutsh can be extended further by looking at the classification created by K. D. Benne and P. Sheats. They provide 12 types of group members' roles under the heading **Group Task Roles**, seven types under the heading **Group Building and Maintenance Roles**, and eight **Individual Roles** which were not related to group needs but went some way to satisfying individuals' wants.

In his book, *Interpersonal Skills*, published by HarperCollins (1991), Professor John Hayes found that by slightly adjusting the Benne and Sheats listing he could use their categories in his observation and analysis of groups.

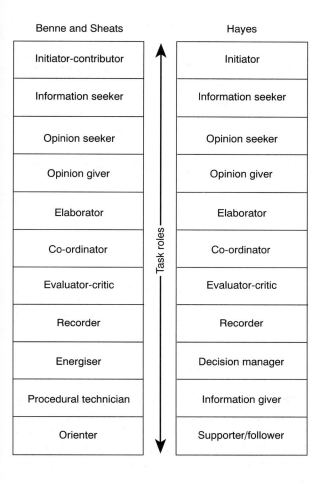

Benne and Sheats	Hayes
Initiator-contributor	Initiator
Information seeker	Information seeker
Opinion seeker	Opinion seeker
Opinion giver	Opinion giver
Elaborator	Elaborator
Co-ordinator	Co-ordinator
Evaluator-critic	Evaluator-critic
Recorder	Recorder
Energiser	Decision manager
Procedural technician	Information giver
Orienter	Supporter/follower

Task roles

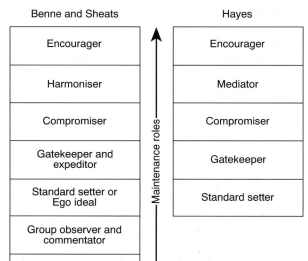

Benne and Sheats	Hayes
Encourager	Encourager
Harmoniser	Mediator
Compromiser	Compromiser
Gatekeeper and expeditor	Gatekeeper
Standard setter or Ego ideal	Standard setter
Group observer and commentator	
Follower	

Maintenance roles

Fig. 36 Task and maintenance roles: A comparison of Benne and Sheats with Hayes

Some of the task roles may be described as:

- An **initiator-contributor** is a person who puts forward new ideas and suggestions for changing the way of doing the job.
- A **co-ordinator** is the person who pulls all the ideas together and makes some sense of them.
- An **evaluator** is the group member who takes it upon him/herself to act as the judge of how well the group is performing.

Some of the maintenance roles include:

- The **encourager**: the cheerleader of the group. He/she keeps the group going and keeps it together.
- The **gatekeeper**: the one who keeps the communication channels open so that everyone may have their say. The gatekeeper can also 'shut the gate' on those who say too much.
- The **harmoniser**: a mediator. He/she will settle differences between group members.

Some individual roles include:

- The **aggressor** who simply likes to disagree with others.
- The **playboy** is someone who just does not want to know and shows it by messing around and making inappropriate and silly points.
- A **help-seeker** is the sad case of poor little me. He/she loves to get the sympathy of others.

WHAT DO THEY MEAN?

Take some of the other roles in Figure 36 and suggest how the behaviour of each would be demonstrated.

Group or individual performance

It may be of interest to look at group functions, but when it comes to making reasoned and reasonable decisions, will a group perform a great deal better than the individual? Or will an exceptional individual outdo the group? According to G. W. Hill, in a 1982 article in the *Psychological Bulletin*, there is no ready answer, as it will depend on the abilities and training of the individual and the group, as well as the task they are doing. Although there may be evidence that, on balance, groups perform better than an individual, in terms of the quality, creativity and acceptability of decisions made, it is clear that not every group will have better decision-making powers than every individual.

The issues to consider are:

- Does the group perform better than the best individual in that group?
- Is the class of decision made by a group of any more distinction than one made by the average individual of the group?

Research by Barbara Maginn and Richard Harris in 1980 came to the conclusion that individuals put less effort into a job where they had to share responsibility for the results with others. They went on to say that if this reduction of responsibility could not be resolved then individual idea-generation or decision-making is preferable.

The social psychologist, Robert Zajonic, in a 1969 article for the American journal, *Science*, provided a number of examples of something called **social facilitation**, which happens in a group setting. This term refers to the phenomenon that living things increase their performance of particular behaviour when with others as compared with the frequency with which they would perform such an activity when alone.

A couple of examples of studies in this area, but prior to Zajonic, include:

- Ants working in groups dig more sand per ant than ants working alone.
- Humans pedalling bicycles go faster when riding in pairs than when riding alone.

Strange though such examples may be, they strongly suggest to some that you get more done when you work together than you do when each individual is working alone. On a frivolous note, adult groups have even suggested that a group of people drinking in a pub consume more per person than one person would consume if drinking alone.

Zajonic reported that the results he observed do not always occur. He said that it is necessary to look at two degrees of **social facilitation:**

- audience effects
- co-action effects

The **audience effect** occurs where an employee is being observed.

Which has the greater impact on our lives?

The **co-action effect** occurs where two or more persons are working on a task as a group.

It seems that if the employee is working on a job with which he/she is very familiar, or on a new task which builds upon or uses the knowledge and skills the employee already has, then he/she does much better when working alongside others or even when people are 'watching'.

If, however, the employee is learning a complex, unfamiliar task, which does not use his/her existing knowledge and skills, then the employee will perform badly when working with others or if someone is looking. The individual does much better if he/she is left alone to master the basics, at least. Take the not so simple act of learning to drive. There is no doubt that sitting there with the driving instructor beside you, you feel reasonably uncomfortable; if you look and see a crowd of people at the bus stop with nothing better to do than watch you make a fool of yourself, you then feel very uncomfortable and make every mistake imaginable.

Zajonic added his own reasoning to previous research which indicated that the mere presence of other human beings is, in some form, physically arousing. He said that when people are aroused they do more of whatever behaviour they are currently engaged in. So if they are working on a task with which they are comfortable, then they will do it even better when others are present, be that working with them or being observed by them. If, however, they are engaged in doing something that they are not sure of, then there will be an increase in mistakes. Zajonic called this the **Dominant Response Hypothesis**.

The examples described above would suggest that a manager must look back to the **boss-centred–subordinate-centred** 'Leadership Continuum' of Robert Tannenbaum and Warren Schmidt. You will recall that this suggests that the style that is preferred is the one that fits the situation in hand.

A situation where there is a well learnt, well practised job is best dealt with by the style at one end of the continuum: close supervision would increase employees' productivity, provided, that is, that the employees did not see the observation as a threat, or think they were distrusted in some way.

Behaviour from the other end of the continuum would best meet the situation where an employee is attempting a new and complex job for the first time. There is no point in getting the employee to work within the framework of a group as yet, and he or she will only make more mistakes if closely observed.

Large or small groups

Is a large group preferable to a small group? Does it make any difference? It would appear that it does, but which is better depends upon the goal of the group. If they are engaged in problem solving then the large group has the edge. If they have to make a decision quickly, then a smaller group is more effective.

What is a large group and what is a small group? 'Large' would be a group of more than 12 people. No group should have more than 15 members. This fact is recognised, for example, by SCOPE, formerly The Spastic Society, in their **team briefing** system (see pp. 49–50) which requires that the briefing group be no more than 15 strong. The smallest group, it is suggested, should be no more than five, or perhaps seven. In small groups it seems to be important that the group be made up of an odd number of people, so preventing a deadlock if the group were reduced to accepting the majority view.

The Japanese have recognised that if a group has more than ten people, it is difficult for the members of the group to maintain personal and emotional linking. Thomas and Fink did some work on 'The Effects of Group Size' and found that the bigger the group, the lower the individual's level of satisfaction.

Another factor in the strength of a group may be the proportion of male and female members. It was L. Libo, in 1953, who suggested that the cohesiveness, or the closeness of a group working together, may be moderated by the male/female mix of the group in relation to the size of the group. In groups of the same sex small groups seemed to be more cohesive than large groups. In large groups a gender mix was more appropriate. These differences are important, as today the balance between males and females in the working population is becoming more equal. As a result, the facility to have single-sex groups is reducing, and in any case such groups may also be regarded as discriminatory.

If one person, working alone, produces 100 units of work per day, will ten people working as a group generate more than, or less than 1,000 units per day?

Research from the 1920s shows that increasing the number of persons in a group has the effect of lowering the performance of each individual within that group. It would be wrong, therefore, to suggest, that ten people would generate ten times the output of one. The reason for this seemingly illogical state is twofold:

1 If a group member thinks that another or others are not pulling their weight, then that member will reduce his/her productivity to re-establish what he/she considers to be a just level of performance. This is what B. Latane, K. Williams and S. Hoskins called **social loafing**.

2 An individual can get 'lost' in a group in that he or she may feel that his/her personal contribution to the group effort has not been recognised.

The manager must therefore create the means whereby the efforts of the individual are known and seen to be known.

Groups are an improvement on individuals on certain occasions, as for example, in the following situations:

1 A wide range of skills, knowledge and experience is needed to address a particular problem.

2 The answer is to be found through an exercise of judgement, rather than an analysis of facts.

3 Decisions made by a group are more likely to be accepted by a much wider audience.

However, individuals are more effective than groups in situations such as where:

1 There are simple and fairly routine tasks to complete.

2 There is a single answer to a problem.

3 The problem requires focused rational thinking to arrive at a solution.

There are other reasons why managers may not wish to use the group process. If speed and cost are important, groups are not favoured. The group process is slower than individual decision-making, as a characteristic of a group, the mutual exchange of ideas, does take time. It also takes time to get a group together. In addition, it can cost a great deal of money to assemble a group,

There are lots of exercises in use which require individuals to list certain given items or statements in priority order. The individual then joins a group and the group repeats the exercise. The results of the individual response and the group response are compared against an 'expert' ranking. The objective is to see which, the individual or the group, is closest to the expert answer. Thus showing if working individually or in a group is better in achieving results. One in common use is the Desert Survival Problem. Meanwhile try this one:

Scope for improvement

If you look back at the activities you undertook on the question of recruitment you will recall that employers look for certain qualities in candidates. Ten qualities are listed below, but not in any particular order. Rank these qualities in order of importance from 1 (most important) to 10 (least important), as they apply to a job which involves working for people with a disability and who need lots of personal care.

First rank these qualities on your own. Then in a group, of between five and seven, discuss and reach a group consensus ranking of the qualities.

	1 Your Rank	*2* Group Rank	*3* 'Expert' Rank	*4* 1–3 Diff.	*5* 2–3 Diff.
a Can deliver messages and take orders					
b Can pacify people					
c Clean and of smart appearance					

d	Clean hands and nails	_____
e	Courteous	_____
f	Dependable and on time	_____
g	Eager to help	_____
h	Keeps calm	_____
i	Sociable and gregarious	_____
j	Trustworthy and honest	_____

Total Column 4 then Column 5   _____

Compare your individual ranking and that of the group with the recommended order given at the end of this chapter. Was the group decision closer to that of the expert than the individual decision? If no then why? If yes then why?

particularly if they are drawn from across departmental boundaries or geographically.

Group cohesiveness

If it is agreed that the best way forward is a group approach, then the group must be held together. In his **functional approach to leadership** John Adair did say that the manager must attend to the needs of the task, the individual and the group. With the group the manager must promote cohesiveness or bonding of the group.

Cohesiveness is the measure of the quality and quantity of what is seen as good behaviour. If this exceeds what is seen as negative behaviour within a group, the group is drawn together to act as a single entity. Cohesiveness makes someone want to remain part of a group.

Laurie J. Mullins in his excellent book, _Management and Organisational Behaviour_, published by Pitman (1989), says that the factors which impact upon cohesiveness and performance within a group can be included under four main headings:

* membership
* work environment
* organisational
* group development and maturity

Membership refers to the size of the group, but also to the compatibility of the members. It is easier to achieve cohesiveness with a group of like-minded people. Cohesiveness improves the longer the group stays together and if it has few changes in its membership.

As previously mentioned, L. Libo showed that the gender mix of a group in relation to its size has an effect on its cohesiveness.

In terms of the **work environment**, cohesiveness is greater where the group shares a common task or is occupied in similar work. There is more cohesiveness if the members of a group work near to each other and also if they have the opportunity to discuss matters and chat freely, without a wall or any other physical obstacle as a barrier.

In **organisational** matters the style of the leader either helps to pull the members of a group together or drives them apart. The more a group succeeds, the closer it becomes. The external threat of a common enemy will bring a group together. The foe may be seen as new working methods or competition with other groups.

The common enemy theory does not always work. If the group does not feel that it can defend itself, that is, it loses its sense of security, then its cohesiveness will not improve. If the very reasons for the group's existence are questioned and if the group members further believe that they will individually be safer from attack if the group breaks up, the group's cohesiveness will come apart.

Group development and maturity is the group equivalent of a person growing up and going through all the trials and tribulations of youth in order to reach a mature responsible state. The more success a group has, the more cohesive it becomes. Success breeds success. For example competition is intense to get into a successful school, college or university, and likewise into a successful company. Once a person gains entrance he or she then feels part of a successful team.

Effectiveness of a group

Just because a group is cohesive, does it follow that it is effective? There are differences between an

Effective groups

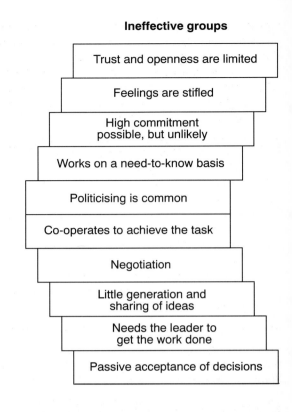

| Trust and openness between members |
| Feelings are aired |
| High commitment |
| Common objectives |
| Good listening skills |
| Conflict is part of the process |
| Consensus |
| Generates and shares ideas |
| Still motivated even in the absence of the leader |
| Interested in participating in decisions |

Ineffective groups

| Trust and openness are limited |
| Feelings are stifled |
| High commitment possible, but unlikely |
| Works on a need-to-know basis |
| Politicising is common |
| Co-operates to achieve the task |
| Negotiation |
| Little generation and sharing of ideas |
| Needs the leader to get the work done |
| Passive acceptance of decisions |

Fig. 37   Group qualities

effective group and a group that is not effective but which appears to be co-operative. The differences can be seen and measured. These lie in both the quality of the way the group works together, its process, and the quantitative measurement – which is the consequence of that process.

The **qualitative** aspects are those that relate to how the group members interact with each other: their trust, feelings and commitment; how they reach decisions; their motivation. These are summarised in Figure 37.

The quantitative measure of the effectiveness of a group concerns the output of work and the longer-term commitment of group members. These aspects are shown in Figure 38.

Groupthink

Another negative aspect of group cohesiveness was found by Irving Janis, who identified a phenomenon in the group process which he referred to as **groupthink**. This occurs where a group is very keen to reach a decision. In principle this is an admirable intention, but if a group pursues this aim by avoiding disagreement and ignoring the pros and cons of alternatives, this group may rightly be accused of lacking creativity and being rather cautious in their views. Such groups tend to be very close knit and this bonding makes them feel safe. They cannot accept that they as a group

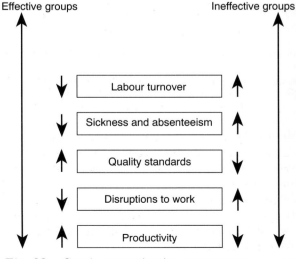

Effective groups   Ineffective groups

| Labour turnover |
| Sickness and absenteeism |
| Quality standards |
| Disruptions to work |
| Productivity |

Fig. 38   Group quantitative measures

would make a mistake. They believe that all their decisions are unanimous and that if someone does not speak when a matter is being discussed, then that person must surely agree with the rest of the group. They would argue away any facts that might make the group feel uncomfortable, and question the worth of the views of 'outsiders'.

GROUPTHINK: THE SYMPTOMS

1 **Invulnerability** they can't touch us.
2 **Rationale** that cannot possible happen.
3 **Morality** we know what is best.
4 **Stereotypes** that other team is stupid.
5 **Pressure** are you with us or against us?
6 **Self-censorship** maybe I should keep quiet, it's not very bad.
7 **Unanimity** can I assume consensus?
8 **Mindguards** our mind is made up; don't let in any other thoughts.

When a group becomes as ineffective as this, where it must have consensus at any price, then Janis did suggest the 'medicine' for recovery:

GROUPTHINK: THE MEDICINE

1 There are always alternatives, make sure they are examined.
2 Encourage an open expression of doubt.
3 Willingly listen to those who call into question firmly held views. Hear those criticisms.
4 Get someone to play the devil's advocate.
5 Look for someone outside the group and obtain their reaction at least, if not their participation.
6 Start up sub-groups of the main group who will then feed their views back to the main forum.

VICTIM OF GROUPTHINK

Have you ever been in the situation where the class seemed determined to reach a particular decision with which you disagreed, but you did not speak up against that decision, not because you were shy but because you felt that you would be shouted down or not listened to?

Have you been in the situation where, after the class made a particular decision, a number of people who did not speak up during the discussion later voiced their disagreement?

Groupshift

When a group makes a decision is that decision more radical or more conservative than one an individual would make, or is it the same? If the group makes decisions that are either more radical or more conservative than those they would make as individuals then the process that has taken place is known as **groupshift**. It was observed by N. Kogan and M. A. Wallach in 1967 ('Risk taking as a function of the situation, the work and the group') that there is a tendency for individuals who hold a particular view prior to group discussion to shift to a more extreme position as the discussion progresses. Conservative types will become more conservative and aggressive individuals will move to a more radical position. Whether the shift results in conservatism or risk depends on the governing norm within the group. Being a member of a group seems to dilute the individual's sense of responsibility for the decision reached by the group. If the decision does not work out as planned then no single individual can be held responsible for its failure.

CHANGE YOUR MIND?

Write down your individual answer to the following questions. Then discuss the questions as a group and agree a response.

'How would you suggest that your success on this module be measured? How would that measurement differ from that for a finance module?'

Did anyone shift their view? Was the shift towards a more radical or a more conservative view?

Synergy

Synergy concerns the situation where the effect of the whole is greater than the effect of its component parts. In terms of the work of a group, synergy is achieved when a group can outdo their best member. The work of Jay Hall in 1971 ('Decisions, decisions, decisions') tells us that an effective group moves in quickly to deal with any points that cause disagreement. By working at and through those areas of conflict, they are able to reach consensus, and synergy.

By contrast, the ineffective group looks for a 'quick fix' in reaching agreement, usually by majority voting or averaging. The ineffective group is more concerned with getting the job done, without too much trouble, than with finding an answer all could share.

Hall provided guidelines for achieving consensus, which he described as: 'A decision process for making full use of available resources and for resolving conflicts creatively.' Some of those guidelines, as they apply to a group member, may be summarised as:

CONSENSUS: HOW TO GET IT
1   Give your arguments as clearly as you can.
2   Listen to the reactions of others and think about those reactions before you react.
3   There are no winners and no losers.
4   If the discussion grinds to a halt, then move on to the next most acceptable answer.
5   Do not alter your views simply to avoid argument or to reach an agreement as quickly as possible.
6   If you all agree quickly then be wary about the quality of that decision.
7   Do not enter into bargaining, such as 'if I give you this, will you give me that?'
8   Do not allow a majority voting system, nor toss a coin.
9   There are bound to be differences of opinion. Seek out those differences and make sure all are involved in the discussions.
10   The wider the discussion the better the chances of reaching a reasoned and reasonable solution.

J. R. Hackman said in 1987 (in *The Design of Work Terms*, Prentice-Hall) that if the individuals within a group behave in ways that enable the group members to learn from each other, then they are certainly increasing the pool of talent within that group. A group therefore needs synergy in order to develop into an effective team, making that group greater than the sum of its individual members. Such a group, it has been said often enough, would be able to change the sum of $2 + 2 = 4$ to $2 + 2 = 5$.

Behaviour in meetings

In thinking about cohesiveness it is of value to observe the behaviour of individuals within a group setting. Andrzej Huczynski and David Buchanan in their excellent book, *Organizational*

Behaviour (Prentice-Hall, 1991) provide the six behavioural categories identified by the social psychologist, Robert Bales. The practical application of these categories is to show that in meetings, or discussions, individuals tend towards certain behaviours. These behaviours of the individual are described as:

1   **Proposing**   a new suggestion, idea or course of action is put forward.

2   **Supporting**   support of or agreement with another is revealed.

3   **Building**   developing or extending an idea or suggestion made by another.

4   **Disagreeing**   criticism is made of another suggestion, idea, or statement.

5   **Giving information**   providing facts, giving an opinion or setting out to explain.

6   **Seeking information**   the individual seeks facts, ideas or opinions from others.

LISTEN AND RECORD
When you next take part in a meeting or discussion group, listen and record the behaviours of the participants. Use a chart similar to that opposite. Each time someone speaks listen and tick which of the six categories of behaviour you think they expressed. Then at the end of the meeting you can total up the scores for each name and each category.
If there is more than one person doing this exercise, compare results, before sharing them with the rest of the group. Does this exercise tell you anything about the group process?

Interpersonal behaviour

When in 1982 A. P. Hare looked at creativity in small groups, his analysis of the research demonstrated four particular measurements of interpersonal behaviour (*Creativity in Small Groups*, Sage, 1982), which are important in group working. They were classified as:

1   Dominant *v.* Submissive
2   Positive *v.* Negative
3   Serious *v.* Expressive
4   Conforming *v.* Non-conforming

A **dominant** style is one in which the autocrat in people is predominant. This person usually talks a lot and tries to control group activities. 'The rat'.

At the other end of the scale is the **submissive**

Category	Names							Total
	Vicki	Jan	Bet	Ian	Avril	Peter	Jo	
Proposing		IIII			II	II	III	11
Supporting		III		IIII		IIII		11
Building				III		IIII		7
Disagreeing	IIIII				IIII			9
Giving information			III				III	6
Seeking information				IIII			III	7
Total	5	7	3	11	6	10	9	51

style. This is the person who looks to the dominant person for help. Such people are rather apprehensive and unlikely to express their views with any force. 'The mouse'.

A person with a style somewhere between the two can act as a good mediator and seeker of a collaborative approach.

Dominant 1 2 3 4 5 6 7 Submissive

Positive behaviour is shown in sympathy towards the needs of the group. This is demonstrated by actions which curtail inappropriate behaviour that would disrupt the group. This style has a friendly and encouraging influence. 'The domestic dog'.

The **negative** person cares little for the group and demonstrates this by continual disagreement and aggressive action which reduce the group's ability to work as an effective unit. 'The hyena'.

Positive 1 2 3 4 5 6 7 Negative

The **serious** type is very interested in getting the job done. Such people engage in any reasonable behaviour that works as long as it gets the job done. 'The fox'.

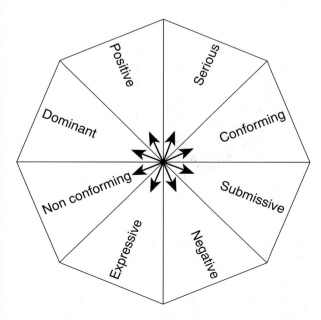

Fig. 39   Interpersonal style web

73

The **expressive** type is very supportive of the group, even at the expense of getting the job done. The job must take second place to the achievement of the group's goals and the maintenance of a happy ship. 'The chimp'.

Serious 1 2 3 4 5 6 7 Expressive

Conforming behaviour is that which matches the standards of the group. Such members are unlikely to stray from the group's established behaviour requirements. They will only change if the norms of the group require such a change. They will think like the group. 'The sheep'.

The **non-conforming** person will not compromise their individuality just to keep the group working as one. 'The domestic cat'.

Conforming 1 2 3 4 5 6 7 Non-conforming

Speaking

Notwithstanding the type of behaviour an individual may follow in a meeting, what effect on the final decision does the actual amount of talking have? Do the persons who shout loud enough and long enough get their own way? What is the truth of the proverb, 'Empty vessels make the most sound'? We are not interested here in the quality of what is said, nor the quality of the person saying it. We are not making a judgement as to the way it is said, we just want to look at **who** is doing the talking, and for **how long**. Then perhaps we can see if it is true, as research suggests, that those who talk the most have the greatest bearing on the decision made. E. D. Chapple conducted research in the 1930s on the amount of talking people did in meetings, timing their participation.

Why is it then that those who talk the most appear to have the greatest bearing on the decision made? Do they use up the available space and time, so that there is little or none left for others? Or is it that those who do the most talking do have the knowledge, skills and experience that the group needs to reach the right decision? What about the quiet ones who have an important contribution to make but find it difficult or awkward to say what they want to say? Perhaps they are not really quiet; maybe it is just that they are ignored by the rest of the group because their contribution is not valued. It may not be valued because of their status: 'Ah, they are new ... what do they know?' or 'Ah, the young ... they lack the experience.' Or perhaps they suffer from being continually put down by others and that in itself will discourage them from making future contributions. J. R. Hackman has said that groups give credence to people because of their greater age and status, even though they may not have the expertise demanded by the task.

Charles Handy in his book *The Age of Unreason* (Arrow, 1990), tells how he, as a young manager in Malaysia, suggested some productivity improvements to his boss, only to be told that the company had been operating successfully for over 50 years. He was asked what made him think that he knew better after only six months. Handy tells us he kept quiet for the next three years.

It is up to the group, including the group leader, to ensure that all members have the opportunity to make their contribution and to be listened to.

When talking does take place, where is it directed? If this can be discovered, then perhaps sub-groups or cliques may be revealed, sub-groups which may be trying to influence the decisions of the main group. Try to map out the direction of communication within a group. Do not forget that communication can take other forms besides speaking. Watch the eyes. Do people look at others first, before launching into speech. If so, perhaps they are seeking permission or approval or support to speak. Do they address all, or a select few? Speech may be directed towards the chairperson, but the eyes may seek out an expected opponent, a hoped-for supporter. However, although interpretation of these signs is very difficult, and should be left to the experts, it may give some clues or indicators as to what may be happening in a group.

This task requires a group of five or seven plus an equal number of observers, one observer for each group member.

The group has to get together to make a decision.

The observers have to watch and take notes on their assigned group member in terms of:

1 When and for how long he/she speaks.
2 Eye contact.
3 Contribution.

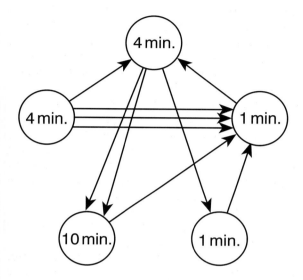

The group has the following task. You all work for a company that sells soft toys. You have been called together to reach a decision on the selection of a supplier of 15 cm pink cuddly pigs. These have been a good seller in the past and you will need 3,000 for the start of the Mother's Day rush in eight weeks. They previously retailed at £9.95 and the price has to be held this year. Quality is very important as the company has a no-quibble money-back guarantee.

The problem is that your usual supplier, Bubbles of Bristol, has gone to the wall, the receiver was called in one week ago. Four suppliers have rushed in to fill the gap. All that has to be done is to decide which one, and it must only be one, that it will be.

1 Tickle Toys of Towcester can provide a 17 cm model at £6.99 each with a minimum order requirement of 3,000. Their toys have an added benefit in that when squeezed the pigs giggle. From order to delivery will be six weeks. For a little extra they can supply them in a presentation box suitable for Mother's Day. Other products they have supplied have met the company's strict quality standards. The problem is that they have been known in the past to change their prices.

2 Boozy Boy Toys of Bangkok can supply a 12 cm model and a 18 cm model, each at £4.50. They can supply, within two weeks of the order placement, if 1,500 of each size is ordered. The samples given appear to be fine but you need time to test the quality. Previous experience has shown that quality may be a problem. The sales representative is keen to get the business and is likely to offer you a personal bonus.

3 Kiddies Choice of Chester say they can meet the order at £5.75 each and their 18 cm pigs will walk. This is a well-known company which advertises regularly on Saturday morning TV. Half the order can be met in five weeks, the remainder in another four. They may even reduce the price if an order of 3,500 is placed. No problems in quality, usually, but a little hiccup last Christmas meant the return of 500 sausage dogs.

4 Bells of Belgrade can supply the order in four weeks at a cost of £4.95. Their pigs will walk, they will go 'oink' if you pull their tails. The 15 cm samples left by the representative appear to be fine. The company has no track record with you or others that you are aware. They are just starting to break into the British market.

Your group has 20 minutes to make up its mind.

Was there a relationship between talking and decision?

There are examples where talking too much can have a negative effect. One barrister took 28 hours to make a closing speech in an attempt to get his client off a fraud charge. Apart from wasting the court's time, he was unsuccessful, as his client was found guilty. The Plain English Campaign have suggested that some barristers start to talk before they know what they are going to say.

GROUP NORMS

Group norms are the shared standards of a group. They are both expressed and implied. Norms tell each person what behaviour is considered acceptable and what is unacceptable in the group. Norms also cover the way a group thinks and feels about people, policies, procedures – they are the group's shared beliefs. Norms also relate to the quality and/or quantity of the work a group produces.

The Hawthorne studies in the 1920s (see p. 24) showed that groups have their own rules which are imposed on individuals within the group. The bank wirers at the Hawthorne Works of the Western Electric Company in Chicago seemed to think that they should not work as hard as they could. They feared that if they worked at optimum level, the company would recalculate the bonus scheme so that they would not earn as much, or even worse, some of them would be made redundant. After deciding amongst themselves the level of performance they should aim for, they became very protective of that group agreement. They showed this by disciplining their own members if they stepped out of line. They were not too honest with management in giving them the daily production figures. They called a group member who made more than the group required, a 'ratebuster'. A 'chiseler' did not produce enough. A 'squealer' was someone who would run to the bosses, telling tales. They were known to exact physical retribution over these miscreants.

Another example of people conforming, or changing their behaviour in order to be in line with the rest of the group, comes from 1952. J. Asch, in *Social Psychology* (Prentice-Hall), gave the results of research which proved that an individual will go along with the group even though his own eyes tell him a different story. In Asch's experiments a series of subjects were asked to identify which of three lines on a card was the same length as a fourth line shown alongside the other three. It was a fairly easy task and very very few people made a mistake. But the results were quite different when those conducting the experiment asked a subject to undertake the exercise in a group setting. The other members of the group were set up by the researchers to give a wrong answer. When the group gave a wrong answer, the subject, disregarding the evidence of his own eyes, went along with them. Subjects who made the right choice, in opposition to the incorrect response of the group, felt and looked rather uncomfortable.

The experiment was repeated again and again and showed that about 35 per cent of the subjects gave the wrong answer and agreed with the rest of the group. Asch demonstrated that a group can go a long way towards pressurising an individual to conform with group standards so as not to be seen as out of step with the group, even though that individual may inwardly disagree.

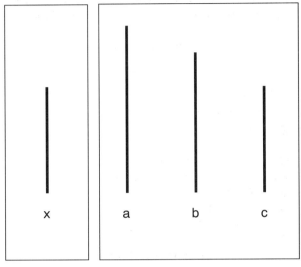

Fig. 40   The Asch study. Line X is the same length as which line: A, B or C?

Implications for management

If the management of a company wishes to change the attitude of their employees, they may try to do so through the group. Their success will depend on the nature and composition of the group as well as the nature of the idea they wish to introduce. If the group is divided in their acceptance of a particular idea, then this approach would not be successful. In this case, the management would be better advised to approach the employees as individuals, away from the influence of the group.

It is clearly of benefit to the management wishing to introduce a change of attitude if the majority of the group agree with the management's goal. In such a situation, researchers suggest, if the management state their wish in a meeting with the group, that would help to influence minority dissidents to accept the desired attitude. D. Kresh, R. S. Crutchfield and E. L. Ballachey, in their 1962 work, *Individual and Society*, suggested that management would be more successful if they were able to encourage the dissidents to declare their new-found attitude to the group. Presumably this public declaration makes it difficult for them to recant later. The thinking resembles that of some religious groups which require their new members to stand up and announce their conversion. Or that of Alcoholics Anonymous where the new member stands up at a meeting to introduce himself by saying, 'Hi, I'm John. I'm an alcoholic.'

Positive group norms

In 1988 J. W. Pfeiffer and A. C. Ballew provided nine criteria which they regard as useful in appraising group norms:

1 Feedback
2 Supportive climate
3 Experimentation
4 Practice and application
5 Goal clarity
6 Group growth
7 Group maintenance
8 Communication
9 Structure and procedure

People learn by acquiring behavioural styles which are strongly influenced by sane and sound feedback about how well they are doing. This **feedback** should:

- be particular and impartial
- only mention what has been noticed
- describe the impact of the behaviour
- relate only to behaviours that can be changed
- be asked for
- not be judgemental

People need a **supportive climate**: to be themselves; to accept feedback; to be able to get angry; to be able to express other emotions.

If people operate within a supportive climate and can accept feedback, then they can start to embrace **experimentation**. This is seen as experimenting with their own personal behaviour within the group, but not playing around with, or manipulating other people's behaviour.

As people develop behavioural patterns resulting from positive feedback and experimentation within a supportive climate they need room for **practice and application**.

Groups need clear goals, although **goal clarity** is a continuing process for the individuals within a group.

Groups need time and help to reach maturity, become effective and cohesive. **Group growth** is perhaps more important within a 'permanent' group than in one with a short life (such as one brought together to carry out a specific task only).

To aid their growth, groups need planned preventative maintenance, rather than *ad hoc* running repairs. **Group maintenance** can help improve skills that aid group facilitation.

Communication is, of course, a skill that needs attention, as, without good communication, it is possible that only a little of what is said in a group situation may be heard or understood by all members of the group.

There is no such thing as an 'unstructured' group; it cannot be a group if it is unstructured. A group's **structure and procedure** must be able not only to meet its present needs for effective and efficient working, but also to change to meet new or revised needs and situations.

DECISION-MAKING

It is perhaps in its ability to throw up vast numbers of ideas or to find the right answer to a problem (when there is one), that the performance of a group may be superior to that of an individual.

When looking at the procedures groups use to reach decisions it is of value to reflect on the work of J. K. Murnighan (1981), who recognised five specific procedural types of group decision-making.

GROUP DECISION-MAKING

1 Ordinary group process
2 Brainstorming
3 Statistical aggregation
4 Delphi technique
5 Nominal group technique

The **ordinary group process** describes the situation where the leader of the group simply sets out the problem for those present and then seeks comments and discussion. This process is similar to that of a fairly standard meeting. What is important, is the role of the leader. As the 'meeting' is largely unstructured, the chairperson must control the group by ensuring that it is not dominated by one person or a sub-group. The chairperson has to keep interest alive and widen the discussion if it begins to focus on narrow issues. If the 'meeting' is chaired effectively, there is no reason why the group cannot work as one, and be committed to whatever decision is reached. Murnighan suggests that this process is suitable for reaching decisions on matters about which the group members are likely to have firm opinions.

Brainstorming is familiar to many students from the start of their secondary school education. This technique brings a group of interested persons together in one place to find a solution to a particular 'problem'. It is at its best when the 'problem' to be examined has more than one possible solution. The technique allows those in the process free wild creative thinking without censorship. Time limits may be imposed on the group, and this pressure, it is felt, will increase creativity and, of course, speed up the delivery of a solution.

The leader of the group puts the question or problem. The group fire back whatever ideas come to mind. Those ideas are listed on a flip-chart or board. Whatever the idea is, it is listed, no matter how crazy it may seem, the crazier may prove the better. It is fast and furious, with ideas bouncing off the walls. The process does not allow an immediate evaluation of the ideas, as this may stifle creativity. However, the ideas have to be evaluated at some time towards the end of the brainstorming session. From a very large quantity of ideas a short list is drawn up and each is considered and fully discussed until a clear 'winner' emerges. Even at the final stages of the session it is of value to look at an idea and think how it may work, rather than think of good reasons why it will not work.

Before the brainstorming session proper begins it is worth taking time on a warm-up exercise.

At 8.00 a.m. each morning, Monday to Friday, a certain person left the apartment they shared with one other. That person got into the lift at the 25th floor, travelled to the ground floor and left the building. At 6.00 p.m. that person returned. This time the person got into the lift on the ground floor and travelled up to the 22nd floor, then walked up the remaining floors.

Why did the person get out at the 22nd floor?
How many plausible ideas can you think of?

Although groups may feel that they have achieved a great deal, and they have enjoyed the process, some researchers suggest that a person working on his or her own can do just as well, if not better, than the group.

JUST FOR FUN. YOUR OWN RESEARCH.

Are many heads working together better than many heads working separately?

This is an experiment which compares the performance of a group with that of an individual.

Divide a class right down the middle. Half acts as the **brainstorming** group, the other half as a collection of **individuals**.

All work on the same problem.

'The class has just been given £1,000 to spend. How will you spend it to benefit the group's educational experience?'

Rules for the brainstorming group

1 Record as many ideas as possible.
2 No censorship of any idea.
3 No evaluation of ideas during the session.
4 No building upon other people's ideas.
5 Fix a time limit.

Rules for the individuals working independently

1 Record as many ideas as possible.
2 Do not confer with others.
3 Do not work within hearing distance of the brainstorming group.
4 Work to the same time limit as the brainstorming group.

At the end of the session

1 Add up the ideas of the brainstorming group.
2 Add up the ideas of the individual group, first removing any duplicate responses.
3 Divide the number of ideas of the brainstorming group by the number of persons in the group.
4 Divide the total number of ideas of the individual group by the number of individuals.
5 Declare the result. Which group produced the greater number of ideas?
6 Keep a list of the results and the lists of ideas. You may need them later.

Where there is a problem that must be solved by a group, but it is difficult to get the group together, and where the solution is one that may be derived from the analysis of numerical information gathered from a quantity of sources, then **statistical aggregation** may be the preferred way to arrive at a decision. The participants do not meet together, nor should they do so, as this may sway the thinking of one or more towards those who may wish to exert undue influence on the decision. The individual participants are required to record what they consider to be the appropriate answer and send it to a co-ordinator. That co-ordinator then aggregates the responses in order to settle on the final solution. However, not many problems are suited to solution by this technique, so its application is limited.

MEAN, MODE OR MEDIAN

Using the **statistical aggregation** method of reaching group decisions, estimate how much it would cost for a party of 30 students from your town/city's Twin European Town/City to take a weekend rail trip, via the Channel Tunnel, to Alton Towers in August.

The estimate you give must be in the local currency of the other country.

The **Delphi technique** is similar to the statistical aggregation technique in that it is time consuming and complex and does not require the group to meet together. It does however take the process a step further. The key is a questionnaire or a series of questionnaires. The co-ordinator puts together the first questionnaire, which clearly sets out the problem and seeks potential solutions. The individuals in the group, away from the influences of other group members, will consider the problem and come up with what they see as one or more likely solutions. The results are compiled by the co-ordinator who then sends a summary back to the individuals. They are asked to review the summary and then provide suggestions as to the refinement of a stated solution or perhaps to make further proposals. The summary helps to spark off ideas and the individual, having seen the contributions of others, may shift or change his/her response. The co-ordinator then provides a second summary and the process is repeated until an agreed solution, or consensus, is reached. This technique is suitable if the group is scattered around the country or the globe. But, it does not, and cannot allow interaction, as would a group which meets face to face.

The **nominal group technique** sets out to address some of the problems of brainstorming, particularly those related to the possibility that, when a group is physically together, some members may exert pressure to make others conform. This technique also takes into account the lack of interplay evident in statistical aggregation and in the Delphi technique. It promotes the best of brainstorming, where creativity is encouraged by the interaction of the group, and the valued parts of the Delphi technique, the opportunity for members to review the opinions of others and the provision of feedback to the individual members. The technique requires that all members of the group meet together, but each individual member is required to work independently of the others. The session starts with the chairperson stating the problem, and restating it if necessary, so that all present understand the problem. When the members of the group feel that they know what the problem is, then there is a period of silence, giving each member an opportunity to think and put down one or more ideas on paper. The chairperson then works round the group, allowing each person to state one of his/her ideas which is then displayed on a board or flip-chart for all to see. Only when each member has had the opportunity to have an idea listed, does clarification and evaluation of all the ideas listed begin. The final stage is voting for the 'winning' solution. This could be done in a host of ways but usually it is done by means of a secret ballot, in which each member ranks, say, four or five ideas in order of preference. The chairperson collects and aggregates the results. If no obvious 'winner' emerges then the results are discussed and a further ranking takes place, involving all group members. The process ends, of course, when the majority favour a particular idea.

Try using the nominal group technique in these two warm-up exercises:

LEG IT

In a small cottage on the cliff tops overlooking the sea lived an old man who had but one leg. One day the post van drew up and delivered a parcel, the stamps on which showed it was from a foreign land. The man rushed inside, as best he could, excitedly ripping open the parcel. Inside, there was a human leg. The man smiled, then laughed. He threw the human leg on the open fire and continued to smile as the flames consumed its grim contents.

What is the story behind this tale?

OR

DEATH IN THE AFTERNOON

Charlie was fine when I left for work that morning. I have no idea why, but I decided to get home early that day. The scene that greeted me when I opened the front door was horrible. Charlie was on the floor, dead. The floor around the body was soaking wet. There was no sign of forced entry. There was lots of glass near the body. There was no-one else in the house, except my pet cat and it couldn't talk.

I do not know what happened. Do you?

Figures 41 to 43 show the potential of the various group decision-making techniques for conflict, group bonding and the feeling of a sense of achievement.

FURTHER READING

You will find mention of all or some of these decision-making procedures in books on management, organisational behaviour, psychology at work and others. Just look in the index for 'decision making' or one of the named techniques. You may find reference to J. K. Murnighan who identified these procedures in his article in *Management Review*, (Feb. 1981), 'Group decision making: what strategies should you use?'

GOALS

Organisations direct their employees to a collective goal but, as organisations are made up of people, it is those people who create or dictate the goals. The top management decide the goals of the overall organisation, and these are translated into goals for departments and in turn goals are given to, and hopefully agreed upon by

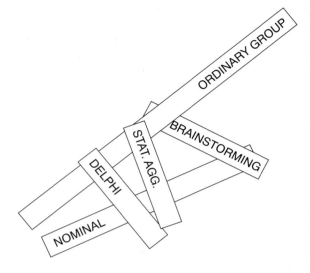

Fig. 41   Potential level of conflict in group decision-making

groups. An effective group therefore has a shared goal. That goal can only be achieved through the co-operation of its members working together and not as a collection of individuals. However, it is clear that individuals within an organisation may have their own set of goals which may, or may not, be compatible with those of the organisation.

Some groups exist simply for the satisfaction of their members and to ensure their own continued survival. It does not follow, however, that a satisfied group is a productive group. A high level of performance does not demand satisfaction,

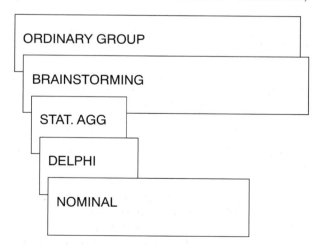

Fig. 42   Potential level of group bonding in group decision-making

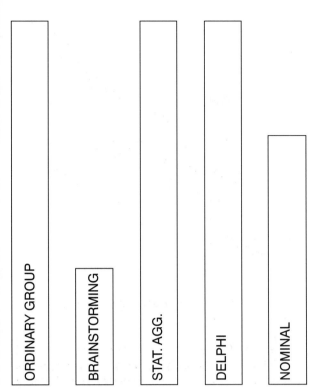

*Fig. 43   Potential feeling of sense of
achievement in group decision-making*

although it will certainly help towards it. The group needs standards and those standards must be clear, not easy, but achievable. The group must have feedback on how well they are doing. Lack of clear standards and feedback will result in low motivation of the group and of the individuals within that group.

THEIR GOAL. MY GOAL.

What do you think the organisational goal of your school or college is? What is your goal in attending such an establishment? Is there a difference? How can you reconcile that difference?

Goals may be formal, in that they are given in writing or orally. They may be informal in that they are merely suggested through the activities of the group. Goals need to be **specific**, have a degree of **difficulty** and be **accepted**.

For a goal to be specific, it should be stated in measurable terms and it must be possible to see that it has been achieved. If a goal can neither be measured nor be seen to have been done, then it is no more than a subjective goal and there is little point in setting such a goal. It is reasonable to ask a group to increase their productivity by 5 per cent but to ask the same group to simply improve their productivity would be too vague a goal.

The level of performance expected, or difficulty level, is important as it must be achievable. There is little point in asking a group to produce 100 widgets a day, as this might be too easy. There is equally no point in asking that same group to produce 3,000 widgets per day, as this may prove to be too difficult.

The group's acceptance of or commitment to a goal may differ according to whether a goal is imposed upon them, or the group has agreed to that goal. In most cases, employees would feel committed to a goal they agreed with their manager, but not so committed if they were simply told to do something.

An example from research of the above principle in action related to the work of a group of drivers loading their trucks with logs to take to a local mill for processing. The drivers were asked 'to do their best', so what they did was to load their trucks to around 60 per cent of capacity. They were then given a goal of 94 per cent of capacity, but they were also told that if they did not achieve that goal no disciplinary action would be taken against them. Over the next three-month period they loaded their trucks up to 80 per cent of capacity, then to 70 per cent and in the third month to 90 per cent. They obviously tried out the no-discipline statement in the second month, but seemed thereafter to accept the goal they were set. The research also confirmed that getting feedback had an important effect on goal setting.

Groups' acceptance of goals is crucial. Groups are very likely to achieve high levels of performance (i.e. if the goals are quite difficult) so long as the goals are agreed but not so likely to do so if the goals are difficult but they have not been agreed. Agreement within a group on a goal, or set of goals, also increases the bonding or cohesiveness of the group.

Earlier in this section it was pointed out that groups are more cohesive if they:

- are small
- have been together a considerable length of time
- have difficult entry and acceptance requirements

- are successful and
- share a common enemy.

But does cohesiveness make groups more productive? The research conducted by Nieva, Fleishman and Rieck suggests not. The norms of the group will play a major part in the measurable productivity of the group. A group with high norms in relation to performance, in terms of quality, quantity, and good relations with those outside of their group, will 'produce' more than a group with lower performance norms. It is the combination of cohesiveness and performance norms that contribute to the level of productivity.

group, and that 'hidden agenda' may not be known to the rest of the group. It is likely that some will use the group to advance their own progress within the organisation; that is their goal. They may wish to spend more time on a particular subject so they may try to manipulate the group to achieve that goal. Individual goals could hinder a group's effectiveness in meeting its goals. Effective groups recognise the existence of a 'hidden agenda' and they encourage individuals to

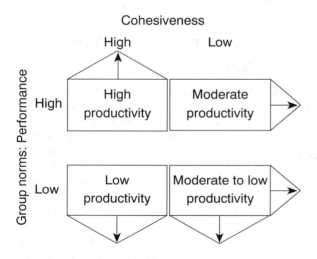

Fig. 44   *Cohesiveness and performance norms and their effect on productivity*

Some goals are different

GOAL

It is a norm, in that it is unwritten, that students are expected to attend class, complete assignments, be on time and take exams.

These expectations are usually in line with expressed goals. If they are not, then there may be problems. Has your educational establishment sat down with your group and set goals? What goals could they set? What goals would you want them to specify, and at what level of difficulty would you accept those goals?

An individual within a group may have his or her own goals that conflict with those of the declare any such goals. The purpose is not to suppress, but to resolve them, in order that a consensus is reached allowing the main target to be achieved: the group goal.

ROLE RELATIONSHIPS

To achieve what the group wants to achieve, the individual, we have seen, must fit in with the actions and relationships of that group. This is seen as a form of **role relationship**.

Role relationships are worked out through the structure of the group, that is, the way a group is organised and the way it organises things. An individual must take on a certain role, a **role identity**, which relates to what are known as situational factors: the requirements of the job, the style adopted by the leader of the group and the form of communications used. It is not often appreciated that people can be quite flexible in their work and can act in a wide range of roles, if it is necessary for them to do so. A rather 'troublesome' shop steward, promoted to foreman, can change from being a militant left-wing defender of the working class against what he saw as the advances of the capitalist class to being an upholder of a rigid style of management.

Role relationships also relate to personal factors such as values, beliefs, attitudes, personality, ability and the way people think they are supposed to act, their **role perception**. In order to work out how they think they should behave in a particular role, people look to others for an example. The data they collect for role models come from what they see, and read on TV, radio, films and in books.

The individual must live up to the role expectations held of them not only by their immediate group, but also by others outside of the group. Every individual has a host of people, ranging from family, friends to bosses and colleagues who expect them to perform different roles. These different expectations can cause them inner conflict.

Roles may be allocated **formally** by the organisation, which gives an individual a **role identity**,

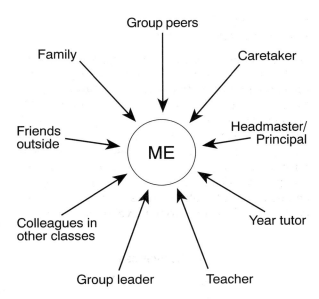

Fig. 45 What do they expect?

in that it tells the person what his/her job is, and that he/she will get a contract of employment. Roles may also be allocated **informally**, by the group. The informal role may not be immediately apparent and may be seen as a contract with the group, but more in the form of a psychological contract. Elements of this 'contract' may include an expected dress code, a common attitude to the teacher or boss, the giving and receiving of support. All of these elements have an important part to play in determining the behaviour of the individual within the group setting and in furthering the achievements of both organisational and group goals.

Role conflict will result if an individual within the group does not understand his or her role or behaves in a way that is alien to the role expectations of others within the group. As a result the group may be less effective and may not achieve its required goals. This discord results from:

- role incompatibility
- role ambiguity
- role overload
- role underload

Role incompatibility can occur, for example, in a situation where the group expects one thing from an individual and the management expects another, or where one teacher is a firm believer in a theory X form of control and another is an equally firm believer in the theory Y approach.

Role ambiguity occurs where insufficient information is available, with the result that the individual does not know or is unsure of what is expected of him/her. An example is the situation where a teacher hands out an assignment and the student or group of students are not sure what is expected of them to reach particular grades.

Role overload results when too much is expected of the group or of individuals within that group. Overload does not mean that there is in total too much work to do, but rather than people find it hard to set priorities among the various tasks they must complete. One example is that of students, who continually complain that they cannot cope as they have so many assignments to complete. What they really mean is that they find it hard to set priorities in order to meet the different expectations of a variety of teachers.

Role underload occurs where a group or an individual feel that they can do much more than is expected of them. They get fed up or bored and when that happens, 'The devil finds work for idle hands to do.'

STRESS

All or some of these role conflicts can result in role **stress**.

Although it is recognised that a certain amount of stress can be a good thing, in that it promotes an increased work performance by, say, imposing the need to meet deadlines, too much stress can be counter-productive. A high level of stress can be harmful as it may lead to frustration and lowering of job performance and job satisfaction. Managers must therefore take all appropriate steps to minimise the occurrence of anything that may cause negative stress in groups and individuals. In this respect, the minimum that a manager should do is:

1   Specify and clarify the formal roles and goals within groups.
2   Recruit groups that are compatible.
3   Tell groups and individuals what is or will be happening.
4   Help to improve the structure of the group, its cohesiveness and attend to any intergroup disharmony.

Even if there is no role conflict or role stress, people may still behave in a way that indicates that there are inconsistencies between the expecta-

tions of the group and those of management, or between those of the individual and those of the group. J. B. Milner, in *Management Theory*, Macmillan, 1971, gives us three reasons for such behaviour:

1   Individuals, or groups distort, misunderstand or are unclear of their role.
2   Lack of motivation on the part of the individual or the group.
3   The group or the individual do not have the knowledge, ability or skills to fulfil the role expected of them.

ROLE CONFLICT WITHIN MINORITY GROUPS

Where a man experiences role conflict with a role he has been given, the role conflict is because of the situation he is in. But does a woman who experiences role conflict have an added dimension if she is filling a role previously only held by men? Does the same apply to the role conflict experienced by those of a different race, or those with disabilities?

FURTHER READING

Read the account of the Hawthorne Studies again to see how the groups had their own goals and how the individuals had to fit into those goals.

CONFLICT

Conflict is like death and taxes: it is inevitable. Conflict is a matter of awareness. It involves two or more persons. If they can see it, or feel it, then it is there. If they cannot see it or feel it, then it is not there. If people hold opposing views, and they are aware of their differences, conflict exists. If people stop others from doing things that they want to do, that is conflict. As dogs fight over a bone, so humans at work fight over resources: that is conflict. Conflict may be deliberately masterminded by one person against another. On the other hand, conflict may not be the result of any deliberate act, it may just be that, whatever people do, in due time their actions will clash with what someone else wants to do.

It used to be thought that conflict must be avoided at all costs. This view considered that conflict was caused by the inappropriate behaviour of people and the easiest remedy was to remove the source of that conflict, that is, the person or persons concerned. This may be an old-fashioned notion but is still in evidence today in organisations with a Unitarist approach. Some still hold the view that conflict in groups must be eliminated in order to make a group effective and productive.

Later, it was realised that conflict is a natural occurrence and should be accepted. It was held that conflict might even assist group productivity.

Present thinking has moved away from simply accepting conflict, to positively encouraging it. Organisations today, it seems, are required to be in a process of continual change in order to grow, or even to survive. Conflict promotes that change. Without it an organisation may believe that its position is satisfactory and that it has no need for anything new. Conflict is rather like the piece of grit in the oyster that creates the pearl. No grit, no pearl. One chief executive is known to have sacked a director because that director could not bring himself to disagree with any of his chief's opinions. I recall attending a directors' meeting of a 'wild cat' organisation where the managing director said that he did not like his executive team to be yes-men. It was very strange to see all of his executive team nod in agreement and in unison! L. David Brown in his work on 'Managing group conflict' suggests that managers should strive to maintain some appropriate level of conflict.

Of course, to be of value, conflict must be positively directed, that is, it should have the aim of moving things forward; such conflict is termed **functional conflict**. But if conflict is used to obstruct or retard the work of the group it can be dangerous; such conflict is called **dysfunctional conflict**.

Stephen P. Robbins, in the fifth edition of his book, *Organizational Behaviour. Concepts, Controversies and Applications* (Prentice-Hall, 1991), provides us with four stages of the conflict process.

- Potential opposition
- Cognition and personalisation
- Behaviour
- Outcomes

IT'S MY BALL AND I'M NOT PLAYING!

Potential opposition

Potential opposition refers to the situation where the ground is prepared and the conditions are such as will enable the conflict to grow. These conditions are problems related to communication, structure and personal variables.

The semantic problems in the area of **communication**, it is suggested, result from differences in background, training and observation and deficiencies in what is known about other members of a group. There can be too little communication or too much. The method of communication can also cause conflict: it is generally agreed that it is bad practice for a manager to chastise an employee in front of others, or for a manager to resort to communicating bad news to employees through memos, rather than speaking to them directly.

Some of the issues related to **structure** which Robbins deals with include the size and leadership of the group, the reward system employed, group compatibility, boundaries and the level of a group's dependence on other groups. It is interesting that the promotion of participative management has the effect of 'encouraging' conflict within a group. This is because the group is 'sharing' in the decision-making process, with the result that differences that need to be resolved are revealed. If the reward system in the group is individually based then this is a clear area for potential conflict; one can easily imagine individuals thinking, 'Why that person, why not me? I do just as good a job.' If one group (A) is dependent on another group (B) but group B is not dependent on group A, then another potential area of conflict is exposed.

The **personal variables** that may give rise to a conflict situation relate to the personalities of the various individuals within the group and their personal values. The person with physical power, the bully, will certainly cause conflict. In Robbins' opinion, the most important personal variable is that of personal values. For example, one employee may hold an extreme racist view but another may believe that this opinion is a prime example of that person's stupidity. In a different sphere, one student at school or college may think a particular subject is a waste of time while another welcomes that field of study. Where there are such differences in value judgements then the wider those are the greater the opportunity for conflict to flourish.

Cognition and personalisation

If people are cognisant (aware) that there is the potential for conflict they can readily identify those situations in which it may arise. On the other hand the potential for conflict may be what Robbins refers to as **felt conflict**. The conflict can only be **personalised** if one or more of the parties feels that conflict: they may become tense or anxious or may experience frustration and hostility towards others. A situation which might give rise to 'felt conflict' is one where, for example, one person has received a sum of money from the organisation's management to pursue a particular action that is denied others. It is only when those others begin to personalise that denial that they may begin to feel frustration or hostility towards the management as the giver or their colleague as the receiver. A similar situation occurs where one student has been given an extension of time for handing in an assignment which is denied others. This is a potential source of conflict but only becomes a real source of conflict when those so denied personalise the situation and experience feelings of hostility toward their fellow student or the teacher.

Behaviour

Conflict may be exposed through the **behaviour** of one or more persons toward one another or others. At its lowest level, an example would be the student expressing disagreement with something the teacher has just said. At its highest (and most serious) level it would be shown if a student burns down the school or college. Most people try to resolve conflict when it is shown through behaviour, rather than by initiating preventative measures at an earlier stage.

Handling conflict

Robbins quotes Kenneth Thomas who has identified basic ways of handling conflict situations. To begin with, there must be a degree of **co-operation**: how far are those involved willing to go to try and placate others in the dispute? But there is also the question of **assertiveness**: how far are those concerned willing to push in order to get their own way?

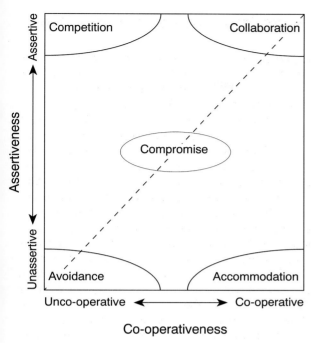

Fig. 46   *Dimensions of conflict handling*
Source: Based on K. Thomas 'Conflict and conflict management', in M. D. Dunnette (ed.), *Handbook of Industrial and Organizational Psychology*, 1976, Rand McNally, p. 900.

Thomas saw five ways of resolving conflict.

- competition
- avoidance
- accommodation
- collaboration
- compromise

Resolution by **competition** occurs where one side considers only their own stance and will not move an inch to meet the other party. They see themselves as competing and therefore they consider they must dominate to win. They care little about the impact their victory will have on others. Their attitude is assertive and most certainly uncooperative.

Thomas suggests that resolution by competition is advisable in the following situations.

1   When an action has to be taken without unnecessary hesitation.
2   On big issues where unpopular decisions have to be implemented.
3   Against those who take advantage of non-competitive behaviour.

COMPETITION ELSEWHERE

Can you suggest other situations where resolution by competition would be appropriate?

Resolution **avoidance** occurs where people can see that conflict exists but in order to prevent direct confrontation they withdraw to their respective camps, unharmed but still feeling hostile. If such people must continue to work together then they are very likely to try to suppress their feelings. The conflict remains unresolved, and may arise again at a later date. This approach is unassertive and uncooperative.

It is suggested that avoidance is suited in situations where:

1   The issue is trifling or the participants have something better to do with their time.
2   There is little chance of winning.
3   Resolution of the conflict is not worth the argument.

AVOIDANCE ELSEWHERE

Can you suggest other situations where resolution by avoidance would be appropriate?

A dispute is resolved through **accommodation** where one party would willingly sacrifice his/her own interests in order to keep the peace with the others. An example at the personal level is that of two people going out in the evening and disagreeing as to which film to go to see; one will give in to the other to keep him/her happy, doing something he/she would rather not do. This approach is unassertive but co-operative.

Appropriate situations for the use of accommodation would be:

1   When you know you are wrong.
2   When the issue is much more important to others than to you.
3   To build up a store of credit 'brownie points' for possible use in future negotiations.

ACCOMMODATION ELSEWHERE

Can you suggest other situations where resolution by accommodation would be appropriate?

Collaboration occurs where both sides go out of their way to reach a mutually agreed solution, one that will satisfy the needs of both sides. The aim is to agree the common ground, make clear the differences, then work on those differences by focusing on the cause of those differences. It is not a case of accommodating the differences, but of valuing those differences. By using a counselling skills approach the parties may then reach a solution beneficial to both. This approach is assertive and co-operative.

A collaborative approach is recommended when:

1   It is important to bring to the fore the deep understanding of those holding differing opinions.

2   It is important to obtain a common pledge by bringing together different concerns into a consensus.

3   It is vital to work at, and through, any feelings that may have an unfortunate impact upon a relationship.

COLLABORATION ELSEWHERE

Can you suggest other situations where resolution by collaboration would be appropriate?

In a **compromise** solution there is no winner, nor is there any loser – although some may suggest that a compromise is a loss for both sides. Each party has to meet the other half-way. A true compromise is where both parties give up something of some value. This is quite different from the old style negotiations between union and management, in which it was important that both parties be seen to reach a compromise after days of deliberations. The reality of that situation was generally that both union and management took a ridiculous initial stand and ended up very close to where they actually wanted to be. That sort of behaviour is to be expected when there is lack of trust. This approach is a half-way house between assertiveness and being co-operative.

A compromise approach is suitable when:

1   When both parties have equal force, but opposite views. and no-one will make concessions.

2   When time is short.

3   When collaboration or competition fails.

COMPROMISE ELSEWHERE

Can you suggest other situations where resolution by compromise would be appropriate?

Conflict outcomes

If the handling of an open and obvious conflict results in progress this is a functional outcome. If, however, the results continue to hinder the progress of the group, this would be a dysfunctional outcome.

A **functional outcome** contests the view that 'it's always been like that'. Such an outcome improves the quality of decision-making, as it demands that a wide range of views are heard. It can be a remedy to combat Groupthink (see pp. 70–1). Bureaucratic departments or organisations tend not to like conflict, as it can promote innovative solutions.

It is recognised that a heterogeneous group, made up of many different types of individuals, who possess a variety of qualities, backgrounds, experiences and skills, produces better quality work than a homogeneous group, where the similarity of the members means that the variety of input is likely to be limited. The former group will experience conflict and, if it is functional, it will progress. The latter group, having no conflict, may take a rather bland approach to their work.

Where there is a **dysfunctional outcome** the results are plain to see. The group falls apart. It is no longer cohesive. Individuals want to leave the group. This is the result of uncontrolled conflict.

Robbins presents two views on functional and dysfunctional conflict. The first is that an excessive manifestation of conflict is never, or at the very best very rarely, functional. It is functional if it is astute and controlled and at a low to moderate level.

The second is that, the less control there is exerted on a group as to how they do their work, and the more creative they are allowed to be, the more likely it is that conflict will have a constructive outcome. It is therefore probable that a group of teachers will acquire greater benefits from functional conflict than a group of workers packing the local supermarket shelves.

FURTHER READING

For an in-depth understanding of conflict within a group situation and a very good read, look for Stephen P. Robbins, *Organizational. Behaviour. Concepts, Controversies and Applications*, Prentice-Hall, 5th ed., 1991, Chapter 13.

GROUP DEVELOPMENT

Formal groups do not instantly become fully effective. Some develop to become effective groups, others remain ineffective and inefficient. How long it will take a group to become effective cannot be predicted, although the stages that all groups must work through can be identified. The stages are like steps on a ladder of success; at each step, the group grows in maturity and is then able to move on to the next step. Group members, upon joining, must be prepared to give something up from their own personal agenda in order that the group can move onward. The duration of each stage will depend on the make-up of the group and its leadership. It is also clear that all issues and any worries must be tackled directly, as otherwise the group will simply become apathetic or else dysfunctional conflict will result in the group's demise.

The table in Figure 47 compares some of the main theories of group development. The pages that follow largely examine the work of Tuckman in this field.

Two major dimensions of group development require particular attention: personal relations and task functions (see Fig. 48). The **personal relations** dimension is the combination of all the relationships an individual has with others in the group. This includes all their expectations, responses, pledges, assumptions and any problems they may have with one another. The **task dimension** concerns the group's understanding of how to do or finish the work it has been given. Any movement, either forward or backward, on either dimension must have an affect on the other.

The Bruce Tuckman model is regarded as the fundamental description of group development. His five-stage model looks at:

1 Forming
2 Storming
3 Norming
4 Performing
5 Adjourning

Some other models of group progress (see Figure 47) combine Tuckman's third and fourth stages, and others include yet more stages that could fit in with the second and third stages of Tuckman.

In the **forming** stage (stage 1), within the personal relations dimension, people are busy trying to find out who the other members of the group are. They are anxious. They start to look for differences and similarities. They test the waters. They want to establish their identity in the group, and they want to be accepted by the group. They tend to look for safe and secure behavioural patterns and so look to the leader for guidance on the way forward. They are fairly eager but not overly so. Their expectations with regard to outcomes are good, but they harbour some concerns. They want to keep relationships simple and to avoid any serious topics that may cause friction.

Within the task dimension, forming is a time of orientation. The group's drive at this stage is to attempt to define what the task is, its scope, and how they should go about reaching the goal. They look at the skills needed by the group. They are still very much dependent on the leader.

How long this stage will last depends very much on the group's views on the clarity of the task and how easy it will be to reach the goal. If the task is fairly simple and easily identifiable then the group will spend a relatively short time at this stage of the proceedings. However, if the task is complex then the time will be extended accordingly.

This low stage of development is only complete when the individuals within the group start to see themselves as part of a group.

CHARACTERISTICS OF THE FORMING STAGE

1   There is little sign of structure or involvement in the task.
2   Group members are worried about the job they will have to do.
3   Members do nothing towards the task unless pushed.
4   Members are not sure why they are there.
5   Members are not sure whether they want to stay with the team.
6   Members are a bit distant, watch and are cautious of others.
7   Members are inclined to keep themselves to themselves.

		Charrier	Cooke/Widdis	Spitz/Sadock	Ward	Miles	Hare		
S	1	Polite	Polite/Purpose	Dependence	Orientation	1. Entering the situation	Latent pattern management and tension management	1	S
T	2	Bid for power	Power	Inter-dependence	Power	2. Conflict over goals and expectations 3. Resistance 4. Factional crisis	Adaptation	2	T
A	3	Constructive	Positive	Termination	Cohesiveness	5. Golden glow 6. Getting involved more deeply	Integration	3	A
G	4	Esprit	Proficient		Working	7. Productive work	Goal attainment	4	G
E	5				Termination	8. Deceleration	Latent pattern management and tension management	5	E

Tuckman

1	2	3	4	5
Forming	Storming	Norming	Performing	Adjourning

Fig. 47 Group development

8   Members carefully test the limits of individual and group behaviour.
9   Communication is superficial.
10   Members wonder who is the real boss.

WHEN YOU WERE FORMED

Think back to when you started on a new course of study at school or college. Do you remember the first few days when you met with your class? How did you feel? Try to discuss with the rest of your group what was going through your mind, what initial perceptions you had about the course.

Stage 2, **storming** may be labelled a stage of dissatisfaction, competitiveness or resistance. In the personal relations dimension individuals try to sort out what they want from the process.

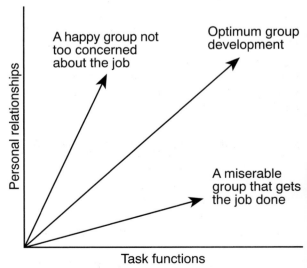

Fig. 48 Two main dimensions of group development

Individuals' hidden agendas are brought to the fore and these may cause controversy when they are seen as being in opposition to the goals of other individuals and those of the group. This can be an uneasy stage in group development as it involves conflict. Hostile reactions are common as some members fight against control by other group members. Individuals have to bend to the will of the group. The discomfort of the group will result in some members remaining quiet and others becoming very domineering. Individuals' original expectations will clash with the reality of the situation. Some will not like the fact that they may be dependent on the leader. They may be frustrated or angry. They may even feel lost or confused or believe that they are incompetent.

The task dimension will at this stage show a questioning of who does what and what the rules are. The work will be held back if there are negative feelings among members. The group structure will be questioned. Members may realise that the job they have to do is much more difficult than they originally expected.

In order to move on the group must move from a testing and proving way of thinking to problem solving. They must concern themselves with the direction of the group and the means to manage the conflict within it. Just because conflict does not reveal itself, it does not mean that the conflict does not exist, it is under the surface waiting to rear its head. Groups need to develop their ability to listen in order to move from this low to moderate level of development. Some groups will never move out of this stage and the reason may be that they like arguing, stirring; they are satisfied simply with complaining. The true measure as to when this stage is complete is when it is clear who controls the group; the dominance problem has been resolved.

CHARACTERISTICS OF THE STORMING STAGE

1. Group members show competitive and confrontational behaviour.
2. Members seem to get easily irritated.
3. Communication is one way.
4. One or two in the team attempt to dominate the rest.
5. Members watch their backs and attend to their own interests.
6. Sub-groups and alliances begin to form.
7. Members may become frustrated at the lack of progress on the task.
8. Some members may wish to impose too rigid a structure and too tight controls.
9. Members may challenge the goals of the organisation and the group.
10. Some members may act alone without regard to the rest of the team.

WAS IT REALLY AS BAD AS THAT?

Think back to when you first formed into small groups in order to complete a group project. What happened? Was there any conflict? If so, how did it reveal itself?

The **norming** stage (stage 3) is the stage of resolution. With regard to the personal relations dimension, the members become less dissatisfied as the means of working together becomes clear. Leadership becomes a shared activity and cliques begin to disappear. The group is actively engaged in recognising the contribution of each member and in resolving group issues. The members are able to reconcile their original expectations without the realities of the situation with which they are faced. They begin to acquire trust, harmony and respect. Negative feelings towards others are filtered. Members start to feel better about themselves in relation to the task and other group members. The group is achieving cohesion.

As far as the task dimension is concerned, the group begins to share ideas, give feedback and explore ways of meeting the demands of the task. They become creative. A framework or structure is in place to deal with issues such as who does what. Work towards completing the task improves as skills and understanding develops.

If, however, a group is unable to work through its problems by agreeing norms and processes that will improve the members' ability to work together, and value the differences of individuals within the group, then that group will either dissolve or remain at the storming stage of dissatisfaction. Although the group may have a new-found feeling of confidence in the cohesion of the group, in this moderate to high level of development, this cohesion may be delicate. If the group steers clear of conflict or fails to address all the differences that exist then its effectiveness will be curtailed. A group's effectiveness could also be limited if at this stage the group was deflected from its purpose and concentrated their efforts on maintaining a friendship group rather than a work team.

CHARACTERISTICS OF THE NORMING STAGE

1 Members are concerned for the needs of the rest of the team.
2 Members work for a friendly sociable atmosphere.
3 Members try to avoid conflict.
4 Competition changes to co-operation.
5 Members start to belong and feel part of a close-knit team.
6 Members wish to conform.
7 Members start to trust others.
8 Members start to respect the views of others.
9 Members start to relate to a structure.
10 Members' original expectations are reconciled with the realities of the situation.

GETTING IT TOGETHER

Think again about that group where you formed and stormed. How did the group resolve the conflict, or is it still unresolved? How would you judge the group's performance? Would you work in that group again?

Not all groups reach stage 4, **performing**. At this stage members can function as individuals working towards the group goal, in sub-groups, which are similarly active, or as part of a whole united force. They are able to adjust to changes in the needs of the individual and the group. In the personal relations dimension they work well together and are not dependent on the 'appointed' leader; they are autonomous. Their communication is open and they do not fear ridicule or discord. Their need for approval is gone and individuals become self assured. Their energies have moved away from dissatisfaction and fighting back. Feelings are positive and they are keen to be part of the group. They feel supported and can give support.

On the task dimension there is an increase in skills, knowledge and confidence in getting the job done. The task becomes easier as the group is more productive. The group's effort is concentrated on experimental problem solving, which moves them towards finding the best solution and focuses on peak group development. The structure of the group is fully operational and accepted.

At this high developmental stage there may be some feelings of dissatisfaction but these are modest compared with those experienced at earlier stages. The group is both task and person oriented, being concerned both with individual performance and co-ordination. Many teams do not reach this stage, but those which do have had to wrestle with the demands of relationships which reduce productivity; and with the demands of productivity which detract from relationships. Groups that reach the performing stage have achieved synergy.

For permanent groups, performing is the final stage. However, for temporary groups which have a limited task to complete there is a fifth stage: **adjourning**. In this stage, on the personal relations dimension, group members start to think about the forthcoming demise of the group. There will be feelings of regret about the splitting up of the group. Some may contain their feelings by not attending meetings or they may express dissatisfaction. Nevertheless, members often have feelings of satisfaction about what they have achieved.

The group's activity on the task dimension will decrease, although there may be a spur to action to meet a deadline or to compensate for the loss of an individual or the breaking up of the group.

Generally, groups become increasingly effective as they pass through the stages identified by Tuckman. This may, however, not always be the case as groups do not necessarily behave in the manner that is expected of them. Productivity may be high in a group where conflict is rife and such a group performs better than a group that is in Tuckman's third or fourth stage. Conflict can be a useful spur to a high level of productivity.

Anthony Montebello and Victor Buzzotta run an organisation in St Louis, USA, called Psychological Associates. In 1993 they wrote in the journal *Training and Development* that their research had helped them to develop a new group behavioural model. Their model is two-dimensional,

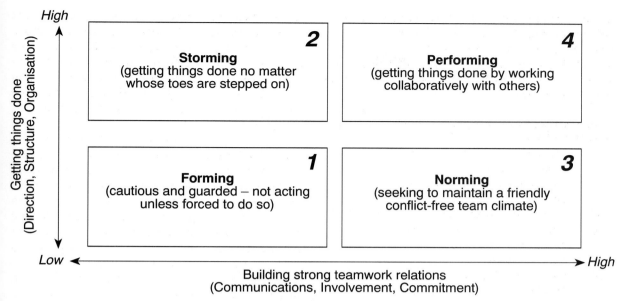

Fig. 49   *The dimensional model of teamwork patterns*
Source: A. R. Montebello and V. R. Buzzotta, 'Work teams that work', *Training and Development*, March 1993, p.63.

the dimensions being: **getting things done** and **building strong relationships**. It is rather similar to the personal relationships and task relationships model which we looked at earlier. However you can see (Figure 49) that they have managed to incorporate Tuckman's stages of group development into their model.

Over a two-year period, Psychological Associates looked at 32 teams. The teams consisted of 'established' groups in successful organisations. What they found was that these teams, far from being established at stage 4, performing, demonstrated behaviour from all the Tuckman stages. Some of the teams (39 per cent) displayed behaviour that indicated, as would be expected that they were at stage 4. Other teams (19 per cent) showed behavioural patterns that were more akin to those of a team just starting out, and still in stage 1, forming. Quite a high percentage of them (33 per cent) revealed behaviour that would be expected from groups at stage 2 of their development, storming. The remaining teams (9 per cent) displayed behaviour appropriate to stage 3, norming.

In the opinion of Montebello and Buzzotta, groups do not progress logically through the Tuckman stages. Although the behaviour of groups resembles the behaviour characteristic of the Tuckman stages, the degree to which any group's behaviour follows these stages depends on the task in which they are engaged. Each task calls forth a different behavioural mix. If a group is simply left alone to get on with the task, it will alternate between stages, taking much longer than it need do to reach the final stage of group development. Such a group needs **guidance**. That guidance should be continuous and should include training so that the group may identify and work on the **S**trengths, **W**eaknesses, **O**pportunities and **T**hreats.

Turning to another approach to **team building**, Phillip S. Wilson, a manager with British Telecom, writing in *Executive Development* in 1992, said that in building a team he started with a 70-hour five-day residential workshop. This method, he believed, was far superior to taking the team away on an outward bound course, an approach favoured by many as an excellent means of team building. Wilson, together with the consultants David Shaw and Associates, looked at indivi... learning styles (see the reference to H... Mumford, *Learning Styles* i... Individual) and team styles (se... p. 96, for another view of te... came up with a few golden ru... teams.

WILSON'S FIVE GOLDEN RULES

1 It is essential that each team member understands the goals and objectives.
2 Look at the whole and decide what work should be done by individuals, sub-groups and the full team.
3 Look at what an individual is able to do and what he/she should do.
4 Agree the decision-making process.
5 Make sure that the mechanism is in place for the team to communicate effectively.

In Wilson's opinion, successful teams are those that adopt and work with these golden rules. He points out that to do so effectively takes time, energy and commitment.

FISHBONE

Wilson, in his article, says that during the training course the group made extensive use of Force Field Analysis and the Fishbone techniques.

What are these techniques and how may they best be used?

Wilson was leading a team at the time when British Telecom were shedding staff. The company realised that they needed to produce twice as much but with half the staff. US West Communications Inc. had had the same experience: they adopted policies, such as early retirement programmes, which were designed to reduce staffing levels to enable them to compete in the increasingly competitive market place. They recognised that in doing so they lost experience and expertise, but they gained in that there were fewer people left who would resist the move for change. As far as the task was concerned groups, it was claimed, saw that standardisation enabled them to work more efficiently. As would be expected, groups faced with the real prospect of redundancy were not too keen to streamline their operation. So they engaged in stalling tactics, either doing very little or, if they considered it necessary, even putting a spoke in the wheel. One team that was created was concerned with the implementation of some of the downsizing changes. Steven C. Tarr and William J. Juliano,

managers at US West, related in the October 1992 issue of *HRM Magazine* how they kept their team productive and happy. They created the visions and the confidence that the team could reach their goals through the construction of a strong group culture and by having expectations of personal authority and responsibility.

It was not easy to get into the Tarr and Juliano team. They wanted people who desired to do something significant for the organisation and something significant for themselves. Those not selected were seen to have what they referred to as a 'victim mentality'. Such people seemed to blame everyone else for their ills, believing that they had no control over their own destiny (*see* 'Locus of control' on pp. 111–14). Tarr and Juliano needed to create a positive culture and give the team the resources to do the job. That included a bright clean working environment and up-to-date equipment. One way they fostered the team ethic was to require all members to work together on the part construction of a house for a charity, called Habitat for Humanity. The team members ate together and played together. The boss evaluated the team members, the team members evaluated each other and the boss. People were given the necessary responsibility and authority to achieve their goals. The time that some would otherwise have spent on monitoring and exercising tight control of the group's work was spent instead on customer-related activities. Two comments made by Tarr and Juliano could be open to misrepresentation, however. They were of the opinion that people should have fun at work and, unlikely as it may seem, at times they told the group, 'You will now begin to have fun.' They claimed that they built up a very cohesive team, with the result that, they said, 'when it's time for one of our staff to move on, we have a hard time getting them to go'. Tarr and Juliano provided a series of recommendations for creating a productive team.

CREATING A PRODUCTIVE TEAM

1 The immediate manager has the greatest effect on productivity.
2 Do not accept the company line if it prevents you from achieving your work goals.
3 Concentrate upon that which you can control.
4 Do not waste your time on something that is beyond your control.

5 Task systems should make team interaction positive and interesting

6 Excellent planning leads to the achievement of milestones and delivery of products.

7 Remember that business is a lot more than making money and getting results.

8 Make work a healthy positive experience for the staff.

Empowerment

Tom Peters, in his 1989 book, *Thriving on Chaos*, Macmillan, 1989, said that we should 'turn the world upside down'. To achieve flexibility people need to be empowered. To aid management, Peters, supporting the idea of working in teams, provided ten conditions necessary to obtain the goal of empowerment.

PETERS' CONDITIONS FOR EMPOWERMENT

Set forth to

1 Involve everybody in everything.
2 Use self-managing teams.

Support it by

3 Listening, celebrating and recognising.
4 Spend time generously on recruiting.
5 Train and then train again.
6 Give incentive pay to everyone.
7 Provide employment security.

Drastically change by

8 Simplifying and reducing the structure.
9 Recreating the middle manager's role.
10 Getting rid of bureaucratic rules and humiliating conditions.

At a time when organisations are moving rapidly from tall structures to flat structures and are 'downsizing' their workforce there is a need to examine the responsibilities and authority of those still gainfully employed. There is a need for teams to operate at peak performance with a much lower level of management control. There is a need to give power to the team and the individual within that team. This is **empowerment**. It is the methodical allocation of power and authority down the hierarchy. Empowerment gives a team freedom of action by removing the earlier management style of telling them not only what to do but how to do it. Through empowerment, teams use their judgement for the benefit of the organisation and the customer. Empowerment has become an 'in' word with many layers of meaning, including a redistribution of the available work within a reduced workforce and people acting up, down and across the organisational structure. The late W. Edwards Demming, who was associated with the development of the practice of total quality management (TQM), considered the concept of empowerment was likely to fall out of favour quite quickly. He believed that the most important thing for most people is that they know what their jobs are.

CHARACTERISTICS OF EMPOWERMENT

1 All in the team are working towards synergy.
2 The environment is such that it nourishes teams by giving them the resources and freedom to act.
3 Management should build up the team's confidence by giving positive feedback.
4 Those responsible for supervising a team should be positive – praising them for correct actions rather than looking out for and criticising errors.
5 A team should not be left to work in isolation; they should be told how their success impacts upon the whole organisation.
6 A team should be encouraged to innovate and take risks. Making a mistake is a learning experience. The person who never makes a mistake, never does anything.

WHERE HAVE I HEARD THIS BEFORE?

Before you tackle this do some reading on empowerment. Then start to think back to Theory Y, System 4 and other styles of management and consider if empowerment is a repackaging of previous theories.

FURTHER READING

Jane Pickard, in her article, 'The Real Meaning of Empowerment', in the November 1993 issue of *Personnel Management*, shows how three companies are successfully using empowerment.

Quality circles

Although American in origin, quality circles are usually associated with Japanese management, which has used them since the 1960s. They have been used extensively in America from the 1970s and in this country since the 1980s. A quality circle consists of a small group of employees who do similar work. They meet together at regular intervals on a voluntary basis with a group leader in order to look at problems they have identified. The circle will examine the causes of the problem and come up with recommendations to give to their management. Where feasible they will also implement their own recommendations.

Quality circles may be seen as a means of empowering people. They therefore need the full support of management, staff and unions. Quality circles are all about getting the people who do the job to solve the problems they are experiencing.

INTRODUCING QUALITY CIRCLES

1 A quality circle needs between three and twelve people. The preferred number is seven or eight.

2 The circle must consist of people who have similar experiences and skills and who work together.

3 There should be no 'outside' experts in the circle as they may be seen as different, and therefore not a natural part of the group.

4 Management must allocate time for quality circles to meet. They should not be asked to meet in their own time.

5 Membership must be voluntary. People should not be required to join a circle.

6 The circle must be allowed to select the problems it studies. Circles are not allocated problems by management.

7 As circles look at their own problems and put suggestions forward to management, they must be allowed to introduce such agreed recommendations.

8 Circles must be provided with training in group dynamics and problem solving techniques.

EA WITH LOTS OF RESISTANCE

seem such a simple idea in that it is
the work who will have the best
how to do it better. But some

managers do not like quality circles. Why do you think that is?

FURTHER READING

A great deal has been written on this subject. Just look for books on general management. The indexes of these should contain references to quality circles.

Team roles

In 1981 Meredith Belbin wrote *Management Teams: Why They Succeed or Fail*. This book, which has become increasingly popular, presents the results of his research into the team roles that are necessary to make a group effective. The role any individual plays seems to be determined by his/her personality. Belbin's work has continued and he has since written *Team Roles at Work* (1993).

Belbin suggested that each of us has a **dominant** role. This principal role is one in which we feel very comfortable and which we display most of our working day. But we also have other roles that we can play, and one of those will be our **supporting** role, one with which we feel quite at ease. None of the roles Belbin identified have anything to do with the service a person renders because he or she has particular technical skills. Belbin identified nine roles.

BELBIN'S NINE TEAM ROLES

1 **Plant**   the intelligent introverted ideas person.

2 **Resource investigator**   the extroverted moulder of others' ideas.

3 **Co-ordinator**   the self-confident orchestra conductor.

4 **Shaper**   the impatient action seeker.

5 **Monitor evaluator**   the serious-minded shooter of kite flyers.

6 **Team worker**   the diplomatic listener.

7 **Implementer**   the methodical doer.

8 **Completer**   the conscientious crosser of 't's and dotter of 'i's.

9 **Specialist**   the single-minded supplier of expert knowledge.

The **plant** is a serious-minded person who is unorthodox in actions and behaviour. Such people have the intellect and imagination to solve difficult problems. They are seen as talented individuals who have the knowledge and can usually be relied upon to get it right. They are the ideas people. However they cannot work with details or be relied upon to work within the rules. They are likely to make silly careless mistakes. They not like criticism and may be resentful if criticised.

The **resource investigator** is the person who builds up a network of contacts and looks for opportunities. Such people like to examine new ways of doing things, they are very curious and enthusiastic. They are very likeable people. They can see the relevance of the plant's ideas, but will not implement them. They are excellent contributors in a team and good at improvising. They keep the team in touch with what is happening elsewhere. Resource investigators may be too optimistic and can lose interest once their initial interest is satisfied. They tend to become bored when on their own, so they are forever out seeking new ideas.

The **co-ordinator** would prove to be an excellent chairperson. Good delegators, they keep everyone on track. Through their maturity and confident behaviour they encourage and welcome all participants and their contributions. In their role as co-ordinator they may be seen as manipulative. In terms of creativity and intellect their rank is around the average.

The outgoing, dynamic **shaper** works well under pressure. Such people are able to encourage a high level of performance from others. They reject contentment and apathy. They have the ability to leap over obstacles, and get others to recognise those obstacles. In the process, however, although shapers may influence people, they would not necessarily be liked. They can provoke people through their impatience and expressions of mild anger. They thrive on argument, but do not hold grudges. Shapers may suffer bouts of paranoia, and are particularly sensitive to the possibility of conspiracy.

The sober **monitor evaluator** can see the larger picture. Such people have excellent analytical skills and judgement, but they think logically rather than laterally. They are generally unemotional. As it is their nature to be critical, monitor evaluators are unlikely to inspire or create a climate that would motivate a group.

The mild-mannered **team worker** can be relied upon to help to sort out any problems in a group. As they are aware of what is happening around them they can respond to differences between people and work towards team building. They are socially oriented and good listeners. They can stand up to the shaper, the plant and monitor evaluator. Their contribution is sorely missed when they are not there. The problem with the team worker is that he/she can be too pleasant, over-worried with the concerns of others and rather indecisive in a crisis.

The **implementor** turns ideas into action. Such people are self disciplined, have plenty of common sense and their reliability is further demonstrated by their hard work and organisational skills. Their work is methodical and systematic and they are trusted to get jobs done. The implementor does prefer the *status quo* and can be rather unresponsive to new, unproved, ideas.

The **completer** is the perfectionist. Such people get things done on time in an orderly fashion. They seek out anything that is wrong or missing. They keep the group focused on the task they are there to do. But completers can find it hard to delegate. They also worry too much about detail and will not let matters out of their hands until they are confident that everything has been completed correctly. All has to be done 'by the book' and this approach can irritate other, more impatient group members.

The **specialist** is the one with the specialised knowledge and skills that are needed by the group for a specific task. Such people are single minded and dedicated to their field. Because of their specialist role, however, they may fail to appreciate the bigger picture, and they tend only to contribute within their field of expertise.

Belbin's theory is that a group containing a mix of the roles identified above will act as a successful team. He claims, as others have also done, that teams are at their best when a range of roles are present in a group. This view must, however, be contrasted with that which sees the homogeneous group as more effective than the heterogeneous one. With regard to the ideal size of a group which we have seen earlier is recommended as five or seven, at first sight there may appear to be a problem in fitting the full range of Belbin's nine roles into the ideal team. But, as each person has a supporting role in addition to the primary role it is possible to have within a small group the complete range of Belbin's roles.

Look at the descriptions of each role: which do you think you fit into? That is what you think. People do not always act in the way that they think they do. So what is needed is for others, the more the merrier, to say which role they think describes the way you behave.

You will find reference to Meredith Belbin in many texts dealing with teams or groups. However it is preferable to get hold of the original texts, *Management Teams: Why They Succeed or Fail,* published in 1981 and *Team Roles at Work,* published in 1993. Both books are published by Butterworth-Heinemann.

Symbolic lenses

Organisations, like life, can be very complex. There are so many things happening in them that it is difficult to remember them all. An easy solution is to pigeonhole things, put them in boxes; for each box we can keep a mind map to lead us through its contents. If we cannot find an item in one box, we need not be worried: we will find it in another box with a different label. So with the operation of groups: the leader and the rest of the membership need to relate their experiences and problems to manageable boxes; they may get out their map and see where they have been or perhaps where they are going. Terry Deal and Lee Bolman put those mind, or cognitive maps into frames which they called:

- structural
- human resources
- political
- symbolic

A considerable amount of attention is paid to the **structural** and **human resources** frames – in the opinion of Deal and Bolman, perhaps too much. To make a good team a great team, they advise, it is necessary for organisations to reframe and look at politics but more importantly at the Symbolic aspects of teams. This change is not just a way

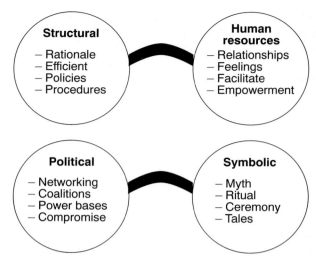

Fig. 50   Deal and Bolman frames

of looking, it is a way of thinking. Think politics, advise Deal and Bolman, and then work on the power and conflict that holds back a group.

Symbolic thinking is an art, not a science. It is intuitive, not calculative. It involves lateral, not linear thinking. It is not too much to say that it is magic, it is faith. It is turning the world upside down to shake out its meaning.

Deal and Bolman state eight symbolic principles that help to make a successful team.

1 'How someone becomes a team member is important': **how badly do you want to join?**

2 'Diversity gives a team a competitive advantage': **mad is not bad.**

3 'Example rather than command holds a team together': **do as I do, not as I say.**

4 'A specialised language fosters cohesion and commitment': **we know what we mean.**

5 'Stories carry history and values, while reinforcing team identity': **myth and legend.**

6 'Humour and play reduce tension and encourage creativity': **carry on laughing.**

7 'Ritual and ceremony renew spirit and reinforce values': **spiritual cleansing.**

8 'Informal cultural players make contributions disproportionate to their formal roles': **everybody needs a 'tribal priest'.**

How badly do you want to join. The message here is that you must want to join the team. You will want to join it so badly that you will give things up in order to join. You will pay the price for entry. That includes forgetting all about contractual hours, weekends, a full family life. It is a two-way process: the group must also want you. This concept should be familiar to us from the idea of 'group development and maturity' which we mentioned earlier when considering group cohesiveness. In that context, it was suggested that people want to join successful groups, be they schools or organisations. The competition is severe to join such groups and the entry requirements are high.

Mad is not bad. The group needs to have a wide range of personalities, talents and styles of working and behaving, as well as people with the right knowledge, skills and experience to do the job. People in groups who all act the same, think the same and behave the same are collectively boring, producing boring things. A good mixture of people is likely to produce a more interesting result. The idea is similar to what was said earlier on functional outcomes of conflict, where heterogeneous groups will do much better than groups that are homogeneous.

Do as I do, not as I say. This is the recognition of the hero as team leader. While it is accepted that there must be rules, this precept suggests that teams should only attend to those rules that are absolutely necessary. A team leader leads by example and it is that example that holds the team together. A team leader need not be there in body all the time, but his/her presence must be felt all of the time.

We know what we mean. Groups have their own culture and to a certain extent, their own language. Words and sayings that mean something to the group will be incomprehensible to the outsider. The effect of this is that a person can speak and understand the language only if he/she is a member of the group. Such a culture helps to bring and keep a group together.

Myth and legend. A group develops its own reputation. People joining a group bring their own reputation with them. The successes of the group, or those of people joining the group, are associated with their behaviour. Their behaviour is seen to be the measure of their success. What seems to be, becomes what is. The personal values, or what are seen to be the personal values, of each member of the group are an important factor in giving

the group an identity that clearly separates it from other groups. You will recall that it has been suggested that personal values are the most important, and oft-ignored, contributory factor in conflict.

Carry on laughing. In tense work situations, where difficult decisions have to be made and delicate actions undertaken, as in a hospital operating theatre, it is sometimes possible to relieve the tension by humour. Humour can allow people to cope with the very serious nature of their job. An effective team has humour and play as essential elements of group life. Some of the humour may appear to the outsider to be childish, but one should remember that children are creative. Work is serious, school is serious. Why should these and other institutions be so serious, asks Robin Prior, a management consultant, when humans are the only animal to have been given the gift of laughter? Prior, in his article in *Training and Development* (March 1993), tells of a clinic that treats patients with stress-related illnesses through laughter. He says that you can tell more about organisational culture through the cartoons stuck on the walls and the jokes people tell, than through any in-depth survey that asks the conscious mind to respond. The cohesiveness of groups is improved by empowering individuals, giving light where there was only gloom. He says that we should treat humour as a precious gift. Work and school may then be fun.

Spiritual cleansing. A group has customs and customs have rituals. These activities have a much deeper meaning than appears at face value. When I was a work study practitioner in a team of seven, we used to summarise the week's activities in a pub on the banks of the Tay. The completion of a project was signalled by a team pitch and putt championship. These rituals were all part of maintaining the uniqueness and cohesiveness of the group. You will recognise the rituals that take place when a group member is leaving, but how often do you see a ritual welcoming a new group member?

Everybody needs a 'tribal priest'. The informal roles that people play can influence the group as much as, if not more than, their formal roles. Team members need someone to confide in, a counsellor, a 'tribal priest'. The person who fulfils this role not only listens to team members, but also advises them about what their superiors want from them, what their requests mean. The 'priest' knows that team members have a separate existence away from work. The priest is able to meet the needs of the person when it means getting near to that person and not keeping a safe distance away. The priest does not believe, as some managers still do, that people should leave their personal lives outside the front door when they come into work.

The Deal and Bolman view on developing top teams would then be:

TOP TEAMS

1 It is more than finding the right people.
2 It is more than devising the right structure.
3 It is more than negotiating agreements and political manoeuvrings for forever scarce resources.
4 It is more than attending to people's needs and motives.
5 It is the rise of an order of believers.
6 It is a group with a shared conviction and culture.
7 It is a search for the essence within the group.

'Peak performance emerges as a team discovers its soul.'

ASSIGNMENTS FOR SECTION 2, THE GROUP

1. Something you prepared earlier

Take the notes you made when you were working on 'The Style Show' (p. 38). Analyse the notes in the light of what you have learnt in this section, looking at the performance of the group in terms of:

- Group cohesiveness
- Groupthink
- Groupshift
- Synergy
- Behaviour in meetings
- Interpersonal behaviour
- Speaking
- Group norms
- Positive group norms
- Decision-making
- Role relationships
- Handling conflict
- Group development
- Team roles
- Symbolic lenses

2. The pyramid game

Your assignment is to submit a bid to the Pharaoh for the construction of one or more pyramids. The bid will take the form of a presentation lasting about five minutes.

1. Groups

You will work in groups of four or five.

2. Observers

There should be one observer per group. The role of the observer is to examine the group process. They may like to observe from the viewpoint of Tuckman's work model and/or John Adair's action-centred leadership model.

3. Resources

In addition to the team members only the following resources may be made available:

a Paper for your calculations and writing your slogan

b Card for building your scale model of the pyramid or pyramids
c Scissors, glue, ruler, felt-tip pens, flip-chart paper, calculator

4. Task

Your organisation specialises in building pyramids. You have been approached by the 50-year-old Pharaoh who has not been feeling well lately, although available statistics indicate that he is expected to live another ten years. The Pharaoh wants an impressive monument to leave his people as a reminder of him during his earthly rule. He is not sure if he wants one big pyramid or two small ones; it is up to you to make recommendations. He is not sure where he wants to site the pyramid(s); it is again up to you to make recommendations. He thinks that the pyramid should be square based with equilateral faces. There are a couple of minor problems:

a He has a budget of ten and a half million gold pieces. If you go over budget then you will all be executed
b He wants to see the completed pyramid(s). Should he die before it is completed he has left instructions that all your team be entombed with him

5. Presentation

For the presentation you will use the scale model(s) and flip-chart paper. On the flip chart you will show your calculations and any other data you deem appropriate. In summary your presentation will include:

a Site proposed
b Size of the pyramid(s)
c Time it will take to complete
d Total cost
e Scale model(s)
f A sales slogan promoting your organisation, which will convince the Pharaoh that yours is the organisation he should choose
g Anything else that will help you win the contract

6. Data

The following data will be useful if you want to produce a feasible bid.

a *Employees*. Employees are commonly known as slaves. They work seven days per week. They do not get a wage, but you do have to feed them at a cost of half a gold piece per day for each slave. If you do not feed them they will die, or at the very least their productivity will fall drastically.
b *Available workforce*. Although the construction industry is coming out of recession you still only have a maximum of 1,000 men available to hire.
c *Productivity*. Productivity of the slaves is important as it takes, according to the efficiency experts, 20 men to move each block of stone.
d *Size of pyramid*.

Length of side measured in paces	No. of blocks needed
70	80,000
80	120,000
90	170,000
100	240,000

e *Costing*. Price per block:
Odan Quarry: 50 gold pieces
Mepash Quarry: 30 gold pieces
d *Transport and erection*. Time includes transportation and erection of each block.
Mepash to site A: 3 days
Odan to Site A: 1 day
Mepash to site B: 2 days
Odan to site B: 4 days

You may agree the time to be taken for this assignment. However as a guide you should take no longer than one hour for the calculations and construction. The presentations will take five minutes per group. The summing up should take approximately 30 minutes.

The Pyramid Game was originally written by Jill Bayley, who developed the game for Roger Hawes, Walker's Crisps Ltd.

MULTIPLE CHOICE AND QUESTIONS

1 A group may be described as a collection of people who:
a Are working for the same organisation.

101

b Have a common boss and are working towards a common goal.

c Interact with each other to achieve a goal.

d Share in the decision-making process.

2 The Harvard professor who drew our attention to working in groups through the Hawthorne experiments was:

a Elton Mayo

b Frank Gilbreth

c Fred. W. Taylor

d John Adair

Questions 3, 4 and 5 each define one of the following Hofstede value system dimensions. Which dimension (*a–d*) relates to each definition?

a Power distance

b Uncertainty avoidance

c Individualism

d Masculinity

3 The quality of working life is seen as important.

4 The measure of acceptance of inequalities.

5 A preference for flexibility and vagueness.

6 Give three reasons why management would want people to work in groups.

a _____

b _____

c _____

7 Give three reasons why individuals would want to work in groups.

a _____

b _____

c _____

8 Formal official groups that are permanent may be referred to as:

a Task groups

b Command groups

c Project groups

d Kinship-friendship groups

9 Describe an informal network group.

_____

10 What are the three functions that Bernard Bass said take up a group's space, time and effort?

a Task, interaction and self-oriented behaviour

b Task, group and individual work activities

c Direct, indirect and task behaviour

d Initiator, encourager and gatekeeper activities

11 What did Robert Zajonic call the increase of behaviours of a particular type when in the presence of others?

a Social facilitation

b Self orientation

c Group orientation

d Iceberg effect

12 What did Zajonic mean by the dominant response hypothesis?

_____

13 What is the 'preferred' size of a group?

a 5 or 7

b 15 to 20

c 8 or 10

d 2 or 3

14 Social loafing is:

a An individual reducing his/her productivity because he/she feels others are not pulling their weight.

b An individual reducing his/her productivity because he/she thinks the reduction will not be noticed in a group situation.

c An individual who has a greater incidence of absence because he/she is working in a group and thinks the absence will not be noticed.

d An individual who tries to hide his/her lack of skills within a group setting.

15 Give one good reason why a group is better than an individual.

_____

16 Give one good reason why an individual is better than a group.

_____

17 Which of these qualities describes an effective cohesive group?
- **a** Limited trust and openness
- **b** Lots of negotiation
- **c** They co-operate to achieve the task goal
- **d** Conflict is part of the process

18 Groupthink may be described as:
- **a** The method groups use to reach decisions.
- **b** The avoidance of disagreements and examination of alternatives through self-censorship.
- **c** Encouraging open expression of doubt.
- **d** The use of a devil's advocate.

19 Describe Groupshift.

_____

20 Group synergy is:
- **a** $2 + 2 = 4$
- **b** $2 + 2 = 3$
- **c** $2 + 2 = 5$
- **d** $2 + 2 = 2$

21 A way of achieving consensus may be described as:
- **a** A decision process for making full use of available resources and for resolving conflict.
- **b** Reaching agreement through the majority decision.
- **c** The status of an individual is related to the weight of his/her argument
- **d** The breaking down of a problem into manageable elements and voting for each in turn.

22 Group norms are:
- **a** The goals set by management and agreed by the group.
- **b** The expressed and implied shared standards within the group.
- **c** The sharing of rewards in relation to individual effort.
- **d** The specification set by management for those wishing to join the group.

The following information relates to questions 23 and 24:
- **a** Brainstorming
- **b** Delphi technique
- **c** Nominal group technique
- **d** Statistical aggregation

23 What is the decision-making technique that is best suited for an answer that is the result of a collection of numerical information?

_____

24 What is the name of the technique that does not require the group to meet together as all is done through a series of questionnaires?

_____

25 The following two statements refer to the achievement of group goals:
- (i) A high level of performance does not demand group satisfaction.
- (ii) Lack of clear standards and feedback will result in low motivation of the group.
- **a** (i) is True   (ii) is False
- **b** (i) is True   (ii) is True
- **c** (i) is False   (ii) is False
- **d** (i) is False   (ii) is True

26 When the group expects one thing from an individual and the management another then this may be seen as:
- **a** Role overload
- **b** Role ambiguity
- **c** Role incompatibility
- **d** Role underload

27 Conflict that is used to obstruct or retard the work of the group is:
- **a** Functional conflict
- **b** Dysfunctional conflict
- **c** Felt conflict
- **d** Personal value conflict

28 K. Thomas provided five ways of resolving conflict. One was collaboration. Provide two further ways:

_____

_____

29 List four of the five stages in Tuckman's group development model.

_____

_____

_____

_____

103

30 Which of these is not to be recommended when forming quality circles?

  a A circle needs between three and twelve people. The preferred number is seven or eight.

  b The circle must consist of people who have dissimilar experiences and skills who do not work together.

  c A circle should include 'outside' experts.

  d Management must allocate time for circles to meet. They should not be asked to meet in their own time.

SCOPE FOR IMPROVEMENT

The opinion of the 'Expert'

		3 'Expert' rank
a	Can deliver messages and take orders	___10
b	Can pacify people	___ 7
c	Clean and of smart appearance	___ 8
d	Clean hands and nails	___ 9
e	Courteous	___ 5
f	Dependable and on time	___ 1
g	Eager to help	___ 3
h	Keeps calm	___ 6
i	Sociable and gregarious	___ 4
j	Trustful and honest	___ 2

REFERENCES

Asch, J., 1952, *Social Psychology*, Prentice-Hall.

Bass, B., 1962, *Manual for orientation inventory*, Consulting Psychologists Press.

Belbin, M., 1981, *Management Teams. Why they Succeed or Fail*, Butterworth-Heinemann.

——, 1993, *Team Roles at Work*, Butterworth-Heinemann.

Benne, K. D., and Sheats, P., 1948, 'Functional roles of group members', *Journal of Social Issues*, Vol. 2.

Boshear, C., and Albrecht, K. G., 1977, *Understanding People, Models and Concepts*, University Press.

Chapple, E. D., 1940, *Measuring Human Relations: an introduction to the study of interaction of individuals*, Genetic Psychology Monographs 22.

Deal, T., and Bolman, L., 1993, 'What makes a team work?', *Organizational Dynamics*.

Demming, W. E., 1986, *Out of the Crisis*, Cambridge.

Deutsh, M., 1949, A theory of co-operation and competition', *Human Relations*, Vol. 2.

Hackman, J. R., 1987, *The design of work teams. Handbook of Organizational Behaviour*, Prentice-Hall.

Hall, J., 1971, 'Decisions, Decisions, Decisions', *Psychology Today*.

Handy, C., 1990, *The Age of Unreason*, Arrow.

Hare, A. P., 1982, *Creativity in Small Groups*, Sage.

Hayes, J., 1991, *Interpersonal Skills*, HarperCollins.

Higgs, M., and Rowland, B., 1992, 'All pigs are equal', *Management Education and Development*, Vol. 23/4, p.355.

Hofstede, G., 1984, *Cultural Consequences*, Sage.

——, 1991, 'Motivation, leadership and Organization: do American theories apply abroad', *Cultures and Organizations: Software of the Mind*, McGraw-Hill.

Huczynski, A., and Buchanan, D., 1991, *Organizational Behaviour*, Prentice-Hall.

Janis, J. L., 1982, *Groupthink*, Houghton Mifflin.

Kogan, N., and Wallach, M. A., 1967, 'Risk taking as a function of the situation, the person and the group', in Newcomb New Directions. *Psychology III* 1.

Kresh, D., Crutchfield, R. S., and Ballachey, E. L., 1962, *Individual and Society*, McGraw-Hill.

Latane, B., Williams, K., and Hoskins, S., 1979, 'Many hands make light work: the causes and consequences of social loafing', *Journal of Personality and Social Psychology*, Vol. 37.

Likert, R., 1961, *New Patterns of Management*, McGraw-Hill.

Maginn, B., and Harris, R., 1980, 'Effects of Anticipated Evaluation on Individual Brainstorming Performance', *Applied Psychology*, Vol. 65.

Milner, J. B., 1971, *Management Theory*, Macmillan.

Montebello, A., and Buzzotta, V., 1993, 'Work Teams That Work', *Training and Development*.

Mullins, L. J., 1989, *Management and Organisational Behaviour*, Pitman.

Murnighan, J. K., 1981, 'Group decision making. What strategies should you use?', *Management Review*.

Peters, T., 1989, *Thriving on Chaos*, Macmillan.

Pfeiffer, J. W., and Ballew, A. C., 1988, *Presentation and Evaluation Skills in Human Resource Development*, Vol. 6, University Associates.

Prior, R., 1993, 'Humour in Business', *Training and Development*, March.

Robbins, S. P., 1991, *Organizational Behaviour. Concepts, Controversies and Applications*, 5th ed., Prentice-Hall.

Tarr, S. C., and Williams, J. J., 1992, 'Leading a team through Downsizing', *HRM Magazine*, Oct.

Thomas, K., 1976, 'Conflict and Conflict Management' in M. D. Dunnette (ed.), *Handbook of Industrial and Organizational Psychology*, Rand McNally.

Tuckman, B. W., 1965, 'Development sequences in small groups', *Psychological Bulletin*, 63.

Wilson, P. S., 1992, 'Management Team Building: An experience at BT', *Executive Development*.

Zajonic, R., 1969, *Social Facilitation. Readings in Organizational Behaviour on Human Performance*, R. D. Irwin.

The Individual

This section sets out to meet the requirements of 11.2 'Investigate the effects of motivation on performance'.

On completion of this section you will be able to:

1   Research people's attitudes to work
2   Analyse the factors affecting motivation
3   Explain the types of individual performance that motivators can affect

---

INTRODUCTION

If, as was said at the end of Chapter 2, 'Peak performance emerges as a team discovers its soul', what then of discovering the soul of the individual to promote peak individual performance? Psyche is a Greek word meaning 'soul', from which we get the word 'psychology'. Nowadays psychology is seen to be the scientific examination of an individual's behaviour, emotions and thoughts. Psychology may be applied to those within a working environment, in order to look at the attitudes and motivation of people at work.

However, before tackling such issues as individual values, personality, and so on, it may be useful to look first at matters that some may consider to be quite common and everyday matters.

COMPOSITION OF THE WORK-FORCE

In any reasonable-sized organisation you will find young employees and old employees; male employees and female employees; married employees and single employees. Some of these will have dependants, that is children and/or relatives that need care. Some of the employees will have been with the organisation for a long time, others not.

Before starting to look at psychological reasons as to how and why people behave in particular ways at work, we may look at more obvious differences between employees. All of these are easily identifiable or easy to find out by looking at personnel records.

MEMO

To: Personnel Dept.
From: The Desk of the Boss
Subject: <u>Productivity, Absence Labour Turnover and Job Satisfaction</u>

I am concerned about the above. Look up your records and get a breakdown of:

1. **Age**
2. **Gender**
3. **Married** employees and **Single** employees
4. Employees with dependants. That's **Parents** or **Kids**.

When you have collected this information then find out which group has more time off; which will produce more work; which are likely to leave and which will be satisfied with their job.

Age

What about young and older employees? Organisations discriminate unfavourably against the older worker; just look at the job adverts. Such discrimination is not against the law, although there are pressures to make it so. It is commonly thought that employees become less productive as they get older. There is no evidence to suggest this is true, but there is evidence from research in the late 1980s and early 1990s, that shows that it is not. That should please organisations, especially as it is a fact that the average age of the working population is increasing.

The older worker is not as likely to move jobs as frequently as younger workers. This lower turnover may be due to there being fewer opportunities for older workers to freely move around the job market. There are also practical and financial reasons for older workers to remain in one job.

The older worker is less likely than the younger worker to suffer from the 7 a.m. syndrome, that is, waking up at seven and saying, 'I can't be bothered', then going back to sleep rather than going to work. But the older worker will be absent from work more frequently and for longer periods if he/she is genuinely ill.

The older worker is more likely than a younger person to be satisfied with his/her job. Provided workers are retrained in the event that technological change makes their present skills obsolete, there is no reason why job satisfaction should vanish.

EMPLOYING OLDER AND YOUNGER WORKERS

Give three reasons why you would recommend the employment of:

a The older worker – try and define what you mean by 'older'.

b The younger worker – what is the age range of 'young'?

Gender

There is no difference. No argument. It is against the law to discriminate on grounds of gender.

But, are you an androgynous person? You may be aware that the *andro* bit means male and *gyne* means female. The whole means the bringing together of what have been seen as male and female characteristics. A man can be tough and tender, as a woman can be tough and tender. An androgynous person is someone who can solve problems with the use of logic and with intuition. Such a person can handle power and influence, as well as help and appreciate others.

It has been suggested that differences between men and women have been learnt. As these cultural norms do not pay attention to individual preferences and needs, they can easily create problems rather than solve problems.

Males are reputed to be competitive, Herculean, dominant and tough and destined to rule. Males are said to be logical thinkers who do not express their emotions and most certainly do not cry, as this is a sign of weakness. On the other hand they are seen as obstinate, overbearing and brutish. If they suffer from high blood pressure and ulcers, is this because of their maleness?

Women are reckoned to be caring, sharing, sensitive beings who look after others. They are thought to be intuitive thinkers who express how they feel. However, they may also be seen as clinging, incompetent and feeble. Women may suffer from a lack of self-confidence and psychological problems.

Stereotypical male or female behaviour, if allowed to run unchecked, can lead to sex discrimination and has done so. At work this may be revealed in discrimination in recruitment, promotion and remuneration and even in sexual harassment.

Macho management, a male form of stereotypical behaviour, much to the fore in the 1980s, has been condemned, not least by Rhiannon Chapman, the director of the Industrial Society, who said that 'sooner or later that type of behaviour gets its nemesis'. The message seems to be that people should not be locked into male or female stereotypical behaviour, as this limits their ability to meet changing situations at work as well as in society generally.

To encourage androgyny at work is not to say that people should be reduced to sameness or some form of unisex behaviour. People should have the ability at work to be themselves, but to have the freedom and indeed be encouraged to call upon a range of behaviours appropriate to specific situations at work.

If the so-called male/female behavioural characteristics are learnt, one learning environment would be at school and college. What evidence can you point to that reinforces stereotypical behaviour, or is it now a problem of yesteryear?

Marital status

As with gender, organisations are not permitted to discriminate in the employment of people on the basis of whether they are married or single. Research has shown, however, that married persons have less time off work, stay in their job longer and are happier in their job than single people.

IT'S OBVIOUS

Is it obvious why married people stick longer in one place, have much less time off and appear to be comparatively content in their job? What about those living together?

Dependants

When it comes to dependants, there is no conclusive evidence, one way or the other, to give organisations a good reason to employ or not employ those with dependants.

WHAT DO YOU THINK?

Do you think an employee with, say, three kids is likely to have more time off work than others? Do you think that an employee with dependent relatives is more likely to stay with the organisation rather than look around for other opportunities? I have found that all responses to these two questions always begin: 'It depends . . .'.

FURTHER READING

There are still at least a couple of issues that require your attention when you are looking at the visible or easily discernible things that help to distinguish people at work. What about the behaviour at work of people who have a disability? What about the behaviour at work of people from different ethnic

backgrounds? Don't ignore these matters. Identify local organisations that deal with the issues involved, and invite them to come and speak to your group.

PERSONALITY

Individuals are different from one another, all are unique. It cannot be repeated often enough that individuals are unique, even though there are constant attempts to corral people into groups, called types. Our psychologist friends have a long way to go to discover what might be called the behavioural DNA. Although, to be fair to them, the personality traits they have described are put on a scale, so individuals do not simply have a particular trait, they can have it in degrees.

TRAIT OR TYPE?

What is the difference between a trait and a type? Does it make any difference to anyone other than the psychologists?

We have looked at some easily identifiable differences between people. There are a host of other ways to distinguish between people but the one that we are now interested in is personality.

Personality may be described as the total pattern of the various qualities that demonstrate a person's ways of thinking, feeling and behaviour as they relate to others or things. Personality is not supposed to be quantitative, although it is commonly said that some people have lots of it, and others lack any of it.

Personality traits are fairly static, in that a person will tend to react to a particular situation in a certain way, each time that situation arises. So, if someone has a single outburst of temper because another is really irritating them, this does not mean that this person has a tendency to temper tantrums. However if that distinctive behaviour is seen to occur quite a lot, then this would be identified as a personality trait.

You may blame, or praise, your parents for your personality. You may blame, or praise, where, how and when you were brought up and the way you reacted to that upbringing. Whatever gave rise to your personality, and the experts are still arguing about it, be it nature or nurture, or a bit of

Personality – who needs it?

both, what is sure is that the situation in which you find yourself will make a difference.

You may have discovered when looking at recruitment and selection in another module that although personality tests are quite widely used, these have no practical use in predicting how individuals behave within the working environment. Such tests may prove useful, however, if they manage to reveal someone who is at the extreme of a particular trait.

DO YOU RECALL?

Do you remember that, when looking at Recruitment and Selection, you considered the Cattell 16 personality factors (16PF)? If not, check your notes.

Extroversion and neuroticism

It is to the work of Hans Eysenck that you need to look first when considering the trait personality theories. His theories, and the work of those who followed, are of importance when we think about the behaviour of people at work. His extroversion scale ranges from complete extroversion to total introversion. Most people fall somewhere between the two extremes.

An **extrovert** person is one who is more interested in what goes on around him or her and in other people; such people may also be lively and sociable. An **introvert** person is so busy thinking about his or her own inner thoughts and feelings

that they may be shy and find it difficult to communicate with others.

Eysenck's other scale is concerned with the degree to which people are **neurotic**. Extreme neuroticism is characterised by anxious, obsessive behaviour and low self-esteem. Putting the two scales together gives the following descriptions of the extremes.

1 *Extrovert with high neurotic score:* highly strung, excitable, unstable, friendly, sociable, dependent.
2 *Extrovert with low neurotic score:* composed, confident, trusting, adaptable, friendly, sociable, dependent.
3 *Introvert with high neurotic score:* highly strung, excitable, unstable, cool, shy.
4 *Introvert with low neurotic score:* composed, confident, trusting, adaptable, calm, cool, shy.

The value of the findings of Eysenck and others is that they can be applied to the working situation.

DANGEROUS DATA ON EXTROVERTS/INTROVERTS

1 Extroverts prefer practical and people-oriented subjects. Introverts prefer theoretical subjects.
2 Extroverts work well with distractions. Introverts do not.
3 Extroverts are more likely to have accidents at work, or going to it and coming from it, than their introvert companions.
4 Motivate an extrovert with a carrot. Motivate an introvert with a stick.
5 Extroverts go for the 'Employee of the Month' type of acknowledgement. Introverts do not.
6 Extroverts like good, honest, regular feedback for good work – a pat on the back. Introverts need to be reminded that stepping out of line is not nice – by a gentle cultural caressing of the throat.

NB: None of the above should be applied without the use of a safety net, that is, lots of research, lots of training, then a lot of experience.

DANGEROUS DATA ON NEUROTICS

1 Low neurotics like the practical subjects. High neurotics prefer people-oriented subjects.
2 Both high and low neurotics are susceptible to

109

stress, particularly those with high scores.

3 The higher up the neurotic scale the more likely a person is to have accidents.

4 A highly neurotic introvert will respond to both carrot and stick, but will perform better if the stick is kept visible.

5 A highly neurotic extrovert will respond to both the carrot and stick, but will perform better the bigger the carrot.

NB: None of the above should be applied without the use of a safety net, that is, lots of research, lots of training, then a lot of experience.

Extroversion v. introversion with neuroticism

The following short questionnaire is for example only. The results are not very accurate. So don't get elated or miserable.

Answer YES or NO to the following 12 questions.

1 Do you sometimes feel happy, sometimes depressed, without any apparent reason?

2 Do you have frequent ups and downs in mood, either with or without apparent cause?

3 Are you inclined to be moody?

4 Does your mind often wander while you are trying to concentrate?

5 Are you frequently lost in thought even when supposed to take part in a conversation?

6 Are you sometimes bubbling over with energy and sometimes very sluggish?

7 Do you prefer action to planning for action?

8 Are you happiest when you get involved in some project that calls for rapid action?

9 Do you usually take the initiative in making new friends?

10 Are you inclined to be quick and sure in your actions?

11 Would you rate yourself as a lively individual?

12 Would you be very unhappy if you were prevented from making numerous social contacts?

Score: Questions 1 to 6

If you say YES then give yourself 1 point; if NO then 0 points. This is your Neuroticism score. 6 would

indicate a person who is very unstable emotionally and 0 one who is very stable emotionally.

Questions 7 to 12

If you say YES then give yourself 1 point. If NO then 0 points. This is your extroversion v. introversion score. 6 would be an extreme extrovert and 0 an extreme introvert.

Remember it was just for fun.

Source: Hans Eysenck and Glenn Wilson, *Know Your Own Personality*, Temple Smith, 1975.

There are lots of interesting things to read on this area. Work your way through books on behaviour at work and psychology at work; look up H. J. Eysenck and Extroversion/Introversion. Try to get hold of *Know Your Own Personality* by Hans Eysenck and Glenn Wilson, Temple Smith, 1975.

Perception

At work, as in life, what is real is not important. What is important is what people think is real, people's perception. **Perception** is the seeing or recognition of things, people using their senses. All those messages captured by the senses are organised and then interpreted to create order in a person's mind about the world around us. We do not all perceive the same thing; some think the organisation or the school/college is great, others that it is the biggest waste of space they have seen for a long time.

Three things influence perception:

- perceiver
- object
- situation

The **perceiver**, that is you and I, observes different things. The other week an acquaintance of mine bought and showed off an old Jaguar, red and plush. Since then I have seen lots of old Jags, red and plush; strange I did not notice them before. Someone working in a shoe shop is likely to see and judge what people put on their feet. Someone taking a hairdressing and beauty course is very likely to see and focus on the hair styles and make-up of others. Machiavellian types (see pp. 114–5) are likely to see others as being as scheming and devious as themselves. Insecure employees will see plots to remove them from their position. A personnel officer will perceive things quite differently from an engineer and both of them quite differently from an accountant. Where we came from, our past, what we do, our job, and our interests, all and more come together to help us see what we see. The problem is that sometimes we only see what we want to see.

WHAT DO YOU SEE?

What do you see first about a person you have met for the first time?

The **object** of observation is not looked at on its own. Whatever surrounds it is also observed. If you see someone from a particular school/college or organisation, then you think of that place as well as observing the person. If you meet someone and find out that that person is an accountant, then you may classify him/her with all other accountants and believe their stereotype image of being boring. The problem with stereotyping is that there is a tendency to accept such stereotypes without criticism. If someone belongs to a successful team, then you may automatically ascribe success to that individual.

GROUP THEM TOGETHER

In what way do you perceive persons with:

- cerebral palsy
- epilepsy?

The **situation** in which we find things is of importance. If you see someone at a rock concert do you then perceive them to be a 'headbanger'? The working surroundings in a school/college or organisation will alter your perception. Is it clean and spacious, does it have good lighting? All these factors come into play when you think about the people working in such a place.

You have already detected that perception is important when it comes to interviewing. Perception is also important to a manager when he/she judges employees at their annual appraisal, on matters such as their loyalty to the organisation and the effort they put into their performance.

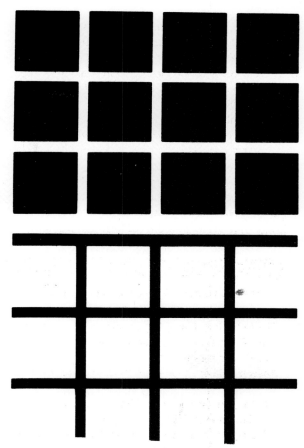

The grey spots that you see where the lines cross are not there.

Locus of control

Who is controlling your life? Do you get up in the morning and read your stars in the daily paper to see if you are going to 'have a nice day'?

If, for example, students achieve good grades on an assignment, they may think it was due to the fact that they worked hard and they deserved the grades, it is the result of their own efforts. However they may think that they were rather lucky to get the grades and that the person marking the assignment must be an easy touch. The difference between these two people is where they place responsibility for something that happens to them. Julian Rotter developed a theory that people explain what happens to them as a direct result of their past experience. He called this **locus of control**.

The main plank of Rotter's argument is based   111

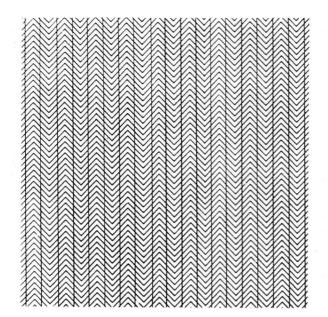

How many straight lines do you see?

on the existence of two extremes, or types. One extreme Rotter called the **internaliser** and the other extreme the **externaliser**. People who believe that they control their own fate, that is, internalisers, will behave differently from people referred to as externalisers.

It is suggested that, as children, internalisers worked out that they were punished for bad behaviour and rewarded for good behaviour. Externalisers however, had a different set of experiences, where punishment and reward did not seem to relate, at all times, to the way they behaved. Externalisers believe that their fate is controlled by the throw of the dice, lady luck, or, more usually, other people whom they see to be more powerful than themselves. Most people will not see themselves as extreme, one way or the other, on this IE scale but they will have a tendency towards being an internaliser or an externaliser.

There has been a great deal of research to show that internalisers, or those who believe they control their own destiny, make up the entrepreneurs of the world. It makes no difference at all whether they are male or female, the common factor is that entrepreneurs are internalisers.

Other research, such as that by G. Blau, 'Locus of control as a potential moderator of the turnover process', in the *Journal of Occupational Psychology* (1987), showed that among people who had thought about leaving their job it was the internalisers who were more likely to do something about it and leave. The externalisers talked about it but did nothing.

What is it?

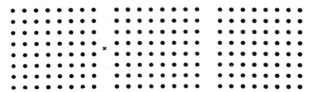

Look at X. Are the dots in Block A in a row and the dots in Block C in a column?

P. Storms and P. Spencer, in their 1987 study, 'Relationships of organisational frustration with reported behavioural reactions: The moderating effect of locus of control', in the *Journal of Occupational Behaviour*, found that externalisers were more likely than internalisers to express their frustration at work by becoming aggressive and engaging in other forms of dysfunctional conflict.

WANTED

People who:

1 Need little motivation to get on with the job.
2 Know it is their own efforts that will produce results.
3 Realise that their success will result in job satisfaction.
4 Want to participate and get on with the job.
5 Will not be sensitive to stress.
6 Will be able to demonstrate initiative.

INTERNALISERS ONLY NEED APPLY

With regard to safety at work, research has suggested that internalisers are more likely to be safety conscious than externalisers. Other research has indicated that older workers, females, members of the working class and those politically to the left tend to behave as externalisers. Externalisers are more likely to remain in a dissatisfying job although it is claimed that they are not very responsive to financial incentive schemes – but they would welcome the extra money of such schemes. Externalisers perhaps respond better to, and prefer, closer control by management as this is what they have grown to expect.

In the opinion of Rosabeth Moss Kanter, in her 1985 work, *The Change Masters* (Allen & Unwin), if you are able to see yourself as being in charge of your own destiny, then you are likely to see change as being innovative and exciting. So the internaliser likes and welcomes change. I wonder how many internalisers have managed to remain as such when subjected to redundancy more than once, as many have been.

P. Spector, in an article, 'Behaviour in organisations as a function of employee's locus of control', in the *Psychological Bulletin* (1981), seems to say that much of the work on organisational theory that recommends particular styles and applications appears to be designed for internalisers only. This may lead some to conclude that such 'good practice' may not be right for externalisers, as they have grown to expect and react to what we tend to think of nowadays as inappropriate management styles.

AN EXTERNALISER – MADE BY OTHERS

Disadvantaged groups, such as people with a disability or those who are black, but also other groups on account of their age, sexual orientation or gender, all suffer from various forms of direct and indirect discrimination. Does it then follow that, as they have had negative experiences at the hands of others, they will then tend towards behaviour associated with an externaliser?

ARE YOU IN CONTROL?

Look at the following statements and record if you agree with Statement A or Statement B.

1   A   To make pots of money you have to be in the right place at the right time.
　　 B   You only get promoted at work through working hard and determination.
2   A   There is a direct relationship between how hard someone works and how he/she progresses.
　　 B   Managers are inconsistent in the way they reward hard work.
3   A   The continued rise of single-parent families is an indication that people do not work at maintaining partnerships.
　　 B   That partnerships stay strong is mainly a matter of good luck.
4   A   It is no good trying to change a person's basic attitude.
　　 B   I know when I am right I can get others to see things my way.
5   A   Getting a good grade on this course is a matter of being slightly luckier than others.
　　 B   Grades on this course relate to ability.
6   A   If you know how to handle people then you can make them follow you.
　　 B   There is not much that can be done by me to alter someone's behaviour.
7   A   The grades I have received to date are all based on the efforts I have put into the assignments.

B Although I work at a consistent level this does not seem to be reflected in my grades.

8 **A** I switch on my TV and see all the trouble in the world and know perfectly well that if I and others like me take the trouble we can do something positive about it.

B I cannot possibly influence in any way events nationally.

9 **A** A lot that happens to me and others is a matter of fate.

B People control their own fate.

10 **A** To get on with people you have to work at it.

B It is too difficult to please some people I know.

Based on Julian Rotter, 'External Control and Internal Control', *Psychology Today*, June 1971.

Score: One point for each of the following: 1B, 2A, 3A, 4B, 5B, 6A, 7A, 8A, 9B, 10A.

The lower your score below 5, the higher is your tendency towards an **external locus of control**. The higher your score above 5 the higher your tendency towards **internal locus of control**.

Remember it was just for fun. It is difficult to have a reasoned analysis on so few questions.

Self-fulfilling prophecy

If a teacher wants a student to fail, then the best way to go about it is to tell him or her that they will fail. Tell them often enough, and with conviction, and the student will believe it. Then *voilà*, the student will fail. It is the same with an employee. Tell the employee that he or she is useless, but make sure the person believes it, then lo and behold, you have a useless employee. The result of all this is that the teacher will claim to have been right and the manager will claim to have been right. The victim, the student, will say he/she expected to fail and the employee that he/she knew they lacked the qualities needed in the job.

The above is an example of a self-fulfilling prophecy, so called by P. K. Morton in 1948. It was said that whatever you hold in your mind, then it will happen. So, if you think you are going to have a lot of problems at school, college or work, then it is very likely that you will have lots

of problems. If you think you are going to be happy at school, college or work, then it is very likely that you will be happy.

1 Believe yourself that you can do it.

2, 3, 4, 5, 6, 7, 8, 9 and 10 are the same as 1.

Repeat above as often as necessary until you have done it. Then succeed in something else.

FURTHER READING

After considering the self-fulfilling prophecy it is a natural move to look at the personality trait: self-esteem. There are many books on the subject, look in any bookshop.

Machiavellianism

A not particularly nice trait is Machiavellianism, so called after Niccolò dei Machiavelli, writer, poet, statesman, patriot, philosopher and scapegoat, who lived in Florence in the sixteenth century. His name is now linked to anyone who uses treachery and intrigue to maintain or get power. Such people use deceit and attempt to plant ideas into the minds of others in order to manipulate them for their own purpose. They do win more than others, are adept at convincing others and are not easily influenced.

It was R. Christie and F. L. Geis, in their 1970 work, *Studies in Machiavellianism* (Academic Press), who revealed the conditions where 'Machs.' will blossom.

THREE CONDITIONS THAT ALLOW A MACH. TO GROW

1 Face to face contacts: 'Let me look into their eyes.'

2 Few rules and regulations: 'No problem, I can improvise.'

3 Others are busy arranging compromises and getting emotionally involved: 'Don't worry, I'll concentrate on winning.'

Do organisations need people with a high Machiavellian score? Yes, but only if ethics and performance do not go hand in hand. If the work

MACHIAVEL.

Each of the above qualities is on a scale, so what is looked for is a score that tends towards one or the other in each of the four measurements. The end result is a grouping into one of 16 types.

THE MYERS–BRIGGS 16

1   ESTJ – Administrators
In touch with their external environment

2   INTP – Architects
Great precision of thought and language

3   ISFP – Artists
Work with dedication and flair

4   INFJ – Authors
They focus on the possible

5   ISTP – Craftsmen
Impulsive people who don't work to a schedule

6   ESFP – Entertainers
Warm and optimistic

7   ENTJ – Field Marshal
They want to lead

8   ENTP – Inventors
Alert and can see what's next

9   INFP – Investigators
Calm, pleasant idealists

10   ENFP – Journalists
They see the possibilities and have a great influence

11   ESTP – Promoters
Active and entrepreneurial

12   ISFJ – Savers
Like to meet the needs of others

13   INTJ – Scientists
They apply the theory

14   ESFJ – Sellers
Sociable and harmonious

15   ENFJ – Trainers
Excellent leaders and followers

16   ISTJ – Trustees
Practical and dependable

of the Machiavellian personality results in an organisation experiencing victims fighting back, holding grudges and engaging in active or subversive retaliation, then it is important for that organisation to identify and prevent the growth of Machiavellianism.

Myers–Briggs type indicator

A popular tool used by many industrial giants, is the Myers–Briggs Type Indicator (MBTI). This is not used in the selection process, but rather to help employees understand themselves and how others see them; those others who may see the world through different lenses. It is not a 'test' in the sense that there is no right or wrong answers. It is an assessment. It can help employees to understand the differences between people, to celebrate, rather than condemn those differences, and to work better with other employees. The MBTI looks at people as:

1   Extroverts or introverts (E or I)
2   Sensing or intuitive (S or N)
3   Thinking or feeling (T or F)
4   Perceiving or judging (P or J)

HOW MACHIAVELLIAN ARE YOU?

Simply indicate the number that is nearest to your attitude.

Statement	Disagree		Neutral	Agree	
	A Lot	A Little		A Little	A Lot
1 The best way to handle people is to tell them what they want to hear.	1	2	3	4	5
2 When you ask someone to do something for you, it is best to give the real reason for wanting it rather than give the reasons that might carry more weight.	1	2	3	4	5
3 Anyone who completely trusts anyone else is asking for trouble.	1	2	3	4	5
4 It is hard to get on without cutting corners here and there.	1	2	3	4	5
5 It is safest to assume that all people have a vicious streak, and it will come out when they are given a chance.	1	2	3	4	5
6 One should take action only when it is morally right.	1	2	3	4	5
7 Most people are basically good and kind.	1	2	3	4	5
8 There is no excuse for lying to someone else.	1	2	3	4	5
9 Most people more easily forget the death of their father than the loss of their property.	1	2	3	4	5
10 Generally speaking, people won't work hard unless they're forced to do so.	1	2	3	4	5

Score:

Add up your score for questions 1, 3, 4, 5, 9 and 10 _____

On questions 2, 6, 7 and 8 score as follows:

Mark of 5 = 1 point. Mark of 4 = 2 points. Mark of 3 = 3 points. Mark of 2 = 4 points. Mark of 1 = 5 points.

The average is a score of 25 points. The higher your score the higher your Machiavellian tendencies.

NB: The scoring has no relation to intelligence.

Source: R. Christie and F. L. Geis, *Studies in Machiavellianism* (Academic Press, 1970).

The title given to each type is not an indication of the type of job for which that type is suitable. It is only an attempt to give that type an easily recognisable label. Nevertheless it is interesting to note that the research of S. Males, 'Police Management on Division and Subdivision' (Police Research Services Unit, 1983) showed that 38.5 per cent of police 'managers' were ISTJ types and 29 per cent were ESTJ types.

The following exercise is taken from a book called *Please Understand Me, Character and Temperament Types*, by David Keirsey and Marilyn Bates. Keirsey has adopted Carl Jung's theory of psychological types and the method of measuring typology developed by Isabel Myers and her mother Katheryn Briggs.

THE KEIRSEY TEMPERAMENT SORTER

Please circle your chosen answer.

1 At a party do you
  a interact with many, including strangers
  b interact with a few, known to you?
2 Are you more
  a realistic than speculative
  b speculative than realistic?
3 Is it worse to
  a have your 'head in the clouds'
  b be 'in a rut'?
4 Are you more impressed by
  a principles
  b emotions?
5 Are you more drawn toward the
  a convincing
  b touching?
6 Do you prefer to work
  a to deadlines
  b just 'whenever'?
7 Do you tend to choose
  a rather carefully
  b somewhat impulsively?
8 At parties do you
  a stay late, with increasing energy
  b leave early, with decreased energy?
9 Are you more attracted to
  a sensible people
  b imaginative people?
10 Are you more interested in
  a what is actual
  b what is possible?
11 In judging others are you more swayed by
  a laws than circumstances
  b circumstances than laws?
12 In approaching others is your inclination to be somewhat
  a objective
  b personal?
13 Are you more
  a punctual
  b leisurely?
14 Does it bother you more having things
  a incomplete
  b completed?
15 In your social groups do you
  a keep abreast of others' happenings
  b get behind on the news?
16 In doing ordinary things are you more likely to
  a do it the usual way
  b do it your own way?
17 Writers should
  a 'say what they mean and mean what they say'
  b express things more by use of analogy?
18 Which appeals to you more
  a consistency of thought
  b harmonious human relationships?
19 Are you more comfortable in making
  a logical judgements
  b value judgements?
20 Do you want things
  a settled and decided
  b unsettled and undecided?
21 Would you say you are more
  a serious and determined
  b easy-going?
22 In phoning do you
  a rarely question that all will be said
  b rehearse what you'll say?
23 Facts
  a 'speak for themselves'
  b illustrate principles?
24 Are visionaries
  a somewhat annoying
  b rather fascinating?
25 Are you more often
  a a cool-headed person
  b a warm-hearted person?
26 Is it worse to be
  a unjust
  b merciless?
27 Should one usually let events occur
  a by careful selection and choice
  b randomly and by chance?
28 Do you feel better about
  a having purchased
  b having the option to buy?
29 In company do you
  a initiate conversation
  b wait to be approached?
30 Common sense is
  a rarely questionable
  b frequently questionable?
31 Children often do not
  a make themselves useful enough
  b exercise their fantasy enough?
32 In making decisions do you feel more comfortable with
  a standards

b feelings?

33 Are you more

  a firm than gentle

  b gentle than firm?

34 What is more admirable

  a the ability to organise and be methodical

  b the ability to adapt and make do?

35 Do you put more value on the

  a definite

  b open-ended?

36 Does new and non-routine interaction with others

  a stimulate and energise you

  b tax your reserves?

37 Are you more frequently

  a a practical sort of person

  b a fanciful sort of person?

38 Are you more likely to

  a see how others are useful

  b see how others see?

39 Which is more satisfying

  a to discuss an issue thoroughly

  b to arrive at agreement on an issue?

40 Which rules you more

  a your head

  b your heart?

41 Are you more comfortable with work that is

  a contracted

  b done on a casual basis?

42 Do you tend to look for

  a the orderly

  b whatever turns up?

43 Do you prefer

  a many friends with brief contact

  b a few friends with more lengthy contact?

44 Do you go more by

  a facts

  b principles?

45 Are you more interested in

  a production and distribution

  b design and research?

46 Which is more of a compliment

  a 'There is a very logical person'

  b 'There is a very sentimental person'?

47 Do you value in yourself more that you are

  a unwavering

  b devoted?

48 Do you more often prefer the

  a final and unalterable statement

  b tentative and preliminary statement?

49 Are you more comfortable

  a after a decision

  b before a decision?

50 Do you

  a speak easily and at length with strangers

  b find little to say to strangers?

51 Are you more likely to trust your

  a experience

  b hunch?

52 Do you feel

  a more practical than ingenious

  b more ingenious than practical?

53 Which person is more to be complimented: one of

  a clear reason

  b strong feeling?

54 Are you inclined more to be

  a fair-minded

  b sympathetic?

55 Is it preferable mostly to

  a make sure things are arranged

  b just let things happen?

56 In relationships should most things be

  a renegotiable

  b random and circumstantial?

57 When the phone rings do you

  a hasten to get to it first

  b hope someone else will answer?

58 Do you prize more in yourself

  a a strong sense of reality

  b a vivid imagination?

59 Are you drawn more to

  a fundamentals

  b overtones?

60 Which seems the greater error

  a to be too passionate

  b to be too objective?

61 Do you see yourself as basically

  a hard-headed

  b soft-hearted?

62 Which situation appeals to you more

  a the structured and scheduled

  b the unstructured and unscheduled?

63 Are you a person who is more

  a routinised than whimsical

  b whimsical than routinised?

64 Are you more inclined to be

  a easy to approach

  b somewhat reserved?

65 In writings do you prefer

a the more literal
b the more figurative?

66 Is it harder for you to
  a identify with others
  b utilise others?

67 Which do you wish more for yourself
  a clarity of reason
  b strength of compassion?

68 Which is the greater fault

a being indiscriminate
b being critical?

69 Do you prefer the
  a planned event
  b unplanned event?

70 Do you tend to be more
  a deliberate than spontaneous
  b spontaneous than deliberate?

ANSWER SHEET

Enter a tick for each answer in the column for a or b

	a b		a b		a b		a b		a b		a b		a b
1		2		3		4		5		6		7	
8		9		10		11		12		13		14	
15		16		17		18		19		20		21	
22		23		24		25		26		27		28	
29		30		31		32		33		34		35	
36		37		38		39		40		41		42	
43		44		45		46		47		48		49	
50		51		52		53		54		55		56	
57		58		59		60		61		62		63	
64		65		66		67		68		69		70	

1⌐   ⌐2 3⌐   ⌐4 3⌐   ⌐4 5⌐   ⌐6 5⌐   ⌐6 7⌐   ⌐8 7⌐   ⌐8

1⌐ ⌐2   3⌐ ⌐4   5⌐ ⌐6   7⌐ ⌐8
  E I   S N   T F   J P

Directions for scoring

1 Add down so that the total number of 'a' answers is written in the box at the bottom of each column. Do the same for the 'b' answers you have ticked. Each of the 14 boxes should have a number in it.

2 Transfer the number in box No. 1 of the answer sheet to box No. 1 below the answer sheet. Do this for box No. 2 as well. Note, however, that you have two numbers for boxes 3 to 8. Bring down the first number for each box beneath the second, as indicated by the arrows. Add all the pairs of numbers and enter the total in the boxes below the answer sheet, so each box has only one number.

3 Compare your score with the Myer–Briggs types. Which of the 16 do you most closely match?

To gain the full benefit from this 'indicator', which is not a test, you will need to devote time and effort to discovering the deeper 'meanings' of the types. Your tutor should be able to help you on your path of discovery.

FURTHER READING

Search through texts on behaviour at work or work psychology to find much more information on the Myers–Briggs Type Indicator and its uses within the working environment. This form of assessment is used in other areas outside work. The search should prove of value particularly if you remember that MBTI is being increasingly used within organisations.

Occupational direction

John Holland, writing in 1971, suggested that people, given the freedom, will move naturally towards jobs that fit their personality. As with many things, the process begins early on in life. People start by having a preference for doing some activities rather than others. This then grows into an interest which, with further maturing leads them to act, think and see things in such a way that they will suit some jobs more than others. He said that people classify jobs under six main headings; he called them 'work environments'. If a human resources specialist can fit a personality into the right job, then there is a good chance that the employee will be happy and satisfied in his/her work.

HOLLAND'S SIX PERSONALITY WORK ENVIRONMENTS

1 **Realistic**   This person prefers a job where he/she can get on and do something. These people may be persistent and not too sensitive but their skills would lead them into work as an Architect, Builder, Engineer or Farmer.
2 **Investigative**   The preference here is for a thinking problem solver. This curious person may be introverted and not concerned with being liked. Such people prefer work that involves analytical research, such as Medicine or a Science.
3 **Artistic**   These creative people seek self-expression. They may be a bit detached from other people but their originality and unconventional ways lead them to work as a Writer, Artist, Designer or Musician.

4 **Social**   Not noted for being good with their hands, these people find success by helping others. Very kind people who may be somewhat inflexible but seek satisfaction in jobs such as Librarian, Nurse, Social Worker, Teacher or in Religious Service.
5 **Enterprising**   These people look for power, they have lots of energy and like a good argument as they can talk fluently. That is why you are likely to find them in jobs such as Lawyer or Estate Agent or in Advertising.
6 **Conventional**   Neat orderly people who prefer to use their self-discipline in a well organised environment. These trustworthy, conscientious but sometimes dependent people seek jobs such as Accountant, Secretary, or Chemist.

WHICH DIRECTION?

Which of the six work environments would suit your personality?

Career anchors

If an organisation is interested in what type of job an individual would prefer then the work of John Holland is worthy of further study, as is the work of Edgar H. Schein. Schein, in his 1990 work, *Career Anchors*, published in USA by University Associates, builds on his previous observations of what guides and holds steady a person's career. When a person has worked out after some experience what he/she sees as his or her own abilities, values and attitudes, and what motivates him or her, that person knows what he or she wants in a job, will not voluntarily give it up, and will not take a job that he/she feels is not right. For this Schein coined the term 'career anchor', which keeps a person steady and prevents drifting. This anchor is something that will not change, to any great extent, during someone's working life. Schein saw eight anchors, with people having a particular preference for one.

SCHEIN AND HIS EIGHT ANCHORS

1 **Technical/functional competence**   These people organise their career through the challenges and actual work they are doing.
2 **Managerial competence**   These people like to solve problems and to lead and control others.

3 **Independence**   These people value freedom and independence.

4 **Security**   Those people want stability and career security.

5 **Entrepreneurial creativity**   These people have a strong need to create something of their own.

6 **Service**   These people want to help others or work for a cause.

7 **Challenge**   These people want to move the immovable and solve the unsolvable.

8 **Lifestyle**   These people want their work to fit their lifestyle. They work to live, not live to work.

It is of value to an organisation if it is able to find out an employee's 'anchor' so it can then work out what may motivate him or her, the appropriate reward system, and the promotion the employee may seek. It may also provide the organisation with some clues as to why some employees lack job satisfaction and have a low level of job involvement.

Schein provided some interesting suggestions as to how prospective employees with each of the different 'anchors' might respond if they were asked about: work, rewards, promotion and recognition.

1. TECHNICAL/FUNCTIONAL COMPETENCE

- **Work:** I want lots of challenging work, with lots of resources to do a good job.
- **Rewards:** I want the same as others doing the same job in other companies. No fancy bonus schemes or profit-related pay.
- **Promotion:** I want professional promotion, just like the managers and an expanded job to go with it.
- **Recognition:** I want praise from my professional equals and those working below me. I do not need praise from some higher-level manager who does not know what my job is about.

2. MANAGERIAL COMPETENCE

- **Work:** Give me lots of responsibility at a high level.
- **Rewards:** I want to be paid a great deal more than those working for me.

- **Promotion:** I am happy to get promotion based on my results.
- **Recognition:** I want even higher levels of responsibility.

3. INDEPENDENCE

- **Work:** I am happy if you tell me what my goals are, but don't look over my shoulder, leave me alone to get on with it.
- **Rewards:** I am fine with pay based on merit, but please, no strings attached.
- **Promotion:** I do not want more responsibility or rank, but I do want more freedom.
- **Recognition:** Give me a medal, a prize, a big 'well done' letter. Anything I can take home, or with me if I join another organisation.

4. SECURITY

- **Work:** I want to work in a nice place, a nice environment and if I can't have a job for life, make it as long as possible.
- **Rewards:** I like a pay scale with incremental points I can climb for each year of service. Do not forget a good pension plan and life insurance.
- **Promotion:** Preferably, promotion is based on seniority, as in some Japanese companies I have heard about.
- **Recognition:** Just note my loyalty and performance.

5. ENTREPRENEURIAL CREATIVITY

- **Work:** I need to create something I can call my own. I really prefer to work for myself. I could work in research.
- **Rewards:** I do not need much pay but I do want to own the patents of anything I invent, or shares in the company.
- **Promotion:** I just want to be able to move in and out of roles that keep my creativity alive.
- **Recognition:** I want to be seen as a major player. I need high-profile recognition.

6. SERVICE

- **Work:** I want to be able to influence policy to accord with my own values in life. I am loyal to the work that I do, not to the organisation.

- **Rewards:** Fair pay and benefits I can transfer to other organisations.
- **Promotion:** I want more influence and to be able to work on my own with little control.
- **Recognition:** To feel that my values are shared and recognised by my fellow workers and management.

7. CHALLENGE

- **Work:** I want to do the impossible and solve the unsolvable
- **Rewards:** It is the challenge I want. I do not want the pay to be other than fair.

- **Promotion:** More challenges.
- **Recognition:** I can test myself.

8. LIFESTYLE

- **Work:** Whatever fits my lifestyle, with a company that respects the fact that I have a home life.
- **Rewards:** Flexible enough to fit in with my life in general.
- **Promotion:** I want to advance, but only if it fits into the way I live my life. I am not willing to move if it has a negative effect on my life in general.
- **Recognition:** Just understand and take into account my way of life.

CAREER ANCHORS

Score as below the answer that best describes your feelings about each of the statements.

Answers

Strongly agree = 4
Agree = 3
Disagree = 2
Strongly disagree = 1

1 I would rather quit than get a promotion outside my field of expertise. ____

2 I am aiming to rise to a general managerial position. ____

3 I look for a career that is relatively free from organisational restrictions. ____

4 I will not accept a job or even promotion if it means moving away from where I live at present. ____

5 To become very highly competent in one particular area is of special importance to me. ____

6 I want to get to a level in an organisation where my decisions make a difference. ____

7 In the career I want I shall look for a job that gives freedom and independence. ____

8 I am willing to give up some freedom to do what I want to do at work in order to keep a job that does not interfere with my personal life. ____

9 I would like to develop my skills so I can build up a new business. ____

10 I look for a career where I could be of service to others. ____

11 I like a job that offers a wide variety of tasks. ____

12 I want to be identified as being with an organisation that has an excellent reputation. ____

13 I shall be motivated by what I have created and can call my own. ____

14 I want to use my skills for the benefit of a cause. ____

15 It is the challenge I want and lots of it. ____

16 I want to be part of a powerful and prestigious organisation. ____

17 I do not mind moving into a management role provided it is in my area of expertise. ____

18 I want to be a generalist rather than a specialist. ____

19 I prefer a job that gives me the freedom to choose the working hours where I am told what to do within very broad guidelines. ____

20 I look for job security with a good pension scheme. ____

21 I want to get lots of money so that I can prove that I am competent. ____

22 Watching others change as a result of what I have done is important to me. ____

23 I am motivated by the variety of work I may be able to perform. ____

24 I want people to know me by the organisation I work for and the job I do. ____

25 I would not like to be promoted outside my area of expertise. ____

26 I would like to manage other people. ____

27 I have no desire to be bound by any organisation. ____

28 I prefer to stay in the general area where I live rather than move to work. ____

29 To create something that is my own is important to me. ____

30 I prefer a job where I can help others. ____

31 Flexibility in a job is what I look for. ____

32 I want status and the title to go with it. ____

33 My main concern is to be known as an expert in one particular field. ____

34 I would prefer a post in general management.____

35 I do not want any organisation to impinge into my personal time and life. ____

36 I seek long-term employment with a company.____

37 I need to use my personal skills in getting on with others in a job that helps others. ____

38 I will aim for a job that gives me variety. ____

39 I want to be known through the job that I do. ____

40 I would rather not be promoted into general management as it would mean moving out of my particular area of expertise. ____

41 I would like a job that brings together my analytical skills and management of others. ____

42 I consider that most organisations are obstructive and prying. ____

43 I like to see that my efforts help others to change. ____

44 I seek a job that gives me one challenge after another. ____

SCORE

Technical competence:	Managerial competence:	Independence	Security/ lifestyle
1____	2____	3____	4____
5____	6____	7____	8____
17____	18____	19____	20____
25____	26____	27____	28____
33____	34____	35____	36____
40____	41____	42____	
Divide by 6 =____	Divide by 6 =____	Divide by 6 =____	Divide by 5 =____

Entrepreneurial creativity	Service	Challenge	Identity
9____	10____	11____	12____
13____	14____	15____	16____
21____	22____	23____	24____
29____	30____	31____	32____
	37____	38____	39____
	43____	44____	
Divide by 4 =____	Divide by 6 =____	Divide by 6 =____	Divide by 5 =____

A higher score on a particular anchor indicates where you would do best. A low score on any one anchor indicates that you will not be happy or too productive and may leave or be helped to do so.

Note that I have combined security and lifestyle and added identity. Identity refers to the situation where a person is more concerned with status, prestige and the badges of a job.

Plot your scores on a graph in an Information Technology session.

Source: Based on T. J. Delong, 'Re-examining the Career Anchor Model', *Personnel*, May/June 1982, pp. 56–7. Copyright © AMACOM.

LEARNING

If an organisation wishes to involve an individual in the process of change then clearly learning will have to take place. There are many definitions of learning, and you may wish to look some of them up, but the best I have seen comes from the pen of Peter Honey and Alan Mumford:

1   Knowing something you did not know earlier and being able to show it.
2   Being able to do something you were not able to do before.

WHAT IS LEARNING?

1 It is a process and an outcome.
2 It involves change in all or some of these:
  • attitudes
  • values
  • behaviour
  • knowledge and
  • skills.
3 It lasts.
4 It can be picked up as you travel through life or you can stop and linger over it.

There is no one **best** way to learn and we all have a favourite way of learning. Some love to sit there, listen to a one-hour lecture and think. Others prefer group work and games.

David Kolb saw learning as four stages of a cycle, and suggested that if the learner wishes to be fully effective, then he/she must be able to adapt to differing learning environments. Learners must be open in their willingness to participate in new experiences without any bias. They must be able to observe and reflect on these new experiences. They must be able to make sense of it all, and draw some theories from it. Then they must be able to use those theories to solve other or similar problems.

From the stages presented in Figure 51, four distinct learning styles become evident. These are: the converger and its opposite number, the diverger; the assimilator and its opposite, the Accommodator. These are presented in Figure 52.

Although it is suggested that the ideal learner should be able to flit in and out of each of the above learning styles, it is only human that most of us have to work hard to do so, as we have a preference for one over the others.

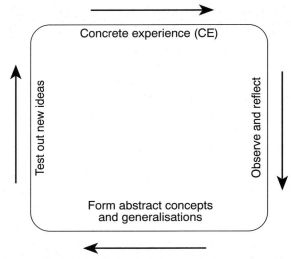

Fig. 51   David Kolb's experiential learning model (1)

FIVE GOOD POINTS ABOUT THE DIVERGER

1 Imaginative and emotional
2 Can see problems from many angles
3 Interested in people
4 Senses opportunities
5 Able to recognise a problem and investigate

The **diverger** can be found amongst personnel managers, those who are interested in counselling and all who have had a humanities, liberal arts and social science background.

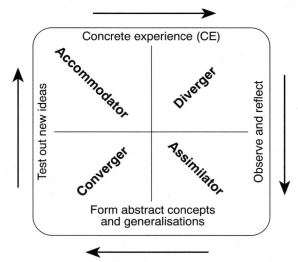

Fig. 52   David Kolb's experiential learning model (2)

1 Can create theoretical models
2 Prefers theory to its practical use
3 Good at comparing alternatives
4 Good at defining the problem
5 More interested in abstract concepts than in people

The **assimilator** tends to have had training in the natural sciences or mathematics and will probably be found in research and planning departments.

1 Good at putting ideas into practice
2 Good where there is a single correct answer to a problem
3 Prefers dealing with things to people
4 Can concentrate their efforts on the problem
5 Good at making decisions

The **converger** is someone who has a narrow interest in the physical sciences and tends to be found in civil/mechanical/electrical/chemical engineering types of jobs.

1 Likes to take risks
2 Prefers the facts to the theory
3 Very adaptable to immediate circumstances
4 Impatient and pushy
5 Likes action and results

The **accommodator** may be found in education, medicine, law, any job that is action oriented, but is very much at home in marketing and sales.

Of course a lot of jobs require a multidisciplinary approach, so this way of looking at learning styles does not mean that one particular style is **the** style for a particular job, it is merely a tendency, not a requirement.

Managers should ensure they discover the preferred learning style of each of their employees. One benefit of doing so is that they may send them on training courses where the delivery suits the employees' own learning styles. But it is up to the employee to discover his or her own learning style in order to be able to gain something from any training situation, no matter what the style of delivery.

Peter Honey and Alan Mumford in their book, *The Manual of Learning Styles* (1986), suggest that if an employee is stuck in one learning style the manager may wish to help that individual to improve his/her range. It is also important that managers recognise their own preferred learning styles as this will be the style that they will tend to prefer their employees to experience.

Honey and Mumford suggest four learning styles, which they refer to as the activist, the reflector, the theorist and the pragmatist.

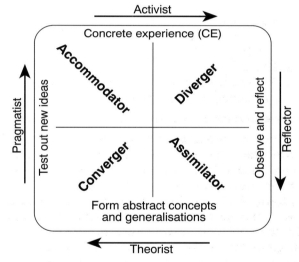

Fig. 53   David Kolb's experiential learning model, with the addition of Peter Honey and Alan Mumford's learning styles

If an **activist** manager sees the value of a training course then he/she is likely to encourage employees to take it, especially if it is a short course. Such managers will probably not want to discuss the details of the course before or after it takes place. Nor will they want to give employees an opportunity to experience a range of learning experiences. What was good enough for them is good enough for their employees. But what of the activist employee?

THREE GOOD AND THREE NOT SO GOOD THINGS ABOUT THE ACTIVIST EMPLOYEE

1 Willing to have a go
2 Will not resist change
3 Flexible and open-minded

1 Acts without thinking
2 Likes to be the centre of things
3 Easily bored

The **reflector** manager will want to discuss what will happen on a training course and then discuss what happened when the employee returns. Such managers are not likely to consider immediately available opportunities for learning such as delegating a job through which an employee may learn, they have to think about it.

THREE GOOD AND THREE NOT SO GOOD THINGS ABOUT THE REFLECTOR EMPLOYEE

1 Very methodical
2 Good listener
3 Careful

1 Slow decision maker
2 Over cautious
3 Not assertive

The **theorist** manager pays attention to Systems Theory and the motivational theories that take a very academic approach to any learning experience. Such managers are not too good at developing those they think to be their intellectual inferiors or those who hold of value a different theory to their own.

THREE GOOD AND THREE NOT SO GOOD THINGS ABOUT THE THEORIST EMPLOYEE

1 Good logical thinker
2 Objective
3 Asks the 'right' questions

1 Not a lateral thinker
2 Dislikes uncertainty
3 Hates those who use intuition

The **pragmatist** manager wants to know if the learning an employee may undertake will have a return for the organisation. Such managers will support any learning recommended by the personnel department. They will not see the benefits of anything that 'will be useful in the future'. If the learning experience is a bit different from the norm, then they are likely to reject the idea.

THREE GOOD AND THREE NOT SO GOOD THINGS ABOUT THE PRAGMATIST EMPLOYEE

1 Practical
2 No nonsense – straight to the point
3 If shown a new system will want to try it out

1 If it cannot be applied, then not interested in it
2 Cannot stand waffle
3 Task oriented not people oriented

A QUESTION OF YOUR LEARNING STYLE

Read the following statements. If you agree with a statement, then tick it. If you do not, then leave it.

1 I like to be absolutely correct.
2 I like taking risks.
3 I prefer to solve problems using a step-by-step approach rather than guessing.
4 I prefer simple straightforward things rather than something complicated.
5 I often do things 'just because I feel like it' rather than thinking about it first.
6 I do not often take things for granted. I like to check things out for myself.
7 What matters most about what you learn is whether it works in practice.
8 I actively seek out new things to do.
9 When I hear about a new idea I immediately start working out how I can try it.
10 I am quite keen on sticking to fixed routines, keeping to timetables etc.
11 I take great care in working things out. I do not jump to conclusions.
12 I like to make decisions very carefully and preferably after weighing up all the other possibilities first.
13 I do not like 'loose ends', I prefer to see things fit into some sort of pattern.
14 In discussions I like to get straight to the point.
15 I like the challenge of trying something new and different.

16 I prefer to think things through before coming to conclusions.

17 I find it difficult to come up with wild ideas off the top of my head.

18 I prefer to have as many bits of information about a subject as possible, the more I have to sift through the better.

19 I prefer to jump in and do things as they come along rather than plan things out in advance.

20 I tend to judge other people's ideas on how they work in practice.

21 I do not think you can make a decision just because something feels right. You have to think about all the facts.

22 I am rather fussy about how I do things – a bit of a perfectionist.

23 In discussion I usually pitch in with lots of wild ideas.

24 In discussions I put forward ideas that I know will work.

25 I prefer to look at a problem from as many different angles as I can before starting on it.

26 Usually I talk more than I listen.

27 Quite often I can work out more practical ways of doing things.

28 I believe that careful logical thinking is the key to getting things done.

29 If I have to write a formal letter I prefer to try out several rough workings before writing out the final version.

30 I like to consider all the alternatives before making up my mind.

31 I do not like wild ideas. They are not very practical.

32 It is best to look before you leap.

33 I usually do more listening than talking.

34 It does not matter how you do something, as long as it works.

35 I cannot be bothered with rules and plans, they take all the fun out of things.

36 I am usually the 'life and soul' of the party.

37 I do whatever I need to, to get the job done.

38 I like to find out how things work.

39 I like meetings or discussions to follow a proper pattern and to keep to a timetable.

40 I do not mind in the least if things get a bit out of hand.

SCORING

For each of those you have ticked put a 1 by the appropriate question number above right.

Activist	Reflector	Theorist	Pragmatist
2	11	1	4
5	12	3	7
8	16	6	9
15	18	10	14
19	21	13	20
23	25	17	24
26	29	22	27
35	30	28	31
36	32	38	34
40	33	39	37
___	___	___	___
===	===	===	===

Now you need to plot the score on the graph below.

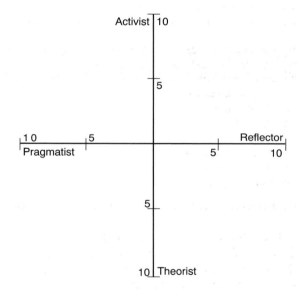

1 Is there one style that is dominant?

2 Do you have a balance of styles?

3 Compare your score with those of the rest of your group.

4 Look back on the group work you have taken part in, and find out the scores of your team members. Do these explain or tell you anything?

5 Does the delivery of your learning agree with your preferred style?

Locate a copy of *The Manual of Learning Styles* by Peter Honey and Alan Mumford (1986). The above is a shortened version of their assessment of learning style.

FURTHER READING

1 Read all about the behavioural approach to learning through the work of Ivan Petrovich Pavlov and his work with dogs. Also the work of Burrhus Frederic Skinner and his work with rats.

2 Read up on the cognitive approach to learning, the work of Edward Tolman and his work with rats.

3 Read Kolb.

4 Read Honey and Mumford.

Individual values

While Rotter suggests that the making of an internal or an external begins when we are young, the work of Morris Massey, *The People Puzzle*, published by Reston in 1979, shows that our early experience has an impact on the values that we hold. Part of the 'baggage' that a new employee brings to a job and organisation is a set of values. Those values are said to influence the attitude and behaviour of the new employee in his or her job.

An employee's values can be described as his or her fundamental beliefs in the way things should be, personally, and for society generally. For example, you may believe that the quality of the burgers you make is of greater importance than the quantity, but your new employer may judge your performance solely on the amount you produce. You will be disappointed with your new job, but ask yourself: will you compromise your values to keep your job?

Research in the 1970s ranked seven values and lifestyles. All, except the first, are values which can be transferred to a working environment.

THE MAGNIFICENT SEVEN VALUES

1 The **reactive** level is not to be found in organisations unless, of course, they employ lots of babies.

2 The **tribalistic** level indicates a traditionalist, at home in a bureaucratic organisation.
Motto: 'I know my place.'

3 The **egocentric** level reveals the hostile and self-seeking person who prefers to work on his/her own. Not at home in a team and the only one that can control such a person is someone more powerful than they are.
Motto: 'I did it my way.'

4 The **conforming** level does not like change and such people are not too happy with others who do not share their values.
Motto: 'You don't want to do that.'

5 The **manipulative** level works towards what he or she wants by the skilful control of others. Such people love to be recognised especially if recognition is combined with material rewards.
Motto: 'Machiavelli was here.'

6 The **sociocentric** level does not share the values of the conformer or the manipulator. Such people seek harmony within themselves and others.
Motto: 'Let's talk.'

7 The **existential** level does not mind others who have different values. Such people do not mind ambiguity, in fact they thrive on it. They value flexibility and are not lovers of authority and status symbols.
Motto: 'Who says all is meaningless?'

It can be seen from the work of Morris Massey that if an employee had egocentric values, then it would be likely that that person would not find job satisfaction within a team framework or in a situation where employees were expected to conform.

Massey suggests that if you can find out what values and ideas were current at the time when a person was ten years old, then you can have a good clue as to what that person's values will be in later life. He believes that it is at the age of ten that people begin to be influenced by what is happening around them in the world, outside their immediate family. The 1960s saw challenge as a theme, when people rejected the traditional values of their elders. The 1970s saw environmental awareness coming to the fore, sexual freedom and gender liberation.

The values of a 50-year-old will be different from those of someone who is 30. Both will have different values from those of someone in their twenties. If a manager is aware of these differences, he/she will be able to lead each person much better and the results will produce a more effective team.

WHEN YOU WERE TEN

What happened in the world when you were ten? What were the values in the UK and world-wide that may be an influence on your values today?

Locke's value theory

In 1976 E. Locke's work, 'The nature and causes of job satisfaction', examined the question of a person's values in relation to job satisfaction. If an employee's values can be determined, then this knowledge may be used to gauge the level of that person's job satisfaction. The more important a value the greater its impact on job satisfaction. So if money is an important value for one employee and not for another, then their level of job satisfaction will differ, as their values are different.

Further, a more detailed examination of the work of Eysenck's scales of Extroversion and Neuroticism will reveal values which, if known, will aid management to focus their efforts in specific areas that, when attended to, will improve job satisfaction. If, for example, introverts high on the neurotic scale valued self-respect and the working environment provided little opportunity for this to develop to any great extent, then such people would not have a very high level of job satisfaction.

FURTHER READING

There are many books which deal with values in depth. Just look up values in the index of management and psychology books. Look at values in relation to a person's personality and the impact they have on that person's working life.

ATTITUDE

At some time a manager will say to a member of his/her staff: 'you have an attitude problem' or 'I do not like your attitude'. What does this mean?

An attitude is the habitual way of regarding another person, a place or a particular situation. It is in the mind, so you will not be able to see it. An attitude can only be inferred by what a person says or how that person behaves. It has been suggested that the strength of the attitude will depend on the kind of experience a person has had. If that experience is frequently repeated, then the attitude will get stronger.

Take, for example, someone who is not satisfied with a course of study. The more that person moans about that course, particularly if he or she thinks there is a good reason to moan, the stronger that attitude of dissatisfaction will become.

Attitudes can, of course, be positive or negative. A person can hold lots and lots of attitudes, hundreds in fact. Attitudes are held about all sorts of things: schools, college, work, teacher, the look of a building, a town and so on.

The structure of an organisation, it has been said, will have an impact on employees' attitude and behaviour.

THREE WAYS THE SHAPE OF AN ORGANISATION AFFECTS ATTITUDE

1 The further up the ladder the more favourable the attitude.
2 The more responsibility and people to control, the more favourable the attitude.
3 The greater the decentralisation of decision-making, the more favourable the attitude of those further down the ladder.

It is believed that an attitude consists of three parts:

- cognitive
- affective
- behavioural

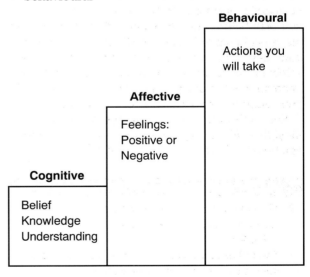

Fig. 54   Three steps to an attitude

The **cognitive** step is the process of getting to know the way in which you learn and the way in which you go about understanding things. So you may believe and understand that in a particular educational module you need to achieve a specific grade overall. You may have been brought up to

129

dislike a particular group in society or you may have been brought up to believe that a particular group in society dislikes you.

The **affective** part is the process of developing good or bad thoughts or feelings about what you understand, have learnt or believe. You may feel good about wanting to achieve a high grade you understand you need. You may have negative feelings towards those you were taught to dislike. You may feel negative towards those that you were taught dislike you. It has been said that you might even be able to measure the affective step by taking a person's pulse or blood pressure when he or she comes into contact with the object of the attitude.

Your **behaviour** is the way we may start to detect your attitude, that is through your actions. It could be in the way you talk, or in your body language. Your behaviour will depend on the strength of your understanding, learning and beliefs together with the level of your positive/negative feelings.

THINK: HOW WOULD YOU BEHAVE?

1 You need a Distinction in this module so that you will have enough D grades to get into the university of your choice. You want to get on to that university course badly. What sort of behaviour would you exhibit?

2 Imagine you have been brought up to dislike a particular group in society and you have negative feelings towards those you were taught to dislike. What sort of behaviour would you exhibit?

3 Imagine you have been brought up to believe that a particular group in society dislikes you and you feel negative towards those that you were taught dislike you. What sort of behaviour would you exhibit?

Behaviour is not attitude. Behaviour is the outcome of the cognitive and affective steps. It is those thinking and feeling steps that make up the attitude. So, when managers or teachers say they do not like someone's attitude, they mean they do not like the behaviour that someone is showing, which they take to be an expression of that person's thinking and feeling. There are plenty of good managers and good teachers, but even they have not been able to tap into the thoughts and feelings of their employees and students.

Behaviour is easy to change. Attitude is difficult to change. Most organisations do not care what attitude you have. Indeed, is it any of their concern? But most companies are very concerned and do care about your behaviour while at work. So an employee's attitude is only of importance to an organisation if it is revealed through behaviour. A person can hold an inappropriate attitude about, say, women at work, or ethnic minorities, or indeed persons with a disability. The behaviour of such a person is, however, moderated at work by the organisation's personnel policies as well as by the law of the land.

The Sex Discrimination Act 1975 and 1986 requires people to behave in a certain way when dealing with gender issues. The Race Relations Act 1976 further requires people to behave in accordance with its provisions. The Disabled Persons (Employment) Act 1944, alas, does not require a person so inclined, to behave other than badly. The laws in the cases of gender and race do not change attitudes but they do change behaviour. The legislation concerning the disabled does neither.

Types of attitudes

Although employees may hold hundreds of attitudes, there are three specific areas of interest when it comes to the working environment. These are:

- job satisfaction
- job involvement
- organisational commitment

An employee has a general attitude to his or her job; this is what is called **job satisfaction**. An employee with a high level of job satisfaction would have a positive attitude, while one with a low level of job satisfaction would harbour a negative attitude.

Job involvement describes the degree to which an employee gets personal satisfaction from his or her job. You may be able to identify someone who actively likes what he or she is doing, so much so that they care how they do their job and get a great deal of personal satisfaction from doing their job correctly. However, just because someone does not score high on job involvement it does not follow that that person will leave. Such a person may like the organisation, and may decide to change jobs within the organisation.

The analysis of research by Stephen Robbins in his book, *Organizational Behaviour*, published by Prentice-Hall in 1991, brought up five elements in work that promote job satisfaction.

ROBBINS' SATISFIED FIVE

1 **Mentally challenging work** Not a lot or you will get frustrated and feel a failure. Not too little, or you will get bored.
2 **Just rewards** A fair day's pay for a fair day's work.
3 **Supportive working conditions** Nice, comfortable working conditions with good equipment.
4 **Supportive colleagues** Nice, sympathetic work mates and a boss who has read all the books on good management practice and follows them.
5 **Personality** A job to fit my personality.

It would be easy to think that just because someone was fortunate to have job satisfaction then that person would be more productive. The research suggests that this might be so for managerial and professional level people, but with others there are so many other factors to consider that the verdict must be 'not proven'. It has been suggested that it is the individual's perception of his/her productivity that leads to satisfaction.

SIX EXTERNAL FACTORS THAT HAVE MADE ME MORE PRODUCTIVE

1 I can't slow down or speed up the machine.
2 I don't control the exchange rates but my product is now cheaper.
3 With this new computer I can do things much more quickly.
4 The market has changed and I am selling a wild cat; the competition are selling dogs.
5 It's a sunny day, so there is a queue a mile long of kiddies wanting a donkey ride.
6 Those business process re-engineering consultants cured the bottlenecks.

When you ask someone what they do, do they also volunteer who they work for? If they do, it may indicate their level of **organisational commitment**. This commitment refers to an employee's loyalty, his or her liking for the organisation, how it operates, the degree of that person's identi-fication with what it does, pride in it and wish to stay part of it. If someone does not identify with the organisation, it is likely that given the opportunity that person will leave, even though he/she has a high level of job involvement. Some researchers suggest that the level of organisational commitment is the best predictor of labour turnover in an organisation.

Attitude change

To change behaviour, an organisation need only impose Draconian penalties on miscreants. At work if someone discriminates unfairly, that person is fired. At school or college if someone discriminates unfairly, that person has to leave the course. But this approach to unacceptable behaviour is frowned upon. John Arnold, Ivan Robertson and Cary Cooper in their book, *Work Psychology: Understanding human behaviour in the workplace*, published by Pitman in 1991, have summarised the research in this area and present some suggestions as to how attitudes may be changed.

EIGHT THOUGHTS ON CHANGING ATTITUDES

1 Make sure any action taken is done by a credible person.
    Watch it: they may shoot the messenger.
2 Extreme changes may be needed, but explain it in moderation.
    It is better to look up to see where to climb than look down to see how far you will fall.
3 There are always two sides to a story – should you tell them both?
    There is this and that. This is better than that.
4 You can't always avoid fear.
    A threat may not work with the majority.
5 It is better to discuss than to lecture.
    Sell not tell.
6 Find out the characteristics of the receiver.
    Know your audience.
7 Make sure they don't know until you are ready to tell them.
    Forewarned is forearmed.
8 Consider working with logic: it's longer lasting than emotion.
    Thinking through the argument is better than just feeling your way through it.

There is more on the subject of change later.   131

T-groups

A further way of attempting to change an employee's attitude is by means of sensitivity training or T-groups. Simply, it is a way of getting 8 to 12 people together in order that each of them may learn more about themselves, and the effect they have on others. It can be an emotional experience which in the wrong hands can do much more harm than good.

FURTHER READING

Find out more on the way T-groups work. Find out about the Johari Window. It is a model that is used to help people understand themselves. It provides four different viewpoints of a person's personality. It is a way of trying to see yourself as others see you.

Myself

| | What is known to me

What others know of me | What I don't know about me

What others know of me |
| **Others** | What is known to me

What others don't know about me | What I don't know about me

What others don't know about me |

Fig. 55   *The Johari window*

Try to discover the uses of which the Johari window may be put within a work context.

Transactional analysis and attitudes

Another valuable insight into attitudes and their effect on managing and the managed, is gained through a glance at transactional analysis (TA). Transactional analysis is a bundle of theories tied up with one ribbon. It is all about the way individuals relate to each other. Positive 'feelings' towards someone or yourself are known as OK

feelings. Negative feelings are known as Not OK feelings. The OK words that are conjured up include: capable, well being, lovable, good self-esteem. The Not OK words include: weakness, incompetence, insignificant, anxious, worthlessness. The idea behind all this is that each of us is of value; we have the right to seek out our own needs; and we are perfectly able to behave in such a way as to get on reasonably with others. It can be loosely summed up from the title of the book on TA by Thomas Harris: *I'm OK, You're OK*.

The drama diamond, so called by Graham Barnes, writing in *Transactional Analysis Journal* in January 1981 under the title, 'On saying hello: the script drama diamond and character role analysis', provides a nice insight into the way TA views:

- attitudes
- behaviour
- emotion

Attitude is seen by TA as our true feelings towards a person or thing. **Behaviour** is how we act towards that person or thing – in a superior or inferior way. **Emotion** is what is being felt inside but not necessarily shown to the outside world. Each of these, attitude, behaviour and emotion, has a positive (OK) and a negative (Not OK) side. If we take the three, attributing to each a negative or positive aspect, then we can reveal a variety of combinations.

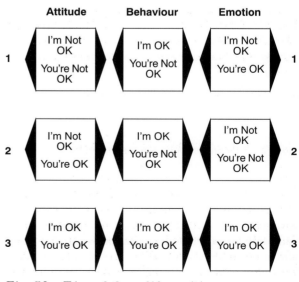

Fig. 56   *TA and three life positions*

The combinations in the first line of Figure 56 would suggest that, where there is an attitude that nobody is capable of getting things right, nothing seems to be going well. Under behaviour, it seems that the individual is one who likes to tell others what to do; this individual would think he/she knew what is best for others. The emotions of such a combination are shame or guilt. The person with this combination will not want to delegate or allow participation. They would prefer to set up more systems so as to save others from failure.

The combination in the second line reveals a bullying manager or indeed colleague. Such people see themselves as not being as good as others. They demonstrate this by tending towards the autocratic behaviour, telling others how to behave. Their emotions are those of despair and hopelessness. Some teachers and lecturers demonstrate this combination when they put down someone who raises a question, making that person feel that it is his or her own fault for not understanding what is going on in class.

The combination in the third line simply means that we are at one with the world.

Transactional analysis was first used in therapy and is now used in training at work. If organisations want their employees to explore their inner feelings and find out how these relate to their attitude about the organisation, managers and others in their group, then they may wish to take a closer look at TA.

FURTHER READING

Eric Berne, *What do you say after you say Hello?*, Corgi, 1975. Thomas Harris, *I'm OK. You're OK*, Pan Books, 1973.

Cognitive dissonance

The problem with trying to change a person's attitude is that the person will experience discomfort. Not physical discomfort, but discomfort of the mind, what is called cognitive dissonance. **Cognitive** is what we have learnt, what we know, what we understand. **Dissonance** means that there is a lack of harmony. Cognitive dissonance then means that something that has happened, or information we have just received, does not agree with what we already understand. There is conflict, and it is within ourselves, we feel uneasy. We need to heal that pain by finding a rational reason for that discomfort.

Take the situation where a vegetarian, or even better a vegan, works in McDonald's. This situation will cause a conflict in the mind. How do such people resolve this conflict, because it must be resolved? They can say that they don't mind others not being vegetarian; if they believe that, then there would be no dissonance. They can say that jobs are scarce and that this is the only job they could get; the dissonance would then be reduced. Whatever they do, they will need to make 'excuses' to themselves in order that they may live with that conflict.

I like the example Charles Handy gives in his *Understanding Organizations*, where he says that the worst thing a male can do is to ask his friend what he thinks of his girlfriend. If the friend gives a less than flattering response, then what does the first man do? The choice he has is to change his own view or to lower the importance of his relationship with his friend.

Another example is that of a mother who tries to change her daughter's attitude about something, but to no effect. The girl may think, 'What does mum know?' Someone else may say the same thing as the mother and suddenly the daughter has a change in attitude. Why? Because the daughter sees that other person as an expert. Persuasion only works if it comes from someone seen as an expert; that way people can rationalise the dissonance. The situation is the same at work: employees may change their attitude if they believe they are listening to an expert.

At work, management most commonly get employees to change their attitude by a financial inducement. If the price is right, then the dissonance is reduced. The employee will change his or her attitude (and behaviour) and explain away the dissonance.

FURTHER READING

Read *Work Psychology: Understanding human behaviour in the workplace*, by J. Arnold, I. T. Robertson and C. L. Cooper (Pitman, 1991). Chapter 8 is all about attitudes at work.

Cognitive dissonance

Attitude surveys

Some organisations sail along thinking that all in their little ocean is lovely. They may, however, be unaware that they are heading towards the Doldrums or Cape Horn.

It is of considerable value for an organisation to find out the views of its employees. After all the organisation expects them to work towards the corporate aims and objectives and to embrace the 'mission' statement. The organisation cannot rely simply on the views fed to it by trade unions and/or management, as both may have good reasons for reinterpreting the facts.

It is no good organisations playing lip-service to an examination of employee attitudes; they have to be prepared to accept the findings and do something about the matter. One organisation I had the pleasure of working with was very concerned about employee attitudes. The chief executive asked the personnel director to undertake an urgent survey. When the results were announced he blamed the messenger. So there are some conditions that must apply if the organisa-

tion and the employees are to get something valuable out of any survey.

1 All managers must show active support.
2 The objectives must be clear and made known to all participants.
3 Employees must want to be and must be involved in the planning.
4 If it is a big or complex survey, it is best to hire experts to undertake it.
5 The organisation must be willing and able to act on the results.
6 The results must be made known to all those taking part and all those they affect.
7 Management must consult the employees on any action proposed.

Before preparing an attitude survey, an organisation may like to look at a few items that should be available within personnel department records. These statistics, in themselves, may well lead the organisation to conclude that all is not well. If the figures suggest that there are a few things that give some cause for concern, then the organisation may wish to undertake an attitude survey.

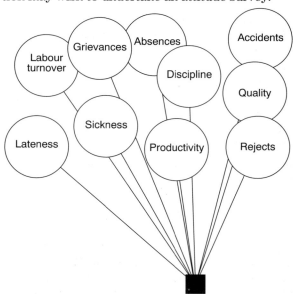

Fig. 57   What's up, Doc.?

There is one questionnaire called the **Cornell Job Descriptive Index** (JDI) which attends to five aspects of an employee's relationship with his/her job.

What do you think about:

1 Your job
2 Your supervisor or manager
3 Your colleagues
4 Your pay and benefits
5 Your promotion prospects?

To conduct a detailed and complex survey of employee attitudes takes time and the services of experts.

A LITTLE SURVEY

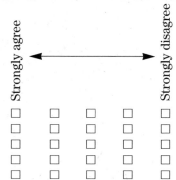

	Strongly agree				Strongly disagree
1 I like my job.	☐	☐	☐	☐	☐
2 I am good at my job.	☐	☐	☐	☐	☐
3 My job uses my skills, experience and knowledge.	☐	☐	☐	☐	☐
4 I get a feeling of achievement in my job.	☐	☐	☐	☐	☐
5 I get recognition for my achievements.	☐	☐	☐	☐	☐

OUT OF TEN

Individually score the following from 0 to 10. The higher the number the happier you are.

1 I am happy with this course.
2 I know what is expected of me in each assignment.
3 I have obtained the grades I deserved, to date.
4 I am happy with my school or college.

Now compare your score with those of the rest of the group. What do the results say about the attitudes within the group?

MOTIVATION

If you want something, then you will behave in a manner which will help you get it. When you get it, then you are satisfied. It is this internal drive that managers have been trying to tap for centuries. At work motivation is the effort that employees put into their work in order to achieve something they want. Management are very interested in how or what motivates their employees. If they could just find out what makes one person work as hard as possible and another as little as possible, if they could only find out what those individual differences are, and why they are present, then they might be able to take steps to improve the lot of the organisation and that of the individual.

Is it all simply to do with money? It would be true to say if an employer did not pay people to work, then no one would come to work. Organisations also indicate the value they put upon labour by the amount of money they pay.

TAKE A POLL

In any class taking this course there are quite a number who have part-time jobs, or who should be encouraged to get part-time jobs. Such jobs are usually within the retail or catering environment. You will find that those working for establishments such as Burger King and McDonald's will be paid much the same, and those working for large chain stores will also get paid about the same. So who pays the best rate? Who do you want to work for? If it is not for the one with the best rate of pay, why is this?

Money may not be the only motivator but if an employee feels that he/she is not getting enough, 135

Tried and tested

for whatever reason, then the lack of it will demotivate. On the other hand a sufficiency may help to motivate. It may not be surprising to learn that a survey showed that young people, and those in non-supervisory jobs, all rated money as an important motivator.

ATTITUDES TO PAY

1 I am reasonably happy if my pay is much the same as that received by others doing the same job as me in this organisation and other organisations.

2 I would be happier if I got more, but if it was suggested that I got too much compared with others, then I would feel guilty.

3 I do know that if I feel I am not getting paid enough I will become dissatisfied with the job.

Money does motivate. However, is it the main motivator? Is there a host of other factors that help to motivate employees? Theories abound, but who and what are the main players and ideas in the field?

SEVEN ON MOTIVATION AND ONE THAT CREPT IN

- Abraham Maslow's **Hierarchy of Needs**
- Clayton Alderfer's **ERG Theory**
- Frederick Herzberg's **Two-Factor Theory**
- David McClelland's **Three Needs Theory**
- J. Stacy Adams's **Equity Theory**
- Edwin Locke's **Goal-Setting Theory**
- Thorndike and Skinner's **Reinforcement Theory** (this is the one that crept in)
- Victor Vroom's **Expectancy Theory**
- plus a little stroking from TA and others

Hierarchy of needs

Abraham Maslow was not thinking about people's working lives when he devised his **Hierarchy of needs**. However, his theory was adopted and interpreted for use at work. Indeed no course is complete until Maslow and his needs have been given an airing. Popular with management and trainers, Maslow's work has not found much support with those in work psychology. It has been suggested that it is popular because the theory is easy to understand and it sounds good.

Maslow's hierarchy originally had seven needs, but these are reduced to five needs, presented in a hierarchical form. The idea is that we start at the bottom and when that need is satisfied then we move up to the next need. Once a need has been satisfied it is no longer a motivator. It is like climbing up a ladder, when your feet are firmly on one rung then you have an inner drive which moves you up to the next rung. But it is not quite as simple as that. Maslow did say that it is possible to get a thirst for a higher-level need before a lower-level need is fully satisfied. Despite this talk of ladders and thirsts, Maslow's work is usually shown in the form of a pyramid.

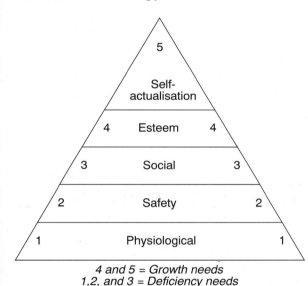

4 and 5 = Growth needs
1,2, and 3 = Deficiency needs

Fig. 58   Pyramid power: Maslow's hierarchy of needs

Physiological needs are seen to be the lowest level of need. They are the most basic things, such as food, water, shelter, sex.

I WANT TO SATISFY MY PHYSIOLOGICAL NEEDS

- Give me sufficient salary to put a roof over my head, food in my mouth, and clothes on my back.
- Don't talk to me about motivation when I can't pay the rent.

Safety needs come to the fore only when the physiological needs have been met. Employees, it is said, look for safety and security from their organisation.

I WANT TO SATISFY MY SAFETY NEEDS

- Give me a safe working environment, safe from any physical harm.
- I want an indefinite term contract of employment.
- Life and accident insurance would be nice.
- Don't tell me things are bad and I am lucky to have this job.
- I would not be happy with a short-term contract.
- I don't want to be bullied.

Social needs are sought when both physiological and safety needs have been satisfied. This is the stage where people see the need for friends, they want to be loved, they want to be accepted by their colleagues.

I WANT TO SATISFY MY SOCIAL NEEDS

- Where can I have a chat with my work friends?
- It would be nice to have a social club so we can have parties, take trips, have a sports day.
- I like to like and be liked.
- If things are not going well for the organisation, at least I might know who my friends are.

The first three needs, physiological, safety and social, are seen as deficiency needs. If these needs are not met then, Maslow suggests, employees cannot develop either physically or psychologically. These needs can be satisfied if the organisation provides money and long-term contracts.

The next tier of needs concerns self-respect: the **esteem needs**, a desire for success and to be seen as being good at what one does.

I WANT TO SATISFY MY ESTEEM NEEDS

- Now I know this may prove difficult as not too many people manage to have this need satisfied.
- What's OK for me might not be OK for others.
- You can call me a 'manager' or an 'executive'.
- What about an 'Oscar' at the annual dinner?
- My photograph plastered all over the place as 'employee of the month' would be fine.
- But then, I am a bit of an extrovert and an internaliser.

If someone has travelled through the four preceding steps then he/she reaches the **self-actuali-sation needs**. These concern a person's need to realise his or her full potential, and the innovative and creative urges.

- Just let me do my own thing.
- Don't interfere.
- It may be difficult because very few reach this level and very few organisations know how to handle this level of need.

It should be noted that a person may be able to satisfy the top two needs outside the organisational environment.

It is generally recognised that Maslow's work is useful in a very general sense, but it does not provide managers and human resource specialists with any particularly valuable information.

Maslow never dreamed his work would be used in management training rooms throughout the world. Although his theory is popular with managers, it is not so with psychologists, who say there is no real evidence to support it. What do you think? Give some good reasons why you think it is valuable and some others why its general application would be inappropriate.

The ERG theory

Clayton P. Alderfer provided a redefinition of Maslow's work. He called it his ERG theory.

- E = Existence
- R = Relatedness
- G = Growth

According to Alderfer, needs are not arranged in a hierarchy requiring the climbing of some ladder or the scaling of pyramids, but can be present all at once. Should one need prove difficult to meet then an employee would turn to another. He also said that an employee may move up and down the needs and that one need may not be satisfied before a person moves on to another.

The **existence** needs are like Maslow's first and second level. They include pay and benefits, a safe working environment and job security.

The **relatedness** needs are those of social concerns and personal relationships, just like Maslow's third and part of his fourth need. These include being accepted for the work that one does, as well as making and keeping friends.

The **growth** needs are in line with Maslow's fourth and fifth level, in that they focus on the search for self-esteem and self-actualisation.

- I know that the G need is almost limitless, because it is like a Chinese meal: lovely to get it but it only leads me to want more, I can never be satisfied.
- If I have problems with the R and the G then I will look at the E closely, so be prepared to review my pay and benefits.

Alderfer has not received the promotion that Maslow has had. His theory is seen as fitting a little better into research results than that of Maslow. However, like Maslow's, the theory has proved very difficult for the psychologists to accept.

The two-factor theory

Frederick Herzberg developed the two-factor theory. The first he called the **hygiene factor**. The second factor he called **motivators**. Both of these have a great bearing on an employee's motivation. Both are of equal importance.

Hygiene means keeping things clean in order to prevent the spread of disease. In this context it refers to certain factors which, if not present, will cause the employee to become ill (dissatisfied), but if they are present the employee will stay healthy (not dissatisfied). Not only are these hygiene factors essential but they have to be there in the right quantity and the right quality. So employees have to get a fair and reasonable rate of pay, and they have to continue to get fair and reasonable pay. It is the same with working conditions: they have to be good, no employee likes to work in a dump. If the pay is bad and or the working conditions are bad, then the employee will be dissatisfied. If the hygiene factors are good it does

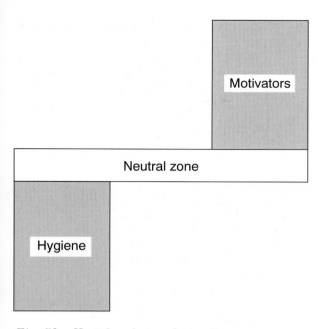

Fig. 59 *Hertzberg's two-factor theory*

not mean that the employee will be satisfied, all it means is that he/she will be less dissatisfied. Good hygiene factors do not motivate employees, as they can only ever reach that stage of being neither satisfied nor dissatisfied, a neutral zone.

HYGIENE FACTORS

- pay
- working conditions
- job security
- supervisors
- getting on with colleagues
- getting on with subordinates
- status

The **motivators** are all connected to the work that the employees undertake. It is only through the performance of the tasks within the job that an employee will achieve satisfaction. Therefore if an organisation cannot offer the employee any of the motivators below, then that employee will be in the neutral zone of being neither satisfied nor dissatisfied.

MOTIVATORS

- the job
- attainment
- advancement
- responsibility

Again, this theory is very popular with managers but poorly received by psychologists. The theory is for the individual not the group, indeed Herzberg thought that the group harmed the satisfaction of an individual's needs.

MASLOW, HERZBERG AND ALDERFER: COMPLETE, COMPARE AND CONTRAST

Maslow	Herzberg	Alderfer
?	Achievement	
Esteem	?	Growth
?	?	?
Safety	?	
?	Wages	?

The three needs theory

David McClelland recognised three needs, his trichotomy of needs:

- achievement
- power
- affiliation

Achievement needs are those held by the employee who wants to do things better than anyone else. Such employees need to succeed. They do not take chances; they avoid any job that they see as too easy or too difficult. They could appear to be hostile and antisocial to those who they feel stand in their way of reaching excellence.

YOUR NEEDS – 1

1 Do you like to solve problems?
2 Are your targets moderate?
3 Do you like to be told how well you are doing?
4 Do you spend time working out how you can get on, in life or work?
5 Do you spend time working out how to improve your performance?

YES?
Then you may have a high need for **Achievement**.

Power needs belong to those who desire to control and influence others. Such needs are, for them, more important than job performance. They want to make others behave differently from how they would normally behave. They want to dominate and be the boss. They are competitive and seek status.

YOUR NEEDS – 2

1 Are you the sort of person that tries to control and influence others?

2 Do you try and take on the leadership role whenever the opportunity arises?

3 Do you like to persuade others to your way of thinking?

4 Do other people think you are somewhat hard to please, forceful and very frank?

YES?

Then you are likely to have a high need for **Power**.

Affiliation is the need to belong, the need to work with others. People with this need want to understand and be understood.

YOUR NEEDS – 3

1 Do you look for situations that provide an opportunity for social relationships?

2 Do you spend time just thinking about the personal relationships you have?

3 Are you concerned about the feelings of others?

4 Are you the sort of person that tries to mend broken relationships?

YES?

Then you have a high need for **Affiliation**.

McClelland has said that those at the top of an organisation usually have a high need for power and only a moderate need for affiliation. It appears that a very high need for achievement has a negative effect on reaching the top and people with such a need have to be content with middle-management level positions.

If you are worried that you are not a high achiever, do not worry; there are lots of courses to help you change your motivation. That also means that employers can train their employees to become employees with a high achievement need.

The equity theory

Employees at work look to see what they put into their job and examine what they get out of it. Then they will carefully look at what they consider others put into their job and what they get out of it. If the difference between them and others is seen to be considerable then the employees will take steps to try and remove any inequalities. They will not just look at their present job and circumstances, they will also look at the past, comparing it with the present. They will compare their situation with those of people in similar positions outside their own company. They will compare notes with their friends outside work.

ME AND OTHERS

Are the grades I get on this course fair in terms of what I put into it? Do they differ from the grades and efforts of:

1 My class mates?

2 Those on other courses?

3 Those doing the same course in other schools and colleges?

If employees think that others are getting a better deal than they are, what might they do about it? They can leave, they can do less. However they are likely to make excuses, by thinking less of themselves and more highly of others, or by comparing themselves with others less fortunate. Or they may engage in **social loafing**, which was raised in Section 2.

IS IT THAT BAD?

OK, I don't think I am getting the grades I should, so what can I do about it?

1 Others are doing less and getting the same grades, so I'll do less.

2 I could try and work even harder to see if that makes a difference.

3 Those others obviously have help not available to me.

4 I am doing much better than some of my friends who did not get on to this course.

5 I am wasting my time, so I'll leave.

What is important is what the employee sees or thinks, not what is actually happening, that is, perception. If an employee sees inequalities, or thinks that they exist, this perception will motivate him/her to reduce these inequalities. Therefore, the management must take steps to find out if their employees perceive equality or inequality in the organisation. They can do so by using a questionnaire which asks them about matters such as pay, the application of rules, the workload. After examining the results of such a survey, the management must do something about the matter, remembering that what the employee thinks about a situation may be quite different from what the management thinks about the same situation. Management must not assume that they are right, they must see the situation from the employee's viewpoint.

Prepare a questionnaire for your class addressing the issue of the effort people put into their work and the results of that effort. Essentially do people see that they are treated equitably?

The goal-setting theory

It was Edwin Locke who suggested that working towards a **goal** at work is a great source of motivation. An examination of the previous section will show that if management agree with an employee what has to be done and if the goals are neither too easy nor too difficult, then the employee, provided with the resources to do the task, will have the willingness and effort to aim for that goal. The goal, although not too difficult, must stretch the individual. This goal-setting theory works well in terms of getting employees to perform but it does not necessarily follow that they will be satisfied with or in their job.

The reinforcement theory

Managers who are not interested in what employees think, but merely in the way they behave, find the **reinforcement theory** instructive. This theory is not concerned with motivating the employee but only with making sure that they do what they should when they should. It is concerned with:

- positive reinforcement
- negative reinforcement
- punishment
- extinction

If an employee behaves in a way that is desirable then the employee will be rewarded with praise and perhaps money. This is **positive reinforcement**, as it actively encourages the employee to behave in a certain way.

There is also **negative reinforcement**, which occurs where punishment is withheld if the employee behaves as he/she is expected to behave. This is a bit like the bully saying that if you do as you are told, then you will not get a beating.

If an employee behaves in an undesirable way then he/she may be punished in order to actively discourage repetition. If, say, your finance teacher or lecturer continually ignores requests for further clarification of a point, so causing one or more persons in the class problems, then soon no one will ask questions. At work this **punishment** could even take the form of an employee being suspended from work without pay.

Extinction is an inactive way of eliminating a form of behaviour that is not desired, and it is done through withholding a positive reinforcement. So at work the employee does not get a bonus until he/she behaves in the way the organisation expects employees to behave.

It is also worthy of note that if the management stops reinforcing desired behaviour, then that behaviour will cease.

However before any organisation feels they should adopt reinforcement theories they may wish to take heed of the advice of S. Jablonsky and D. De Viries who, writing in 1972 in *Organizational Behaviour and Human Performance* on the subject of 'Operant conditioning principles extrapolated to the theory of management', said: tread with care.

TREAD WITH CARE WITH JABLONSKY AND DE VIRIES

1 Don't use punishment as the first step or the main means.

2 Reinforce desired behaviour and try, if possible, to forget the undesired.

3 Do it quickly, don't wait too long.

4 Find out what the individual thinks are negative and positive factors.

5 Explain the desired behaviour in terms of the expected outcome.

The expectancy theory

One of the most favoured theories of motivation is Victor Vroom's expectancy theory. It depends on three factors:

- valence
- expectancy
- instrumentality

Valence is the strength of an employee's want for something. The list of such wants, or rewards, is very long, and an individual's rewards can be very different. There are two types of reward: extrinsic and intrinsic.

Extrinsic rewards are those that surround the job, such as money, promotion, time off, prizes, holidays, private medical cover, and so on. A valence can be negative or positive. One employee may not be interested in the thought of medical insurance as a reward, whilst another would positively leap at the chance of such a benefit.

Intrinsic rewards are those that are part and parcel of the job itself. They include the pleasure of doing a job well; the satisfaction of a person who has high achievement motivation; getting a buzz out of just doing the job well. Intrinsic, then, refers to the fact that the job has to be done and, through the doing, the employee gets satisfaction.

Valence for a specified end result can then be:

1 Positive – I want it.

2 Negative – No thanks.

3 Indifferent – Not bothered one way or the other.

Expectancy can be examined in the following situations. If a manager has promised something that we want, so long as we in turn do something the organisation wants, the next question is: can we do what the manager wants? Have we got the know-how? Can we do it in time? Have we the confidence in ourselves? Is it possible? If the answer to one or more of these questions is a resounding 'No', then no matter what the valence,

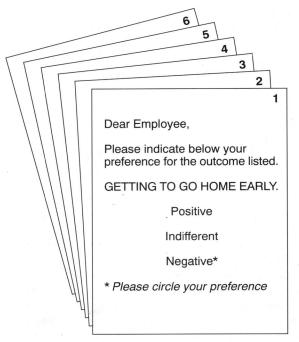

Fig. 60   Valence: Pick a card

the motivation to do whatever is asked will not be high.

Say you work in a warehouse, and part of your job is to load trucks. At lunch time the boss asks you to load one particular truck, and says that as soon as you finish you can go home. Now let us imagine that going home is a good valence for you, in that you would like to go home early. The next point to consider is: can you do it? The answer could be: 'Yes' or 'Yes, with extra effort I can do it'. Or it could be: 'No, I don't have the stamina' or 'No way, who are they kidding?' Whatever the response it is bound to be a positive 'Yes I can do it', or a negative 'No I cannot do it'. If you want to go home early and you can do it, the management are on the right track to aid your motivation. But, let us say that you are not thrilled with the promise of going home early, but you can do the loading very quickly; then, you are not going to be motivated to do the job as quickly as you are perfectly able to do it.

Instrumentality. Having considered the questions of do I want it? and can I do it? we next ask: will I get it? So if you want promotion and you work as hard as you can, then find that you don't receive the promotion, you are not going to be particularly happy. So before you experience that

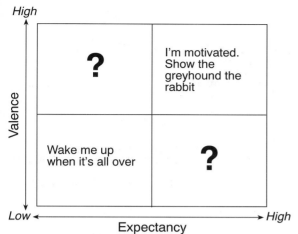

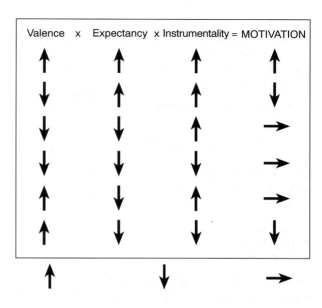

Fig. 61   Vroom's expectancy theory

unhappiness you need to try to work out whether or not you will get the reward. It is not a case of knowing that the reward will be there or not, it is a case of thinking whether it will be, or not. What is the use of working hard to get good grades so that you may go to university, only to find that GNVQ qualifications do not find favour with the university of your choice?

I worked for one boss who promised me an attractive outcome, a rather nice holiday, if I were able to deliver a contract below a particular price. Now, I liked the valence part, the holiday, I liked the expectancy part – I knew it could be done by a lot of hard graft – and as far as instrumentality was concerned I believed that my boss would deliver. I was wrong on the instrumentality part, he did not deliver. He claimed it was a 'joke' in order to motivate me so he could get what he wanted. I had not taken into account that some-times you have a boss with a devious mind, who thinks of a superb way of motivating, but one that can only work once.

Can you suggest replacements for the question marks in the diagram above?

WHICH DIRECTION?

I think that one of the arrows above is facing the wrong way. Which is it? Or perhaps I'm OK. The figure is not complete; consider other combinations.

EXPECTANCY THEORY MUSTS FOR A MANAGER

1 Find out what the employee wants as a reward. If that reward cannot be given by the manager then make sure that the employee is under no illusions. The manager must make sure that the employee is aware what the manager can offer. Use a menu of rewards so the employee may select what is of value to him or her.

2 Find out if the employee believes that his/her effort will produce the required performance. That includes finding out if the employee needs any resources not currently to hand. If the employee feels he or she cannot do the job, then find out why. The answer may lie in training or supervision, or it may be that the task cannot be done within the limits imposed. For example an employee may work very hard but if the equipment does not work properly, the employee will not see the point, as the expectancy to perform well is out of his/her hands.
Improve the opportunity to succeed in tasks. Remove the chances of failure.

3 Find out if the employee believes that he/she will receive the reward if he/she performs well. If the reward cannot be given, the manager must say so. The employee will be looking at what happened to others in the same or a similar situation. Circumstances do change, and if there is such a change, a manager should advise the employee of an altered state, even though it will affect the performance.
Make clear what rewards are linked to what performances.

The expectancy theory recognises that an employee's performance will be based on their personality, skills, knowledge, experience and abilities, with some employees being more suited to their job than others. The theory also sees that some employees will not quite understand what the manager expects of them. It also recognises that employees need the opportunity to perform well.

Stroking with TA

Transactional analysis does not consider that motivation is simply something that a manager does to an employee. It sees motivation as an essential part of the way employees act with each other and their customers. The employee can also motivate him or herself. TA does not call this motivation, TA calls it stroking.

Stroking means recognition. Daily conversation with other employees, customers, bosses and friends means that we are engaged in stroking. A word is a stroke, a facial expression directed at someone is a stroke.

A stroke can be negative or it can be positive. If it is negative, then it makes us feel Not OK about ourselves or others. However, if it is positive then we can feel OK about ourselves or others. It is up to the manager to make sure that an employee gets more OK strokes than Not OK strokes.

OK strokes are not limited to saying pleasant things about, or to, an employee. Criticism can be an OK stroke, so long as it is constructive. Asking someone their opinion is an OK stroke, as is anything that endorses a person's existence, anything that boosts or maintains a person's self-esteem.

Not OK stroking extends beyond the nasty remarks. Everytime someone in a group is invited to feel superior to another in the group, then others will be receiving Not OK strokes. Think of the time the teacher or lecturer singles out one person for praise: '. . . a wonderful assignment . . . best I've read . . . well deserving of a distinction . . .'. Do the others in the class consider that they have been told that they are Not OK?

Whilst the manager must ensure that each employee gets his or her OK strokes, these are usually conditional upon the employee doing something to warrant receiving the strokes. However the manager must also provide unconditional strokes. Unconditional strokes are usually those that are related to the employee as a living breathing person. Asking about hobbies, holidays, family and interests is OK stroking not requiring the person to have done something to 'deserve' the stroke. Managers must therefore think of the employee as a complete person: the person at work requiring work-related conditional strokes and the person who comes to work, requiring personal unconditional strokes.

STROKES – FIVE THINGS WE DO THAT WE SHOULD NOT

1. **Do not give the stroke.** That people are only doing what they are paid to do is no excuse for denying a stroke.
2. **Do not accept the stroke.** To say, I am only doing my job, others can do it as well, is a silly reason for not accepting a positive stroke. It is deserved; so take it.
3. **Do not reject a stroke.** You can reject a stroke. Just because an employee is given an OK stroke it does not mean that it has been for something he/she is looking for. Being complimented on how good you are at word processing your assignment is no good if you looking for strokes on the ideas you have expressed.
4. **Do not ask for a stroke.** It is an employee's and a student's right to ask for and get feedback on the work that they do. If it is not forthcoming, go and seek it.
5. **Do not stroke yourself.** Do not be modest. Pick up your trumpet and blow. If you want to get on, then tell others about your success and achievements.

It would appear that people are quite happy to receive lots of Not OK strokes. Some may suggest that it is better than being totally ignored. Lots of employees and students find it embarrassing to get an OK stroke. They are so used to receiving destructive criticism and have learnt how to react to Not OK strokes. Training courses will have to be run in order that employees and students know how to react to being told: You're OK.

A MANAGER CANNOT MOTIVATE

It has been suggested that employees motivate themselves. Managers can only demotivate. All a manager can do is to create the situation which permits employees to motivate themselves.

What do you think? If you agree, does it not make a nonsense of all that is written on motivation?

The motivational diamond

In October 1992, in the *American HRM Magazine*, Daniel Boyle reported on how Diamond International had made great gains in improving morale and productivity. In an attitude survey he conducted, he found that 65 per cent of the employees said that they were not treated with any reasonable degree of respect by their managers, 56 per cent said that they had a pessimistic attitude to their work and almost 80 per cent said that they were not given enough reward for the job they were doing. Surprisingly, he did not introduce financial incentives to deal with this situation. He introduced what was called the 100 club. The incentive this time was not based on employees doing something more than they were already doing, but giving recognition for something that they should have been doing anyway. This positive stroking included meeting the presently agreed targets in: productivity, quality, attendance and time keeping. There were 15 separate targets to meet and once an employee reached 100 points he/she was given a jacket with the company logo on it.

The 'prize' was not important, what was important was that the organisation began to change its attitude towards the employee. This was summed up by one plant manager, who said: 'We've taken you for granted for as long as you've worked for us, and we aren't going to do that anymore.' A final attitude survey showed that close to 80 per cent of the employees now thought that the organisation showed concern for them as individuals and that they were deemed to be important in the organisation's eyes.

IT'S NOT ON

Do you consider that it is rather silly to reward employees for coming to work on time? Surely that is what they should do anyway.

Performance appraisal and rewards

You may have discovered from the core HRM module that performance appraisals and performance related pay are linked ways of objectively assessing employees, motivating and rewarding them accordingly. There is, however, a body of evidence to suggest that they do not work.

Alfie Kohn, an American writer, psychologist and consultant, said that financial incentive schemes do not work. Speaking at the 1994 British Demming Association (devoted to the works of the writer and guru, W. E. Demming) conference, Kohn said that such schemes only encourage employees to go for the cash, with the result that quality and job involvement suffer. Kohn said his analysis of available research showed financial bonuses do not work. Perhaps his argument is a continuation of that put forward with respect to intrinsic and extrinsic motivators by those who follow the theories of the Herzberg.

Further, you may have already discovered that where performance appraisals, linked with performance related pay, are individually based, then they may well be doomed. Are they destined for failure? If the individual has to work as part of a team and co-operate with others, how can he or she do so when encouraged to focus on individual interests? Banks and other financial institutions are abandoning schemes which reward individuals in favour of those that reward teams.

DON'T YOU JUST LOVE IT?

What do you think about a group assignment where one grade is given for the group's response?

M. Bowles and G. Coates in their article, 'Images and Substance', in *Personnel Review* (1993), quoted D. C. Feldman and B. A. Weitz as saying that individuals use non-performance ways of advancing their career. They do so because individuals see the management as a purveyor of images or impressions inside the organisation to the employees, and outside the organisation to its customers. What this means is that individuals will not spend their valuable time achieving performance objectives, as organisations have problems in objectively measuring performance. They will, instead, spend their time and effort on behaviour that will relate to the images and impressions organisations find desirable.

AN INTERPRETATION OF THE WAY AHEAD IN NON-PERFORMANCE TERMS

1 Do not rely on merit alone.
2 It is essential that you improve social interactions with your manager and team members.
3 Look and talk like a team member.
4 Remember that where you want to go is not the same as where the organisation wants you to go.
5 Being honest and ethical is not always the best way to get that promotion.
6 Objectively assessing your performance is difficult.

FURTHER READING

You should find out about the following topics:

• Cognitive Evaluation Theory.
• Requisite Task Attributes Theory.
• Job Characteristics Model.

Look back to see what was said earlier on Theory X and Theory Y and on goal setting.

ORGANISATIONAL CULTURE

Psychologists spend their time studying the behaviour of people at and outside work, looking at their whole personality and how individuals interact with each other. Sociologists analyse social behaviour, structures and the behaviour of leaders and their followers. Now anthropologists are turning their attention to the culture of organisations.

In 1975 A. A. Etzioni, in *A Comparative Analysis of Complex Organizations* (Free Press), said that there are three types of goal that need attention:

1 Order goals
2 Economic goals
3 Cultural goals

Culture in an organisation may be seen as: the shared beliefs, customs, ideas and values within an organisation which make it different from other organisations. Individuals should be made aware of, or they should try to find out, the culture of the organisation they are trying to join. When a person joins an organisation, he/she not only takes on the job, but also embraces the culture of the organisation. If an individual's values, beliefs and ideas are not the same as the organisation's, then the individual will have to change, leave or be very unhappy.

It is the culture of the organisation that will help it decide how it reacts to its customers, its suppliers, outside agencies and to decide who to recruit and who to avoid recruiting.

There is also the **climate** in the organisation. This is the atmosphere created by the feelings and emotions of the employees. I have often been told of people who have gone for an interview, feeling positive about information received concerning the culture of an organisation, but have walked out of the interview because the climate did not line up with the expressed culture.

You could be forgiven for thinking that, with organisations having missions and visions, they are sounding more like cults. Some cults, remember, need a great deal of deprogramming in order to return to the real world. H. M. Trice and J. M. Beyer in their 1987 work, 'Studying Organizational Cultures Through Rites and Rituals', published in Vol. 9 of the *Academy of Management Review*, give four elements of a culture.

TRICE AND BEYER'S FOUR ELEMENTS OF A CULTURE

1 **Practices**   Rites, ceremonies, ritual.
2 **Communications**   Myths, sagas, legends, folk tales, symbols.
3 **Physical forms**   Artefacts, design, layout.
4 **Language**   Using language in such a way that it excludes 'outsiders'.

Tom Peters, who is not a lover of the rational or the logical, prefers to focus on leadership, vision, people and culture. Peters says that employees will give a great deal to the organisation that gives their lives meaning.

V. Sathe looked at 'Culture and Related Corporate Realities' in 1985, and when E. H. Schein asked the question, 'Does Japanese management style have a message for American managers?' in 1982, he gave three clues on how to partly assess an organisation's culture. It is suggested that concern must be directed to the issues of leaders, crises and deviants. Knowledge about these might enable you to detect the real culture of an organisation.

1 Tell me the background of those that lead the organisation.

2 Tell me of a critical incident that the organisation had to pull through. How did it respond to that crisis and what did it learn?

3 Tell me who the deviants in the organisation are and how the organisations handles such individuals.

Of course there are other more straightforward ways of trying to find out an organisation's culture. E. H. Schein reminds us of some in his work, 'The role of the founder in creating organizational culture'.

1 Get hold of the organisation's philosophy as given out in recruitment literature and promotional materials. From this information you may get a good idea of whether you would like to work there. But remember, rhetoric may be different from reality.

2 Look at the building the organisation occupies and the way the available space is used. Is it open plan or is it a series of little offices? What is the quality of the furnishings and the surroundings? Is it clean?

3 Look at the reward and status system. Find out how the organisation rewards excellent performance. Find out if status is based on rank or achievement.

4 Look at what items the management think it important to measure and control. What do the employees think that their leaders deem to be important and how do those leaders measure success?

5 Look at the organisational structure. Look to see if it is tall or flat.

6 Look at systems and procedures. Look and you may find a bureaucratic organisation lurking beneath the facade.

In *Understanding Organizations*, Charles Handy tells us that there are four main forms of organisational culture. They are:

1 Power
2 Role
3 Task
4 Person

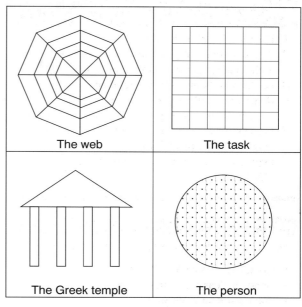

Fig. 62   Charles Handy: Four cultures

The **power culture**, shown as a web, is where person power is within the spider at the centre and resource power is within the web. It is small and can react quickly to changing market situations. It is typical of a new or very young company where the power is still in the hands of the owner/manager. It can also be typical of a large organisation which is split up into small discrete units. It does rely heavily on the power from the centre, if this goes then the culture will go, as it may be absorbed into something larger or it disappears altogether.

If you:

1 Want to be left to get on with the job.
2 Like playing politics.
3 Dislike procedures.
4 Like to be a risk taker.
5 Dislike security.
6 Consider that individuals are better than committees.
7 Recognise that when the spider goes the organisation may be blown away.

The **role culture**, represented by Handy as a Greek temple, is the bureaucratic organisation which has rules and procedures for nearly every eventuality. Such organisations respond slowly to possible changes. Some people may be very comfortable being part of such an organisation. Read again about Max Weber.

SEVEN GOOD REASONS WHY A ROLE CULTURE IS FOR YOU

If you:

1 Like a job description and work to it.
2 Like doing just as required and no more.
3 Think position power is their strong point.
4 Like security and stability.
5 Dislike ambition, creativity and innovation.
6 Dislike personal power and think expert power is only just OK.
7 Like working in a bank or the civil service (exceptions accepted).

The **task culture** symbolised by Handy's net, is the matrix organisation. As it is based on the formation of groups for specific challenges, it is able to adapt fairly quickly to changing situations. Although control is not easy, because work is devolved to project groups, it is supposed to be the preferred culture. However, if that were true all other organisational cultures would be obsolete, but they are not. It is the culture favoured by work psychologists as it is an example of their theories. It is, then, of no surprise that middle-ranking managers yearn for this type of culture.

SEVEN GOOD REASONS WHY A TASK CULTURE IS FOR YOU

If you:

1 Like being rewarded for results.
2 Like working in teams.
3 Like control over your work.
4 Like expert power.
5 Like to work in a competitive market.
6 Like having resources if you can prove you need them.
7 Like the idea of the customer comes first.

The **person culture** is shown as a cluster. The organisation is there to serve the needs of those who work within it. There is hardly any identifiable structure. Partnerships would be a loose example of such a culture, or a group of individuals who have come together simply for the convenience of working under a single banner. The concept of such an organisation is quite fanciful. They rarely exist, as usually an organisation's aims and objectives are greater than the individuals within it.

SEVEN GOOD REASONS WHY A PERSON CULTURE IS FOR YOU

If you:

1 Are self-interested.
2 Do not like being told when and what to do.
3 Like expert power.
4 Do not like being influenced by others.
5 Are not impressed by personal power.
6 Like the organisation to be subordinate to the individual.
7 Like to dream, because for most of us that is all it is.

The idea that if you give employees boring and repetitive work to do, then you will end up with boring and repetitive employees who are not at all happy in their job, was recognised in the 1930s. Two methods of combatting this situation are job rotation and job enlargement. Herzberg and his two-factor theory spawned a further concept, job enrichment.

Job rotation

If employees work on a job that is very routine and repetitive the time will come when that job no longer presents them with any challenge. It is at this time that the management should move the employee to another job. The second job should be one that requires the same level of skill and abilities as the first. This lateral movement cannot work wonders but can have some effect in reducing labour turnover, absence and dysfunctional conduct associated with boredom.

Job rotation may, however, cause problems to some who may feel that they are simply moving from one boring job to another boring job; they may need to be stretched.

Job enlargement

Another idea, developed in the late 1950s, was developing the job horizontally. This means giving the employee more to do at the same level by bringing together, say, a number of tasks previously performed by three employees and getting each of the three to complete the combined tasks.

Employees may, however, see this as simply an increase in the number of boring, routine tasks they have to do. It does nothing to address the problems of those who want a sense of achievement, but it is satisfactory for others who like such activities. It may give people time and space to think and chat to colleagues.

Job enrichment

The idea of job enrichment is to design the job vertically, in such a way as to give the employee the chance for challenge, growth, achievement and recognition. The employee should receive regular feedback on performance; job enrichment should allow the employee more freedom to carry out a complete job rather than just parts of a job.

FIVE GOOD REASONS WHY ORGANISATIONS SHOULD INTRODUCE JOB ENRICHMENT

1 Helps to motivate employees.
2 Reduces sickness and absenteeism.
3 Reduces moans and grievances.
4 Reduces the likelihood of employees leaving.
5 Leads to improved employee performance.

Of course it should be recognised that not every employee will want job enrichment. Some may be perfectly happy with a routine job. Equally not all managers are happy with job enrichment.

FIVE GOOD REASONS WHY ORGANISATIONS SHOULD NOT INTRODUCE JOB ENRICHMENT

1 Knowledge is power. Why lose it?
2 Give them an inch and they will want a mile.
3 Technology has a greater effect on the way a job has to be done.
4 They are not competent to use it properly.
5 It costs in training, equipment and probably more pay.

Herzberg's original idea was developed further by Greg Oldham and Richard Hackman. Writing in the *California Management Review* in 1975 ('A New Strategy for Job Enrichment'), they said that a job can be divided into five core dimensions.

THE HACKMAN AND OLDHAM FIVE CORE DIMENSIONS

1 Skill variety
2 Task identity
3 Task significance
4 Autonomy
5 Feedback

Skill variety refers to all the different skills required for the performance of a job. Management examines jobs to identify these skills. Whereas previously the skills needed to do a job were perhaps spread amongst a number of employees, they can be combined into the role of one employee. In the opinion of some, the wider the range of skills needed in a job the greater the challenge it presents to the employee.

Task identity refers to the situation where an employee carries out the whole job not just bits of it. It is more meaningful for an employee to build the whole TV set rather than to continually construct one part. Employees may feel that the job they are doing 'belongs' to them if they are doing a complete identifiable job. Employees need to 'own' the job they are doing in order for it to have meaning.

Task significance means that the employee can see that what he or she is doing has some impact on others, be that inside or outside the organisation. Employees want to make sense of what they are doing. Too often have I seen employees being asked to provide regular financial or statistical information to another department, but never have they been told why and what use may be made of their efforts. Let employees know who their client is, whether it is another department or someone outside the organisation, and let them know the relationship between them and the work they do.

Autonomy means giving employees some control and some option over what they have to do, and how they do it, expanding their jobs vertically. Where before management had all the control, now they give over some of that control to the employee. The areas where such freedom and independence may be given include: work scheduling, methods of working, fixing tea and lunch breaks, quality control and costing. This represents empowerment.

Feedback is informing employees how well or badly they are doing. Feedback should be given in a timely manner and not too long after the event. It should be given regularly, not as an occasional whim of the manager. Employees want to know how well they are doing so they can make improvements if necessary. Feedback should not be limited to negative comments, as this is a sure way to demotivate employees. Praise must be given where and when due, despite the reserve of the British about accepting praise.

Before embarking on a course of job enrichment the organisation may wish to consider conducting an attitude survey first. Herzberg might not have favoured such a course: he not only thought that groups smothered the satisfaction of individuals, he also suggested that individuals should not participate in deciding the forms of job enrichment that might be introduced, as he did not think that they were always competent to make such choices. This he saw clearly as the prerogative of management.

Job dimensions survey

One way of trying to find out the relative presence of each of the above five core dimensions is to conduct a survey, based on the Motivating Potential Score (MPS) developed by Hackman and Oldham (the five dimensions survey). All that is required is that employees complete a questionnaire about their feelings towards their job, based on the five core dimensions.

Step 1. Score out of ten each of the dimensions below relating to your present 'job'.

Skill variety   Task identity   Task significance   Autonomy   Feedback

$\boxed{?/10}$ $\boxed{?/10}$ $\boxed{?/10}$ $\boxed{?/10}$ $\boxed{?/10}$

Step 2. Complete the following to find your score.

$$\frac{\text{Skill variety} \times \text{Task identity} + \text{Task significance}}{} \times \text{Autonomy} \times \text{Feedback} = ?$$

You will see that the autonomy and feedback dimensions are deemed to provide a greater motivating influence than the other three and this difference is reflected in the previous calculation.

Quality of working life

Job enrichment, and the other techniques mentioned above, were advanced by the neo-human relations school of management thought. They developed into a method of looking at the agreeable and disagreeable aspects of everything relating to a job in an organisation. Under the name, Quality of Working Life, or QWL, the method was widely promoted in the USA and Europe. Not only is QWL concerned with excellence, with regard to employees, it also addresses the economic health of the organisation. QWL is not limited to one technique, it is a blanket idea which covers everything that contributes to bringing a human face to the organisation.

R. E. Walton, in 'Improving the Quality of Work Life' (*Harvard Business Review*, June 1974), devised the eight categories that sum up QWL.

QWL AND WALTON'S EIGHT CATEGORIES

1 An organisation that is seen to be socially responsible.
2 A job that does not interfere with a person's leisure time and family life.
3 An organisation that acknowledges an employee's right to privacy and the right to express his/her disagreement.
4 An organisation that provides security and the opportunity for personal growth.
5 A job that develops an employee's competencies.
6 A safe and a healthy place to work.
7 A fair and adequate day's pay.
8 An environment that gives employees an identity, freedom from prejudice and a sense of belonging.

3

HOW IS YOUR QWL?

HOW IS YOUR QWL?

Relate each of the eight conditions above to a part- or full-time job you may have, or to your life as a student (but with the exception of item 7).

FURTHER READING

QWL is promoted in this country through the offices of the Advisory Conciliation and Arbitration Service (ACAS). Obtain their booklet on the subject.

More on change

Whether the need for change results from internal or external factors, the change will be at three levels: individual, group and organisation. Changes that impact upon an individual will be easier to manage than those that affect the group or the organisation as a whole.

Kurt Lewin, in his *Field Theory in Social Science*, published by Harper in 1951, identified three stages the individual, group or organisation have to go through, whatever the level of change involved. These three stages are also used by practitioners in management services.

LEWIN'S COOL THREE

1 **Unfreezing**   This is the recognition that there is a need to make changes. Advise the employees about it, plan, organise, schedule, arrange training.
2 **Changing**   This is the implementation, where the success and flexibility of the planning etc. will be tested.
3 **Refreezing**   This is the follow-up, making sure the change has continued, is recognised and now is a normal part of the functioning of the organisation.

Of course some employees are resistant to any changes. This resistance is natural, as employees look to see how such changes will affect them personally. Who would want change if it means that chances of promotion are reduced, if it means a move to another location, if it means no pay rise or if it means that there is yet another change amongst many others? J. P. Kotter and L. A. Schlesinger, in 'Choosing strategies for change' (*Harvard Business Review*, 1979), classified the reasons why employees resist change.

FOUR GOOD REASONS FOR RESISTING CHANGE

1 Parochial self-interest.
2 Misunderstanding.
3 Different assessments of the situation.
4 Low tolerance for change.

Parochial self-interest is simply the natural inclination of the employee to put him or herself first, before others or the organisation. It does not matter that the change will be better for the continued success of the organisation, if the individual sees that the change will cause him or her to lose something he or she wants to keep, then that individual will resist. If enough employees feel the same way then they will band together to try and halt any changes.

Misunderstanding is a communication problem. The grapevine may paint a picture that does not please the individual. The manager may give the employees a very inadequate explanation of the reason for the changes. If the employees do not trust the management then whatever that manager says will be taken with a pinch of salt as the employees will be looking for the 'real' reasons that they fear are hidden from them.

Different assessments of the situation. It should not be assumed that, the greater the intelligence of the individual, the less likely that individual will be to resist – greater intelligence does not necessarily mean that people will see the need for such changes. The reverse is likely in that the more intelligent employee will find more reasons to resist. Each employee will assess the situation differently so the management cannot assume that all will be resistant or that all will rush to embrace the change.

Low tolerance of change is particularly applicable to employees who value security and stability. The introduction of new technology may cause concern for some if they feel that they might not be able to cope. It is the job of management to recognise this form of resistance and to give support. There is a fear of change. In times of great change people tend to look back to the so-called security of the past.

Kotter and Schlesinger also provided some suggestions that might help to minimise the resistance to any change.

1 **Education and communication**   Take the time and effort to explain the what, when, where, how, why and who. Even this approach will not work if there is lack of trust.

2 **Participation and involvement**   Make sure that those involved in the change take part in planning the implementation of that change.

3 **Facilitation and support**   Spend time on those who fear the change by giving support and retraining.

4 **Negotiation and agreement**   A manager may have to 'buy' the change. This could mean offering financial or other incentives. But do not rush into this course of action.

5 **Manipulation and co-option**   Identify an employee who has great pulling power over other employees. Get that person on the side of change by giving him or her an important role in the process of change. This is a Machiavellian approach which may not work.

6 **Explicit and implicit coercion**   This stage is the last resort of an organisation or manager who just cannot hold the employees together. This use of power is favoured by the bully manager and unfortunately has to be used to encourage the awkward squad to change. Herzberg calls it KITA (kick in the ass).

Transactional analysis and change

Julie Hay's book, *Transactional Analysis for Trainers* (McGraw-Hill, 1992), shows that TA has reviewed change and its consequences.

It has been suggested that it can take up to four years to adjust to an important change. Individuals are not going to be fully competent in a new job for at least two years. There are seven stages that an individual is likely to go through when adjusting to a change in the working environment, and each will have an effect on the performance of the work done by the individual.

1 **Immobilisation**   'Going into shock', where the individual is rooted to the ground and does nothing.

2 **Denial**   Acting as if things are still to be the same, in that individuals will behave as they have always done. This denial of change will result in others questioning the unchanged behaviour.

3 **Frustration**   The individual starts to blame others for the change. There is an internal fight as to how the individual should continue. Here the individual is working out what to do.

4 **Acceptance**   The individual has worked out what has to be done and realised that he/she must let go of the past.

5 **Development**   The individual begins to develop new knowledge and skills and begins to grow within the changed situation.

6 **Application**   The individual has worked out where he/she fits in, with members of the group, manager, job and organisation. It is a time of consolidation, getting on with what has to be done the way it has to be done.

7 **Completion**   Competent and settled down, no longer comparing the present with the past. The change is complete.

These stages operate regardless of whether the change has been imposed on or initiated by the individual.

Although the above represents the responses of an individual, it is important to try and understand an individual's needs during these stages.

1 **Immobilisation**   Needs reassurance that he/she is still wanted.

2 **Denial**   Needs the organisation, the manager and others to have a little patience while he/she comes to terms with the change.

3 **Frustration**   Needs to recognise that frustration is normal. Needs to be allowed space to scream.

4 **Acceptance**   Needs to redefine his/her identity and review what is important to him/her and others who are close.

5 **Development**   Needs training and coaching and to identify a role model.

6 **Application**   Needs to monitor his/her own progress and receive encouragement.

7 **Completion**   Come on in, the water is lovely.

Those who advocate TA make further suggestions as to how a manager can help an employee to progress through the seven stages as smoothly as is practicable and can meet the employee's seven groups of needs.

The seven acts of a manager to meet the seven stages of change and the seven needs of employees

1 **Immobilisation**   Give employees time and space. Give them information and sources but do not expect them to absorb the data straight away.
2 **Denial**   Do not push. Listen, but keep quiet. Recognise this as the most difficult stage.
3 **Frustration**   Empathise. Tolerate and understand what they are going through. Accept the anger that may be directed towards you.
4 **Acceptance**   Give a little advice, not a lot. Talk of what the employee wants to talk about.
5 **Development**   Give more advice. Provide coaching and training where required.
6 **Application**   Encourage. Encourage. Encourage.
7 **Completion**   That is it. They have arrived. They are safe and well.

FURTHER READING

There are many books on transactional analysis. I strongly recommend Julie Hay, *Transactional Analysis for Trainers*, published by McGraw-Hill in 1992.

Stress

While many employees would suggest that they tend to be satisfied in their job and that they welcome change, such comments will depend on their self-esteem, their satisfaction with life in general and their ability to endure stress. It does not take a great deal of research to find out that a high percentage of employees find their job stressful. Some would love to leave their present job because of the stress they suffer. It would be easy to find, by means of a survey, some who have suffered a stress-related illness. To do so, however, could have a bad affect on productivity.

It may be easy to find these people, but some organisations do not like to admit that stress exists in their place of work. In a survey conducted by Marie McHugh, of the University of Ulster, 70 per cent of managers admitted that employees in their organisations experience stress. It was interesting to note that they also said that the group most vulnerable to stress were themselves, the managers, although they did say that production workers were a close second.

Some use stress as an excuse although to others it is a very real problem. Students claim stress as the reason they cannot possible complete their assignments; after all, they say, those assignments are like buses, nothing for ages then they all come at once.

RESEARCH HAS SHOWN THAT:

1 Sixty per cent of absences from work are due to stress-related illnesses.
2 100 million days per year are lost because employees cannot be bothered going in to work.
3 The CBI suggest that stress-related absences and turnover costs £1,500,000,000 per annum.

Stress is the pressure people feel in their personal lives and at their place of work. It can be likened to a pot of water simmering on the cooker: if the heat is not turned down, it may boil over and burn. Stress can not only do physical harm, it can also be emotionally harmful and it can make it difficult to think straight. As we saw in Section 1 on The Management, stress can arouse the zombie, the bully.

SYMPTOMS OF STRESS IN THE INDIVIDUAL

1 Change, for the worse, in appearance.
2 Stomach upset.
3 Back problems.
4 Irritability.
5 Excess use of alcohol or drugs.
6 Nervousness.
7 Depression.
8 Inability to sleep.
9 Inability to relax.
10 Inability to cope.

There are many more symptoms. Uncontrolled stress can lead to death.

Stress in moderation is good, it is natural and normal. Little or no stress is just as bad for productivity as a high level of stress. It can be short or long term. It is not the duration that counts, it is the power of the individual to recover that counts. Continued exposure without the means or ability to recover will result in **burnout**. This is the term used to describe the situation where employees are no longer able to get their act together and get on with the job. Some occupations have high levels of stress more or less on a permanent basis; working in a critical care ward would be one example.

HIGH STRESS JOBS

Can you think of just three high stress occupations?

An employee suffering at the hands of a managerial bully, or bullying by other employees, suffers from the extreme form of stress called **trauma**. Trauma can also occur as the result of unfair dismissal, redundancy, discrimination or harassment.

TRAUMA CAN LEAD TO

1 Lack of concentration.
2 Alienation.
3 Repeated lateness.
4 Repeated absences.
5 Accident proneness.

There is no such thing as a job without stress, although some jobs are more likely than others to cause stress to an employee. It has also been seen, in Section 2 on The Group, that stress can be associated with the role of employee. An organisation must be aware of the factors that can lead to excessive stress in some of their employees. McHugh's research found that managers and staff both thought that production targets were the greatest cause of stress.

STRESS. WHAT CAUSES IT?

1 Tight schedules.
2 Terrible management.
3 Inadequate resources to meet job demands.
4 Conflict of values.
5 Frustration.
6 CHANGE.

The trouble with stress is that it is a mental problem. It is far easier to deal with an injured leg than an injured mind. So what are organisations doing about stress? After all it costs, in terms of lost time and lost production. Research by Sue Wheeler and Dawn Lyon of the University of Birmingham suggests that British employers are not doing enough. Their report in *Personnel Review* in 1992 said that employee assistant programmes were given high priority in America, where health care, keep fit and stress prevention programmes are provided, but were little in evidence in the UK. They also said that UK organisations do not understand the uses of counselling and therapy. That is not to say that there are no progressive organisations in the UK.

Marie McHugh found that managers in many organisations are guilty of not addressing or recognising the causes and effects of stress.

1 Managers fail to see the great costs of stress at work.

2 Managers do not see stress as a cost, and a cost that must be reduced.

3 Managers are not aware of the very existence of stress in their organisation.

4 Managers do not know what they should do to solve stress problems.

5 Managers do not see employees as a valuable resource which must be protected and supported.

6 Managers do not see that the health of the employee and the health of the organisation are intertwined.

Marie McHugh describes one approach that management may wish to consider, total stress management (TSM). This is a little like total quality management in that it is a philosophy that must permeate the whole organisation. TSM is a four-stage problem-identification and problem-solving loop.

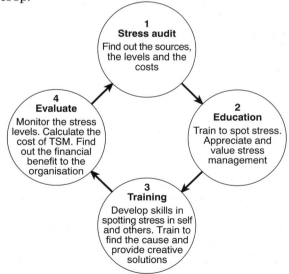

Fig. 63   The McHugh and Brennan TSM loop

Employees doing the same job have different abilities to cope, within themselves, with the same level of stress. This is the **stress threshold**, and represents how much a person can take without behaving in an out of the ordinary way. Valarie Adler, writing in *Psychology Today* in 1989, in an article entitled 'Little Control — Lots

of Stress', concluded that the more autonomy an employee has, the greater his or her ability to handle stress. Organisations and managers should, however, look for those employees who may be predisposed to stress-related behaviour. Such employees may be classified as 'A' types or 'B' types.

What is it?

Type 'A' and Type 'B' people

An 'A' type person is one who appears to be subject to pressures of time and responsibility. 'A' types are very competitive, appear aggressive, uneasy, hurried, impatient. They work hard and play hard. They are also prime candidates for coronary care. They are more susceptible to the physical systems of stress.

A. Furnham, writing of 'The Type A Behaviour Pattern and the Perception of Self' in *Personality and Individual Differences* in 1990, said that 'A' types are more extroverted and neurotic, with greater need of control, than their opposite, the 'B' type. They have also been rated, in research, as angry, domineering, smug, egotistical, insincere and spiteful. However, it is suggested that 'A' types may see these as positive attributes in an attempt to raise their rather low self-esteem.

At work 'A' types are found to be very competitive, giving themselves far too much to do within impracticable deadlines. They are workaholics and see themselves as having a greater and more important workload than the 'B' types. They are, however, no more or less dissatisfied with their jobs than the 'B' type. They may respond well to rewards but that does not mean that they produce better quality work than the 'B' types. If stress were infectious the 'A' types would be very likely to spread it.

M. Friedman and R. Rosenman, in *Type A Behaviour and Your Heart* (Knopf, 1974), provided a number of characteristics of the 'A' type.

1 They don't like other 'A' types.

2 They cannot sit still without feeling guilty.

3 They try to get a quart into a pint pot.

4 They run around like the White Rabbit in *Alice in Wonderland*.

5 They find it difficult to listen.

6 They find it difficult to smell the flowers and see nature.

'B' types on the other hand, are much more calm and casual. They are the opposite of the 'A' types. They can work within the situation in which they find themselves at work and do not find the pressures of time too daunting.

FOUR FEATURES OF 'B' TYPES

1 Not at all like 'A' types.

2 Stay cool.

3 Peace and love.

4 They have no need to blow their own trumpet.

To cope well with stress employees need to have a 'hardy personality'. S. Kobasa, writing in the *Journal of Personality and Social Psychology* in 1979 on the subject of 'Stressful Life Events, Personality, Health: An enquiring into hardiness', suggested that a person needs three qualities in order to cope with the stress of working life, and life in general. These are: commitment, control and challenge.

KOBASA AND THE THREE CS

1 Commitment I know who I am and what I am doing.

2 Control I control my life and can influence others.

3 Challenge Change is the norm, not the *status quo*.

Organisations need to take note of the theory of 'A' and 'B' types and of the idea of the 'hardy personality'. They may see that aiming for the reduction of stress will help towards job satisfaction and higher productivity. Furthermore, taking steps to change the 'A' types to being more like the 'B' types will reduce the problems associated with being an 'A' type.

AN 'A' TYPE STUDENT OR A 'B' TYPE STUDENT?

The more you agree with a statement the higher the score you should give yourself out of ten.

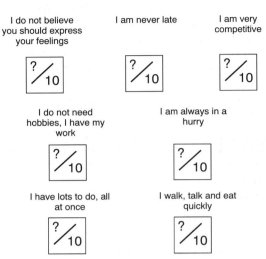

Score of 55 and over shows a definite 'A' type. Score of 40 or less is the take-it-easy 'B' type.

FURTHER READING

There is plenty to read on this topic. Just look up stress in the index of a variety of management books. Try and get hold of a book by John W. Newstrom and Keith Davies, called *Organizational Behavior: Human Behavior at Work*, 9th ed., McGraw-Hill 1993.

NEW AGE THINKING

Continued and relentless change requires new forms of expression. That expression may come from New Age thinking. You must have noticed repeated references to the terms myth, ritual and spirit, all of which may be clues that there is a movement away from the basics of teams, style and communications.

The Japanese, oft-quoted role models are engaged in sending their organisation men (it tends to be men rather than women in Japan) to courses so that they may 'discover' themselves and become more creative in problem solving. Organisations have not forgotten their concern for profit, but are considering ways in which they can develop the inner person for the new art of commercial and industrial war.

There are differences of opinion about New Age thinking and employee training based on new age technologies. Some see them as demonic and dangerous, but others see them as innovative and uplifting. New Age thinking does not involve crystal healing, astrology or past life regression. It does include meditation, neurolinguistic programming, self hypnosis, yoga.

One chief executive officer seems to have been made aware that we are in the New Age where:

employees should be rewarded not only in the pocket but also in the soul.

FURTHER READING

Take a history lesson. To understand what is happening today, find out what happened yesterday. Look up the four major periods of management ideas:

- Rational-economic period, *c.*1900 to 1930+
- Social period, *c.*1920 to 1950+
- Psychological period, *c.*1940 to 1970+
- Entrepreneurial period, *c.*1980 to 1990+

and why not add a fifth:

- Guru period, *c.*1990

From your reading you will find out about the values of society, the development and values of organisations and the values of managers.

You should also examine the Models of Man:

- The Rational Man Model
- The Social Man Model and
- The Complex Man Model

You should be able to fit these round the Management Schools discussed in Section 1.

ASSIGNMENT FOR SECTION 3, THE INDIVIDUAL

1   Take one group or class.
2   Take measurements of absenteeism, timekeeping, grades, non-completion of assignments, late assignments, number in group or class, gender mix, age ranges, ethnicity, persons with a disability.
3   Compare measurements with the norms of the organisation, or best practice. This

would include, say, a requirement for 100 per cent attendance at keynote lectures and if the actual were, say, 60 per cent then clearly something is wrong. The wrong could be unreasonable expectations from those managing the course or the students having a negative attitude to the lectures.
4   Devise an attitude survey questionnaire. You will need prior knowledge of questionnaire design.
5   Analyse the results
6   Make recommendations for improvements.

The whole should be compared with your school or college quality control programme.

MULTIPLE CHOICE AND QUESTIONS

1 An **androgynous** person is someone who demonstrates:
   a   Male characteristics
   b   Female characteristics
   c   Both male and female characteristics
   d   A dislike of male or female characteristics

2 Which grouping would apply to an **extrovert/low neurotic**?
   a   Composed, adaptable, sociable
   b   Excitable, friendly, sociable
   c   Composed, trustful, shy
   d   Excitable, unstable, shy

3 **Perception** is:
   a   What people think is real
   b   What is real
   c   A learning style
   d   A stereotype image

4 **Locus of control** is a person's perception of who is controlling his or her life. Decide whether each of the statements below is true or false:
   (i)   Internalisers are people who believe that they control their own fate.
   (ii) Externalisers are people who believe that their fate is decided by others.
   a   (i)   is True   (ii) is False
   b   (i)   is False   (ii) is False
   c   (i)   is False   (ii) is True
   d   (i)   is True   (ii) is True

157

5 **Machiavellianism** refers to someone who:
 a Follows Theory Y
 b Manipulates others
 c Is a good team player
 d Is a new-age thinker

6 According to Morris Massey, a person whose value level is such that he or she would not be at home in a team setting is:
 a Sociocentric
 b Existential
 c Egocentric
 d Reactive

7 An **attitude** consists of three parts. Which of these three make up an attitude?
 a Cognitive, behavioural, knowledge
 b Cognitive, affective, behavioural
 c Affective, behavioural, actions
 d Beliefs, knowledge, understanding

8 **Cognitive dissonance** is information received which:
 a Conflicts with present knowledge
 b Confirms present understanding
 c Supports current beliefs
 d Provides solutions to problems

9 In relation to the need for an attitude survey, decide if each of the following statements is true or false:
 (i) High levels of lateness indicate a negative attitude problem.
 (ii) Low levels of quality indicate a negative attitude problem.
 a (i) is True   (ii) is False
 b (i) is False   (ii) is False
 c (i) is False   (ii) is True
 d (i) is True   (ii) is True

10 In Maslow's **hierarchy of needs**, the group called the **deficiency** needs are:
 a Esteem, social, safety
 b Self-actualisation, esteem, social
 c Social, physiological, safety
 d Self-actualisation, physiological, safety

11 In the Alderfer **ERG theory**, the needs of **existence** are very similar to which of Maslow's needs?
 a Esteem and self-actualisation
 b Safety and esteem
 c Physiological and safety
 d Social and safety

12 Herzberg's **hygiene** factor includes:
 a Pay and working conditions
 b Attainment and status
 c Security and responsibility
 d Advancement and responsibility

13 David McClelland's **three needs theory** includes:
 a Power, status and achievement
 b Achievement, power and affiliation
 c Achievement, security and affiliation
 d Responsibility, power and status

14 Which statement best describes the **Equity theory**?
 a The best work is shared equally.
 b The pay and benefits received by one are greater than those received by others.
 c What a person puts into a job, and gets out of it, is equal to what others give and get.
 d It is a willingness to remain in an organisation because of the benefits.

Questions 15, 16 and 17 are related to the following information:
 a Punishment
 b Extinction
 c Positive reinforcement
 d Negative reinforcement

Which of the above are described by the following statements?

15 Punishment is withheld.

16 Eliminating a behaviour not required.

17 Rewarding desirable behaviour.

18 **Valence** in Vroom's **expectancy theory** is the:
 a Expectation of achieving a goal
 b Strength of an employee's want for something
 c Satisfaction in meeting an agreed target
 d Belief in receiving a reward for meeting an agreed target

19 Transactional Analysis stroking is:
  a Cognitive dissonance
  b Improved productivity
  c Recognition
  d Goal setting

20 Which group has an analytical interest in **organisational culture**?
  a Psychologists
  b Philosophers
  c Sociologists
  d Anthropologists

21 A **role culture**, according to Charles Handy, is like:
  a A bureaucratic organisation
  b An *adhoc*racy
  c Scientific management followers
  d The New Age approach to management

Questions 22, 23 and 24 relate to the following information:
  a Job rotation
  b Job enlargement
  c Job enrichment
  d Job satisfaction

Which is

22 Moving employees around to different jobs at the same skill level.

23 Developing a job horizontally.

24 Designing a job vertically.

25 Kurt Lewin identified three stages an individual, group or organisation has to go through in the **change** process. Which of these are they?
  a Unfreezing, changing, re-freezing
  b Misunderstanding, low tolerance, self-interest
  c Education, co-option, coercion

26 Which TWO of the following may be symptoms of **Stress**?
  a Depression
  b Excessive use of alcohol
  c Tight schedules
  d Management

27 Give three examples of what could cause **inappropriate stress**.
  a _____
  b _____
  c _____

28 Describe a **type 'A'** personality.
  _____

29 David Kolb provides a **learning cycle** of four stages. Identify TWO.
  a _____
  b _____

30 New Age thinking is all about:
  a Revisiting the classical management theory
  b Providing extrinsic rewards
  c Development of the inner self
  d Total rejection of scientific management techniques

REFERENCES

Adams, J. S., 1963, 'Towards Understanding of Inequity', *Journal of Abnormal and Social Psychology*.

Adler, V., 1989, 'Little Control – Lots of Stress', *Psychology Today*.

Alderfer, C., 1969, 'An Empirical Test of a New Theory of Human Needs', *Organizational Behaviour and Human Performance*, Vol. 4.

Arnold, J., Robertson, I., and Cooper, C., 1991, *Work Psychology. Understanding Human Behavior in the Workplace*, Pitman.

Barnes, G., 1981, 'On saying hello the script drama diamond and character role analysis', *Transactional Analysis Journal*, Jan.

Blau, G., 1987, 'Locus of control as a potential moderator of the turnover process', *Journal of Occupational Psychology*.

Bowles, M., and Coates, G., 1993, 'Images and Substance', *Personnel Review*.

Boyle, D., 1992, 'Employee Motivation that Works', *American HRM Magazine*.

Christie, R., and Geis, F. L., 1970, *Studies in Machiavellianism*, NY, Academic Press.

Delong, T. J., 'Re-examining the Career Anchor Model', *Personnel*, May/June 1982, pp. 56–7.

Etzioni, A. A., 1975, *A Comparative Analysis of*

Complex Organizations, Free Press.

Eysenck, H., and Wilson, G., 1975, *Know your own personality*, Temple Smith.

Friedman, M., and Rosenman, R., 1974, *Type A Behaviour and your Heart*, NY, Knopf.

Furnham, A., 1990, 'The Type A Behaviour Pattern and the Perception of Self', *Personality and Individual Differences*.

Handy, C., 1985, *Understanding Organizations*, Penguin.

Harris, T., 1973, *I'm OK. You're OK*, Pan.

Hay, J., 1992, *Transactional Analysis for Trainers*, McGraw-Hill.

Herzberg, F., 1966, *Work and the Nature of Man*, World Pub. Co.

Holland, J., 1971, *Making Vocational Choices*, Prentice-Hall.

Honey, P., and Mumford, A., 1986, *Manual of Learning Styles*, Honey and Mumford.

Jablonsky, S., and DeViries, D., 1972, 'Operant conditioning principles extrapolated to the theory of management', *Organizational Behaviour and Human Performance*.

Kanter, R. M., 1985, *The Change Masters. Corporate Entrepreneurs at Work*, Allen & Unwin.

Keirsey, D., and Bates, M., 1984, *Please Understand Me. Character and Temperament Types* (5th edn), California, Prometheus Nemesis.

Kobasa, S., 1979, 'Stressful Life Events, Personality, Health: An enquiring into Hardiness', *Journal of Personality and Social Psychology*.

Kolb, D., Rubin, M., and McIntyre, J. M., 1974, *Organizational Psychology. An experiential approach*, Prentice-Hall.

Kotter, J. P., and Schlesinger, L. A., 1979, 'Choosing strategies for change', *Harvard Business Review*.

Lewin, K., 1951, *Field Theory in Social Science*, Harper.

Locke, E., 1976, 'The nature and causes of job satisfaction', in M. D. Dunnette (ed.), *Handbook of Industrial and Organizational Psychology*, Chicago, Rand McNally.

Males, S., 1983, 'Police Management on Division and Sub-Division', *Police Research Services Unit*.

Maslow, A., 1954, *Motivation and Personality*, Harper & Row.

Massey, M., 1979, *The People Puzzle*, Reston.

McClelland, D., 1961, *The Achieving Society*, Van Nostrand.

McHugh, M., 1992, 'Stress at Work. Do Managers Really Count the Costs?', *Employee Relations*, Vol. 15.

Morton, P. K., 1948, 'The Self Fulfilling Prophecy', *Antioch Review*, Vol. 8.

Newstrom, John W., and Davies, Keith, 1993, *Organizational Behavior: Human Behavior at Work*, McGraw-Hill, 9th ed.

Oldham, G., and Hackman, R., 1975, 'A New Strategy for Job Enrichment', *California Management Review*.

Robbins, S., 1991, *Organizational Behaviour*, Prentice-Hall.

Rotter, J., 1971, 'External control and internal control', *Psychology Today*, June.

——, 1982, *The development and applications of social learning theory. Selected papers*, NY, Praeger.

Schein, E. H., 1982, 'Does Japanese management style have a message for American Managers?' *Sloan Management Review*.

——, 1990, *Career Anchors*, University Associates.

——, 1993, 'The Role of the Founder in Creating Organisational Culture' in *Organisational Dynamics*, (publisher unknown).

Skinner, B. F., 1938, 'The Behavior of Organisms: An Experimental Approach', NY, Appleton-Century.

Spector, P., 1982, 'Behaviour in Organisations as a function of employee's locus of control', *Psychological Bulletin*.

Storms, P., and Spencer, P., 1987, 'Relationships of organizational frustration with reported behavioral reactions. The Moderating Effect', *Journal of Occupational Behaviour*.

Thorndike, E. L., 1925, *Behaviorism*, Norton.

Trice, H. M., and Beyer, J. M., 1987, 'Studying Organizational Cultures through Rites and Rituals', *Academy of Management Review*, Vol. 9.

Vroom, V. H., 1964, *Work and Motivation*, NY, John Wiley.

Walton, R. E., 1974, 'Improving the Quality of Work Life', *Harvard Business Review*.

Wheeler, S., and Lyon, D., 1992, 'Employee Benefits for the Employer's Benefit. How Companies Respond to Employee Stress', *Personnel Review*, Vol. 21.

Selective Glossary

Ability   The employee's competence to undertake a job or task to the standards required.

Accommodation   In conflict situations this refers to behaviour where one person has the facility to subordinate his or her stance in favour of the other person(s).

Adhocracy   A fairly free organisational structure which has no strict rules and regulations, it is informal and decentralised.

Androgynous   The bringing together of what have been seen as separate male and female characteristics.

Attitude   The habitual way of regarding another person or place or a particular situation. It is in the mind, so you are not able to see it. An attitude can only be inferred from what a person says or how that person behaves.

Attitude surveys   A means of finding out from employees how they feel about their job, the organisation and the people they work with.

Autocratic   In relation to a manager, refers to one who dictates instruction to employees, not allowing them any participation in decision-making.

Autonomy   In relation to employees, the level of freedom given to them in deciding what, when, where, and how a job should be done.

Avoidance   In conflict situations this refers to behaviour by which a person conceals the conflict, keeping it to him or herself, or steps back from it.

Behaviour   How employees conduct themselves at work and how that response to the working environment affects their working relationship with others and the requirements of the organisation.

Body language   The messages revealed through body movements which confirm or contradict what is being said.

Brainstorming   A problem-solving technique in which a group of interested persons is brought together in one place to find a solution to a particular problem. It is at its best when the problem to be examined has more than one possible solution. This allows those in the process free wild creative expression of ideas.

Career anchor   This refers to the situation where a person has worked out, after some experience, his/her own abilities, values, and attitudes, and what motivates him or her. This person knows what he/she wants in a job, and will not voluntarily give it up.

Cash cows   Organisations with a high market share but a low growth rate and which need little money in order to hold on to their present position in the market.

Centralised   Where decision-making is performed at one central point in an organisations.

Change   Doing things differently from the way they are done at present.

Charismatic   Personality or behaviour of an individual that is very attractive to others.

Cliques   People with a close working

161

relationship in a department or section. They may hold 'meetings' around the coffee machine or huddle together at a canteen table. Cliques are undemocratic and formed for the protection of their membership.

Closed group   A work group that confines itself to the accomplishment of the task, and gives little or no attention to the interaction-oriented function of its membership.

Coercive power   The control over others that has its root in fear.

Cognitive dissonance   The result when something that has happened, or information that has been received, does not agree with what we already understand. There is conflict, and it is within ourselves, we feel uneasy. We need to heal that pain by finding a rational explanation of that difference.

Cohesiveness   A measure of the quality and quantity of what is seen as good behaviour. Where this exceeds what is seen as negative behaviour within a group, that group is drawn together to act as a single entity.

Collaboration   In conflict situations this refers to the situation where each side tries to satisfy the needs of the other.

Command groups   Groups that are permanent, in that they have no predetermined period of existence and are shown on the organisational chart.

Communication   The passing of understandable information from one or more persons to another person or group.

Compromise   In conflict situations this refers to the situation where each side gives up something in order to reach an agreement.

Conflict   A matter of awareness. It involves two or more persons. If they can see it, or feel it, then it is there. If they cannot see it or feel it, then it is not there. If people hold opposing views, and they are aware of this, that is conflict.

Decoding   The receiver of a message retranslating a communication received from a sender.

Delphi technique   A group decision-making technique that does not require that group to meet together. The key is a questionnaire or series of questionnaires prepared and disseminated by an independent person.

Diagonal communication   Transfer of information between people working at different levels and in different departments of an organisation.

Dog   An organisation that has a low share of the market and a low growth and which has little or no profit.

Dominant response hypothesis   This says that a person working on a task with which he or she is comfortable will do it even better when others are present, whether working with them or being observed by them. However if the person is not comfortable doing the task then his/her performance will be worse if working with others or if being observed.

Dysfunctional conflict   Conflict that obstructs or retards the work of a group and/or an organisation.

Empowerment   Enabling employees to assume the authority in the effective performance of a task without continual reference to a higher level of management.

Encoding   Translating a message into a specific format.

Equity theory   Adams' theory that says that employees look at what they put into a job and what they get out of it, compare this with others, and then take action to eliminate any unfavourable variance.

ERG Theory   Alderfer's theory that defines the three needs of an employee as E = Existence, R = Relatedness and G = Growth.

Expectancy theory   Vroom's theory that says that the motivational strength to perform in a particular way is related to the degree to which that performance will attract a desired or undesired outcome, and the expected ability to reach a specified performance level.

Expert power   Power vested in a manager, or a consultant, because of the recognised expertise he or she is believed to possess.

Externaliser   Person who believes that his/her life is controlled by influences outside him/herself.

Extrinsic rewards   Benefits received by employees which relate to matters associated with work, such as pay and working conditions.

Extrovert   A person who is more interested in what goes on around him or her and in other people than in his/her own thoughts and feelings.

Feedback   In relation to an employee, the clear and direct information he or she receives about his/her effectiveness and efficiency.

Felt conflict   Conflict as experienced by an individual.

Financial control companies   Organisations that are concerned mainly with financial performance and not their competitive position.

Flat organisational structure   Refers to an organisation with few levels of management and decision-making conducted at lower levels, thus increasing the power of the middle ranks in the organisation.

Formal communication   Communication that is necessary within a department and with other departments of an organisation in order to aid and ensure co-operation in meeting the organisational aims and objectives.

Formal groups   Groups that are created by management in order to undertake specific activities.

Functional approach   In relation to management action, where the manager balances the needs of the organisation to meet the task in hand, the need to keep the group or team together and the needs of the individual within the team.

Functional conflict   Conflict that is positively directed, with the aim of moving things forward.

Gap searching   The behaviour of the receiver of a communication who is not listening but is busy looking for a 'space' created by the sender, in order that the receiver may express a particular viewpoint.

Goal-setting theory   Locke's theory that says that where there are clearly defined goals that are not easy to achieve the result is higher levels of performance.

Goals   Objectives or aims, both collective, or corporate, and individual. Organisations direct their employees to a collective aim. As organisations are made up of people then it is those people who create or dictate those aims in the form of objectives. The top management decide the goals of the overall organisation, and these are translated into departmental and individual goals.

Grapevine   An informal route used to pass on gossip and rumour. It may be seen as a leakage of bits of information.

Group   Two or more persons who share a purpose and have a leader.

Group development   The stages that a group passes through. Seen by one writer as forming, storming, norming, performing and adjourning.

Group norms   The shared standards of a group, both expressed and implied.

Groupshift   This refers to group behaviour where the group makes riskier or more conservative decisions than the group members would make as individuals.

Groupthink   This refers to the situation where there is a deeply held desire amongst the group to reach a decision. They avoid disagreement

163

and do not look at the pros and cons of alternatives. They cannot accept that they as a group will make a mistake and they underestimate competition.

Hierarchy of needs   Maslow's theory that defines the physiological, safety, social, esteem and self-actualisation needs which form a series of steps. When one need is met, this triggers action to satisfy the need on the next level.

Horizontal communication   Communication between people on the same grade or ranking in an organisation. It may be between teams of employees or with those of similar status in other departments. Horizontal communication is the most common form within an organisation.

Hygiene factors   Items such as pay, working conditions and supervision. If these are good in quality and quantity, an employee will be less dissatisfied with a job.

Individualism   A characteristic of a national culture meaning that people have a preference for an individual approach as opposed to being part of a collective.

Informal groups   Groups that are formed without direct action by management to meet the needs of social interaction, although they exist for more than just social purposes.

Interaction-oriented group behaviour   Part of the group process, whereby the group set standards of behaviour, support each other, sort out any conflicts within the group, reaching agreement for the good of the whole group.

Internaliser   Person who believes that he/she controls what he or she does and what happens to him/her.

Intrinsic rewards   The good feelings an employee gets from doing his or her job.

Introvert   A person preoccupied with his/her own inner thoughts and feelings. Introverts may be seen as shy, and may find it difficult to communicate with others.

Job enlargement   The development of a job horizontally.

Job enrichment   The development of a job vertically.

Job involvement   The value of the contribution of an employee to the work he/she is doing. Think of a Nurse or Aid Worker.

Job rotation   The movement of an employee from one job to another.

Job satisfaction   The degree to which an employee gets a personal buzz from the job he/she does.

Kinship-friendship group   A group that exists for social purposes at and away from work. They share information and gossip.

Large group   A group of 12 or more.

Leadership grid   A method for analysing the style adopted by a manager in terms of the dimensions, concern for production, and concern for people. The grid contains 81 possible styles.

Learning   Knowing something you did not know earlier and being able to show it. Ability to do something you were not able to do before.

Locus of control   The level at which persons believe that they control, or do not control, their own destiny.

Machiavellianism   A character trait typified by a belief that the ends justify the means. A person with this trait is a rational thinker with a very low level of emotional contact.

Maintenance functions   Actions which keep things on a person to person level, and which keep a group working as a single unit, and running at a fast but safe speed. The functions include sorting out disputes and mutual support.

Manager   Someone in an organisation who gets things done through other people.

Marxist perspective   A belief that workers can only achieve their just rewards through the process of continual conflict.

Masculinity   A national culture characteristic referring to the hard-man, 'macho' approach in which the participants like to lock horns in combat. Opposite of the 'softer' or feminine approach which values others and has a high regard for the quality of life.

Motivation   The stimulus that drives employees to put effort into their work in order to achieve something they want.

Negative power   A form of power which is used to stop things happening.

Network groups   Informal work groups in which an individual sees the need to develop contacts throughout the organisation, up, down and across the scalar chain. This networking may extend to customers, suppliers, and other outside business contacts.

Nominal group technique   A group decision-making technique which requires that all members of the group meet together to try to solve a problem. Each individual member is required to work independently of the others. It starts with the chairperson stating the problem and restating it, if necessary, until all present understand it. There follows a period of silence, during which each member thinks about the problem and puts down one or more ideas on paper.

Occupational direction   The idea that people, given the freedom, will move naturally towards jobs that fit their personality.

Official groups   Groups that have a formal structure, and which are organised in order to perform the work given to them.

Ordinary group process   A group decision-making technique whereby the leader of the group presents the group with the problem and then seeks comments and discussion.

Organic structure   An organisational structure that is flexible in its design and has the ability to grow and alter to meet changed circumstances.

Organisational behaviour   The way people behave as part of an organisation. Studies of organisational behaviour look at the impact of the way people behave in organisations in order that such information may be used to improve the effectiveness and efficiency of the organisation.

Organisational climate   The atmosphere created by the feelings and emotions of the employees of an organisation.

Organisational commitment   The strength of employees' loyalty to, and liking of, an organisation and how it operates; the degree to which they identify with what it does, have pride in it and wish to stay part of it.

Organisational culture   The shared beliefs and values of those within an organisation.

Pedantocracy   An organisation that lays excessive stress upon detail or upon the strict adherence to rules.

Perception   The seeing or recognition of things. The use of the senses to reach an understanding of the meaning of that which surrounds people.

Person culture   A culture characterised by a belief on the part of its members that the whole thing is there to serve the needs of those who work within it.

Personal power   Charisma, the power of the personality.

Personality   The distinctive characteristics or qualities of a person, seen in how that person reacts and interacts with others.

Physical power   The might of the stronger person or the one with superior energy.

Pluralist organisation   Organisation that believes and understands that different groups have different ambitions, and that if disharmony results, a solution will be found through compromise.

Position power   The power residing within a manager simply because of the particular position that he/she holds in the organisation.

Power   The ownership of control or command over others.

Power culture   Shown by Charles Handy as a web, where person power is within the spider at the centre and resource power is within the web.

Power distance   A national characteristic concerned with the measure of the acceptance of inequalities.

Quality circle   A small group of employees who do similar work and who meet together at regular intervals on a voluntary basis with a group leader in order to look at problems they have identified.

Quality of working life   The degree of excellence of working life as defined by the extent to which organisations take measures to ensure that employees are allowed to share in the decisions that affect them at work.

Reinforcement theory   Thorndike and Skinner's theory that says there are four possible actions which confirm the repercussions of behaviour: 1. positive reinforcement; 2. negative reinforcement; 3. punishment; 4. extinction.

Resource power   The influence retained by a manager who is able to give and decline, say, a pay rise because he/she has financial control.

Role   A person's expected function, or way of behaving, in relation to the position he/she holds.

Role culture   The environment in which a person carries out his or her role, that is, the bureaucratic organisation.

Sapiential authority   The influence and power

given to an employee over others on the same hierarchical level because of his/her expertise or wisdom within a particular area of work.

Scalar chain   The term used to describe the chain of command or authority from the top to the toe of the organisation.

Self-fulfilling prophecy   One in which expectations of likely behaviour directly influence actual behaviour, as where there is a strong positive or negative view that a person will behave in a particular way to a given set of circumstances, and those expectations are met, with the behaviour matching that expected.

Self-oriented group behaviour   Behaviour characterised by a concentration of time and energy on satisfying the individual's own needs, even though such actions may well conflict with the needs of the group.

Situational leadership model   A model in which the behavioural style of the manager relates and reacts to particular aspects of the employee, known as the follower and his/her readiness to follow. This is expressed on a two-dimensional model comprising task relationships and people relationships.

Social facilitation   The characteristic whereby people increase their particular behaviours when with others above the level they would perform when alone.

Social loafing   A form of behaviour in which a group member, who thinks that another or others are not pulling their weight, reduces his or her productivity to re-establish what he/she considers to be a just level of performance.

Statistical aggregation   A group decision-making technique used where a problem needs a group solution, but it is difficult to get the group together and where the solution is one that can be obtained by the analysis of numerical information gathered from a quantity of sources.

Stars   Organisations with a high market share and a high market growth and with enough profits to pay for further growth.

Strategic control company   An organisation that tries to balance both the competitive and financial objectives.

Strategic planning organisations   Organisations that attempt to gain the greatest lead in their own particular field of operation.

Stress   An internal reaction to a situation the outcome of which is both important and uncertain.

Stroking   Recognition. Daily chatting with other employees, customers, bosses and friends means that we are engaged in stroking. A word is a stroke, a facial expression directed at someone is a stroke.

Style   The manner of doing something. In connection with management, it refers to the way in which a manager behaves to an employee or team of employees.

Sub-clique   The inner circle of a clique, which has control over the clique.

Synergy   The situation where the whole is greater than the sum of its parts.

System 1   In Likert's model of management influence, this refers to the exploitive and authoritative manager.

System 2   In Likert's model of management influence, this refers to the benevolent and authoritative manager.

System 3   In Likert's model of management influence, this refers to the consultative manager.

System 4   In Likert's model of management influence, this refers to the participative manager.

Task culture   One that is based on the formation of groups for specific challenges, so that it is able to adapt fairly quickly to changing situations.

Task functions   Those activities which assist the group to reach their work goals.

Task groups   Temporary groups that are usually formed to start and finish a task within a set time.

Task-oriented group behaviour   Behaviour that concentrates on the achievement of group objectives or goals.

Team briefing   The process of cascading key information from management down the scalar chain.

Theory X   McGregor's theory that says that workers are naturally lazy and need to be coerced into working effectively.

Theory Y   McGregor's theory that says that employees are capable of self-control, are creative and seek responsibility.

Three Needs theory   McLelland's theory that says individuals have three needs: achievement, power and affiliation.

Trait   Long-lasting characteristic that typifies a person's behaviour.

Transactional analysis   A bundle of theories tied up with one ribbon that concern the way individuals relate to each other. Positive feelings towards others or oneself are known as OK feelings. Negative feelings are known as Not OK feelings.

Two-factor theory   Herzberg's theory that says two factors, the hygiene factor and motivators, have a great bearing on an employee's motivation. Both are of equal importance.

Type 'A'   An aggressive individual who wants to achieve more and more in less time.

Type 'B'   A laid-back individual who is the opposite of Type 'A'.

Uncertainty avoidance   A national characteristic typified by a range from those with a preference for flexibility and vagueness to those with a preference for a more bureaucratic structured approach.

Unitary organisation   An organisation that believes that all employees work towards the company goals, with loyalty and complete acceptance of the structure and systems.

Value systems of national cultures   Four particular dimensions were identified as being of importance: 1. power distance; 2. uncertainty avoidance; 3. individualism; 4. masculinity.

Value theory   Locke's theory which says that if an employee's values can be determined, then this knowledge may be used to gauge the level of that individual's job satisfaction.

Values   The fundamental belief that things should be organised in a certain way and that this arrangement is preferable to an individual, or to society generally.

Vertical communication   The transfer of information either down the organisation scalar chain, from the top to the bottom, from the manager to the employee, or up the organisation, from the employee to the manager.

Wild cats   Organisations that have a low share of the market but a high growth rate and which require much more money to be put into the business than the profit they are currently making.

Index